Rebecca Sitton's ••• Spelling Sourcebook 3

Your Guide for
Teaching
and Extending
High-Use
Writing
Words
401–800

ISBN 1-886050-02-3

©1995—Rebecca Sitton

South 2336 Pittsburg, Spokane, WA 99203

15 14 13 12 11 10 9 8 7 6 5 4 3 2

Dear Educator,

I have created the *Spelling Sourcebook* Series for you as an alternative to traditional workbook spelling. It is your source for teacher-customized spelling instruction designed to complement the writing-rich classroom. You can develop your own research-based, spelling-for-writing program using the *Spelling Sourcebook* options and resources.

Begin with *Spelling Sourcebook 1.* This specific guidebook tells you how to develop and implement your own spelling program using high-frequency writing words. The seventeen Articles of Part 1 include options for dividing the high-use words across the grades, organizing a flexible schedule for teaching the words, and establishing practical expectations for spelling accountability in writing; guidelines for effectively using research-based procedures, informing parents and involving them in the new program, and handling lower and higher achievers; and suggestions for authentic and performance-based spelling evaluations. Part 2 of *Spelling Sourcebook 1* is the reference section. It features 1200 high-frequency writing words listed in their order of frequency of use, practical spelling rules, game and writing ideas, and a review of valid spelling research with a complete bibliography. The final section, Part 3, has your blackline master forms for instruction and record keeping.

Spelling Sourcebooks 2, 3, and *4* are your activity books. They provide abundant suggestions for teaching and extending the high-use words within a literature-based, language-centered classroom. *Spelling Sourcebook 2* includes ideas for words within the frequencies 1–400. This book, *Spelling Sourcebook 3,* includes ideas for words within the frequencies 401–800. *Spelling Sourcebook 4* follows *Sourcebook 3,* with ideas for words 801–1200. There are no student books. You don't need them with the *Spelling Sourcebook* Series.

I invite you to participate in the *Spelling Sourcebook* methodology. This nontraditional, commonsense approach to spelling will help your students learn to spell where it counts . . . in their everyday writing!

If you have questions, contact me. If you'd like to share your experiences using the *Spelling Sourcebook* Series, contact me. Or if you'd like information on the spelling seminar I present to educators that highlights the concepts of the *Spelling Sourcebook* methodology, contact me. I'd like to hear from you.

Sincerely,

Rebecca Sitton
South 2336 Pittsburg
Spokane, WA 99203
(509) 535-5500

About the Spelling Sourcebook Author

Rebecca Sitton is an internationally recognized authority on spelling instruction. She applies research-based spelling strategies to instruction within an integrated, language-centered curriculum that offers students many opportunities for writing.

Rebecca has experience teaching in both regular and special education, was a Chapter I teacher, and served as a school district Language Arts Coordinator. Currently, she is a free-lance educational consultant and staff development trainer to numerous school districts and regional education agencies. She serves as an instructor for the Bureau of Education and Research, providing seminars to educators throughout the United States and Canada. She teaches at the university level and is an author of numerous published educational materials.

Published Materials by Rebecca Sitton

Spelling Sourcebook Series, Northwest Textbook, 503 639-3194

Spelling Sourcebook Video Series, Northwest Textbook, 503 639-3194

Increasing Student Spelling Achievement — seminar guidebook, Northwest Textbook, 503 639-3194

Increasing Student Spelling Achievement Audio Tape Program, Bureau of Education and Research, 1 800 735-3503

Spelling Workshops Series correlated to HEATH READING, D.C. Heath, 1 800 235-3565

Instant Spelling Words for Writing Series, Curriculum Associates, Inc., 1 800 225-0248

Stop and Think— Life-Skills Literacy Series, Curriculum Associates, Inc., 1 800 225-0248

QUICK-WORD™ materials, Curriculum Associates, Inc., 1 800 225-0248
   QUICK-WORD™ *WORDSHOP Activity Series*
   QUICK-WORD™ *Handbook for Everyday Writers*
   QUICK-WORD™ *Handbook for Everyday Writers* (Canadian Edition)
   QUICK-WORD™ *Handbook for Everyday Writers* (Spanish Edition)
   QUICK-WORD™ *Handbook for Beginning Writers*
   QUICK-WORD™ *Handbook for Practical Writing*

Story Pictures Plus Series, Curriculum Associates, Inc., 1 800 225-0248

Storybooks Plus Series, Curriculum Associates, Inc., 1 800 225-0248

Your Guide to the Contents

About Spelling Sourcebook 3

What is the purpose of Spelling Sourcebook 3?

Spelling Sourcebook 3 lists Core Words 401–800 in their order of frequency of use in everyday writing (see *Spelling Sourcebook 1* pages 77–82 for the complete *Sourcebook* word bank of 1200 Core Words and discussion of how they were compiled). Following each of the 400 Core Words, multiple activities are suggested for teaching the words and "springboarding" to related language learning. Here is a sampling of the activity idea options.

What kinds of activities are included?

literature—books and follow-up activities that reinforce and extend the Core Words

writing—motivational writing ideas that require students to apply their spelling skills in writing activities

vocabulary building—activities that "springboard" from the Core Words to introduce other forms of the words, synonyms, antonyms, homophones, homographs, prefixes and suffixes, roots, multiple meanings, clipped words (plane/airplane), and words often confused (then/than)

research activities—ideas to stimulate research, writing, and oral reporting

visual activities—visual discrimination and perception activities

word origins—activities that encourage an understanding of word histories, eponyms, and foreign words and phrases

dictionary skills—activities that promote competent use of dictionaries and other writing references, including lessons on alphabetical order, multiple meanings, pronunciations, and syllabication

phonetic analysis—activities that reinforce sound-symbol correspondence of consonant, vowel, and digraph sounds; and awareness of silent letters

structural analysis—activities for exploring compounds, contractions, double letters, and palindromes; affixes and word parts; and patterning activities

thinking skills—activities that help students explore word relationships through sequencing, analogies, and sorting; exercises that encourage students to discover multiple meanings of words; and creative and expository writing

spelling rules—activities that teach reliable rules, or generalizations, with opportunities to apply the rules to new words

Why is it most effective to present words in the order of their frequency of use in writing?

For the tightest bond between spelling and writing, the Core Words should be taught in their order of frequency of use in writing, just as they are listed. This ensures that the words with the greatest long-term spelling power are learned before words with less utility in writing (see *Spelling Sourcebook 1,* Article 2, page 9).

What are the grade levels of the Core Words in Spelling Sourcebook 3?

The grade levels to which these Core Words can be assigned varies. Dividing the words into grade levels is a decision for the program developers to make as they customize *Spelling Sourcebook 1's* Core Word bank to meet the needs of a specific group of program users (for guidelines for grade level options see *Spelling Sourcebook 1,* Article 2, page 9 and Article 16, page 67).

How will the activities challenge better spellers?

Many of the activities in *Spelling Sourcebook 3* are designed for better students who are minimally challenged by learning to spell the Core Words on their spelling pretests and posttests or previews and reviews (for an explanation of the Self-Corrected Test and guidelines for administering it, see *Spelling Sourcebook 1*, Article 4, page 21). The activities in *Spelling Sourcebook 3* extend learning beyond the Core Words to word banks, skills, and application opportunities that develop understandings about our language and its effective written use (for additional ways to challenge better students, see *Spelling Sourcebook 1*, Article 11, page 49, and Article 12, page 51).

How will the activities meet the needs of less able spellers?

Some of the activities in *Spelling Sourcebook 3* are included for typical learners, but there are also activities for students who need extra reinforcement with spelling and language concepts (for additional ways to meet the learning needs of students with spelling problems, see *Spelling Sourcebook 1*, Article 13, page 53). These students will particularly benefit from the activities that develop visual skills. Though many skills are interwoven for spelling facility, the visual modality is the dominant skill for spelling success (for additional visual development ideas see *Spelling Sourcebook 1*, Article 7, page 29). These students also benefit by being included in the discussion of the language-learning activities and projects generated by the typical and more-capable learners. Language facility is acquired through example and practice.

Is it necessary to teach all of the activities?

No one should teach all the suggested activities in *Spelling Sourcebook 3*; there are too many. Rather, the activity ideas are a menu of options from which to choose as an integrated spelling and language program is taught. The most effective instruction for most students would employ a variety of activities so that the students receive a balanced curriculum of skills and their application.

How should activities be selected for instruction?

The teacher makes the activity decisions, just as the teacher decides how many Core Words to include in a unit and the time frame for teaching a unit (see *Spelling Sourcebook 1*, Article 2, page 9). The instructional philosophy of the teacher and the needs of the students should provide the guidelines for activity selections—which activities to include in the program, which students should be assigned which activities, and the format of the activities.

Are the activities designed for independent seatwork or teacher-directed instruction?

Spelling Sourcebook 3 does not stipulate the instructional format for the activities. Teachers may choose to assign activities as independent work for individual students or students in small cooperative-work groups; or use the activities as teacher-directed instruction to individuals, small groups, or the whole class. An activity that would be appropriate for independent work for some students might also only be effective with teacher direction for other students. The teacher, not the program, makes this decision.

How is review achieved?

The activity ideas incorporate systematic review of concepts and words, especially those that routinely present a persistent spelling challenge. However, teachers can increase the review as necessary by teaching activities for previous words that were not selected for initial instruction and systematically including selected review words on current spelling preview or review tests. This review complements the built-in *Sourcebook* system for review and mastery of specific words students misspell or misuse in their writing (see *Spelling Sourcebook 1*, Article 8, page 33, Article 9, page 39, and Article 11, page 49).

What are student expectations for accurate spelling and use of words in the writing activities of Spelling Sourcebook 3?

As writing activities are assigned from the suggestions in *Spelling Sourcebook 3*, students should be reminded to proofread their work. Which words are unacceptable for students to misspell or misuse in their writing? The answer depends upon the kind of writing lesson it is.

The *Spelling Sourcebook* suggestions for writing consist of everyday writing experiences and topics for writing-as-a-process assignments. In both situations, students are afforded spelling references for the words for which they are accountable—words unacceptable to misspell or misuse. However, selected activities could be used for a "no-reference" writing piece in which a spelling reference is not provided to students (see *Spelling Sourcebook 1*, Article 10, page 45).

Spelling accountability for everyday writing is for the current list of Core Words, any technical reference words (see *Spelling Sourcebook 1*, Article 3, page 17), as well as students' Priority Words (see *Spelling Sourcebook 1*, Article 8, page 33, and Article 9, page 39). One hundred percent accuracy in spelling is not expected on everyday writing pieces for developing writers. However, writing-as-a-process assignments progress through various stages of refinement to the final copy—a perfectly proofread piece void of all errors. In most instances, the teacher can decide which format to employ as writing is assigned. In general, when a class-made or student book is a suggested activity, a "published" work is developed through writing-as-a-process toward an error-free final copy.

Which activities in Spelling Sourcebook 3 provide the best information for spelling assessment?

Grading the activities that are selected for instruction from *Spelling Sourcebook 3* is a small factor in total spelling assessment. In fact, most of the activities aren't designed to be completed for a grade. Among the activity options, the most important evaluative information would be derived from students' spelling on the assigned writing activities. Spelling mastery, as defined by the *Sourcebook* methodology, is achieved only in writing. The writing activity ideas offer opportunities for authentic evaluation, as well as for performance assessment (for spelling evaluation guidelines see *Spelling Sourcebook 1*, Article 10, page 45).

How does Spelling Sourcebook 3 complement Spelling Sourcebook 1 to ensure spelling mastery?

Spelling Sourcebook 3 provides abundant language-integrated ideas for making spelling instruction a meaningful complement to the writing-rich curriculum. But the activities do *NOT constitute a total spelling program*. The activity options simply support the *Spelling Sourcebook* methodology outlined in *Spelling Sourcebook 1*. Implemented together, *Spelling Sourcebook 1*, the program design; and *Spelling Sourcebook 3*, the support activities for words 401–800, offer commonsense strategies for ensuring language learning and spelling growth where it really counts—in writing.

Activities to Teach and Extend High-Frequency Core Words 401–800

401 *round*

Other Word Forms,
Vocabulary Skills,
Writing Questions and Answers

❖ Have students brainstorm for common other word forms of *round: rounded, rounding, rounder, roundest.* Discuss unfamiliar words. Have students write the other word forms in sentences that ask a question. Then have students exchange papers and answer the questions using the same word forms of *round* in the responses.

Sound-Symbol Awareness,
Writing Words

❖ Have students write *round* and underline the *ou.* Have students write the following words and underline the *ou: though* (330), *brought* (327), *course* (317), *group* (295), *young* (256), *enough* (209), *should* (156). Then have them find and write more *ou* words. Point out that the *ou* is an unreliable spelling pattern, as it stands for a variety of sounds in words.

Antonyms

❖ Ask students to identify the antonym of *round,* the word *square.*

Idiomatic Usage,
Writing Explanations

❖ Have students explain in writing what they think it means to say these expressions (then discuss):

round numbers	like a square peg in a round hole
to round something up	round trip (See literature entry below.)

Book Tie-In, Making a Poster

❖ Use *Round Trip* (Ann Jonas, Morrow, 1983), a unique description of a day-trip to the city past farms and silos. Turn the book around and return to the country in the dark. Students can have fun making the round trip in this tale, a turn-about story with turn-about art. Follow up with students making a turn-about poster featuring coming and going on a round trip.

402 *dark*

Other Word Forms, Vocabulary
Skills, Alphabetical Order

❖ Have students brainstorm for common other word forms of *dark: darker, darkest, darkish, darkening, darken, darkened.* Discuss unfamiliar words. Have students write the other word forms in alphabetical order.

Antonyms

❖ Ask students to write the antonym of *dark,* the word *light* (227).

Book Tie-In,
Writing a "Pourquoi" Story

❖ Use *A Promise to the Sun: An African Story* (Tololwa Mollel, Joy Street, 1992), a *pourquoi,* or "why," story that explains why bats fly only after dark. Follow up with students writing a *pourquoi* story that provides a fictional explanation of a scientific fact. Then have students research and write about animals that are nocturnal, such as bats. Nocturnal animals are active after dark.

Book Tie-In, Writing Poetry,
Creating a Book

❖ Use *Nightmares: Poems to Trouble Your Sleep* (Jack Prelutsky, Greenwillow, 1976), a book of scary poems to make anyone afraid of the dark. Creatures featured in the poems include a wizard, ghoul, ogre, werewolf, and skeleton. Ask students to invent and describe in writing their own "Creature to Trouble Your Sleep." Compile the stories into a class-made book (see page 138, Creating Classroom Books). Have students read their scary descriptions aloud to the class.

403 *past*

Homophone Usage, Book Tie-In, Writing Riddles ❖ Introduce the homophone of *past,* the word *passed.* Have students write the homophones in sentences to differentiate them. Then use *Hey, Hay! A Wagonful of Funny Homonym Riddles* (Marvin Terban, Clarion, 1991), a collection of brainteasers in which the answers are all homophones— sometimes two, three, and four words that sound the same. Follow up with students writing their own silly riddles using homophones.

Antonyms ❖ Ask students to identify an antonym of *past,* the word *present.*

Book Tie-In, Writing a Journal ❖ Use *Dreamplace* (George Ella Lyon, Jackson, 1993), which uses dreamy watercolor paintings to tell a tale of the past Anasazi culture in Mesa Verde, Colorado. Have students follow up the reading by writing a journal entry about one day in the life of a typical Anasazi cliff dweller of long ago.

404 *ball*

Idiomatic Usage, Writing Explanations ❖ Have students explain in writing what they think it means to say these expressions (then discuss):

    to drop the ball   on the ball

    to get the ball rolling   That's the way the ball bounces.

Writing a List, Book Tie-In, Research and Writing, Public Speaking ❖ Have students list sports and games that use a ball (bowling, basketball, football, soccer, golf, handball, ping-pong, volleyball, baseball, tennis). Then have students research a person who has excelled in one of these sports. Resources could include *Sports Great Joe Montana* (Jack Kavanagh, Enslow, 1992), *Magic Johnson: Champion With a Cause* (Keith Greenburg, Lerner, 1992), and *Zina Garrison: Ace* (A. P. Porter, Lerner, 1992). Have students report their findings in writing and orally to the class.

Writing Words ❖ Have students play Spelling Baseball with selected troublesome spellings (see **Spelling Sourcebook 1**, page 91).

Multiple Meanings, Writing a Definition, Writing Explanations ❖ Remind students that some words have more than one meaning. Have students write a definition for the meaning of *ball* as used in the story of Cinderella. Have them locate the ball of the foot. Students knowledgeable of baseball and softball may write an explanation for the calls *strike* and *ball.*

Homophone Usage, Vocabulary Skills ❖ Introduce the homophone of *ball,* the word *bawl.* Contrast *bawl* with *brawl.* Discuss the word meanings.

Visual Skill-Building ❖ Write the word *balloon* on the chalkboard. Have students write the word and underline the word *ball* inside.

405 *girl*

Other Word Forms, Suffix Practice, Writing Questions ❖ Have students brainstorm for common other word forms of *girl: girls, girlish, girlhood.* Discuss the suffix *hood.* Have students brainstorm for other words with the *hood* suffix. Choices may include *boyhood, childhood, neighborhood, priesthood, statehood.* Then have students write the other word forms of *girl* in sentences that ask a question, exchange papers, and write answers to the questions.

Antonym ❖ Ask students to write the antonym of *girl,* the word *boy* (205).

Sound-Symbol Awareness, Writing Words ❖ Have students write *girl* and underline the *ir.* Then have students find and write more words that contain an *ir* as in *girl,* such as *first* (74), *bird, circle, third.*

406 *road*

Other Word Forms,
Writing Sentences
❖ Have students brainstorm for common other word forms of *road: roads, roadblock, roadside, roadway.* Have students write the other word forms in sentences.

Homophone Usage
❖ Introduce the homophones of *road,* the words *rode* and *rowed.* Have students write the homophones in sentences to differentiate them. Then have students find and write more homophone sets. Next, have students play the game Mystery Words using the homophone sets (see *Spelling Sourcebook 1,* page 89).

Writing Abbreviations
❖ Introduce the abbreviation for *road (Rd./rd.).* Ask students to research and list abbreviations for more street names, such as *St., Blvd., Ct., Ave., Hwy., Ln.*

Sound-Symbol Awareness,
Sorting Words
❖ Have students write *road* and listen to the long *o* sound. Then have students collect more words with the long *o* sound to note the most frequent spellings for long *o* (most common: *o* [*no*], *o*-consonant-*e* [*those*], *ow* [*show*], *oa* [*coat*], *old* [*cold*], *oe* [*toe*]). Create a list of long *o* words. Have students write the words in categories sorted by the spelling for the long *o.* Have one category for "other" to accommodate less common spellings.

407 *blue*

Homophone Usage
❖ Introduce the homophone of *blue,* the word *blew.* Have students write the homophones in sentences to differentiate them.

Idiomatic Usage,
Writing Explanations
❖ Have students explain in writing what they think it means to say these expressions (then discuss):

    out of the blue   once in a blue moon
    talk a blue streak   blue Monday (See literature entry below.)
    to get the blues   to fly the red, white, and blue

Book Tie-In, Writing Days of the
Week, Writing Abbreviations
❖ Use *Blue Monday and Friday the Thirteenth* (Lila Perl, Ticknor, 1986) to explore fact and fantasy concerning each day of the week. Have students write the days of the week and their abbreviations.

Multiple Meanings,
Writing Sentences
❖ Brainstorm for meanings of *blue.* Then have students check a dictionary for verification. Review words that can be used in different ways, such as *will* (46), *through* (102), *too* (112), *right* (116), *point* (272), *draw* (338), *letter* (344), *state* (371). Have students write the words in sentences to illustrate their different meanings. Then have students play Password using words that have more than one meaning (see *Spelling Sourcebook 1,* page 89).

408 *instead*

Synonyms, Creating a Book
❖ Have students create booklets of synonyms for selected words (see page 138, Creating Classroom Books). Choices may include the overused words *nice, said,* and *walk.* Title the booklets "Instead of <u>Nice</u>" (or <u>Said</u> or <u>Walk</u>). Encourage students to use their "Instead of" references as a resource for synonyms as they write.

409 *either*

Visual Skill-Building, Writing Sentences

Write *either* on the chalkboard, and draw an outline around it to accentuate its shape. Provide students with graph paper (or use the blackline master on page 108 of *Spelling Sourcebook 1*). Have students write the word in the boxes and outline its shape (see Letter Grid Games on page 88 of *Spelling Sourcebook 1*). Then have students make word shapes for review words, exchange papers with a partner, and see if the partner can fill in the boxes with the appropriate words. Next have students write sentences using these words.

410 *held*

Other Word Forms, Writing Sentences

Have students brainstorm for common other word forms of *held: hold, holds, holding, holder, holders.* Have students write the other word forms in sentences.

Writing a List

Have students list different kinds of holders. Choices may include a pot holder, candle holder, magazine holder, and pencil holder.

Sorting Words

Have students play Word Sorts (see *Spelling Sourcebook 1*, page 92) using these words: *old* (144), *here* (134), *high* (224), *horse* (385), *world* (191), *children* (200), *hold* (370), *wild, healthy.*

411 *already*

Word Analysis, Dictation and Writing, Writing Sentences, Word Meanings

Have students write *already* and *all ready*. Differentiate the words. Then dictate these partial sentences for students to write and complete:

When the food is all ready to eat, _____ .
I've already learned _____ .
It's already too late to _____ .
The team is all ready for the game when _____ .

Then discuss and have students write in sentences *always* (183), *all ways, altogether,* and *all together.*

412 *warm*

Other Word Forms, Writing Questions and Answers

Have students brainstorm for common other word forms of *warm: warms, warmed, warming.* Have students write the other word forms in sentences that ask a question. Then have students exchange papers and answer the questions using the same word forms of *warm* in the responses.

Other Word Forms, Writing Words

Have students play All in the Family (see *Spelling Sourcebook 1*, page 86) using the other word forms of *warm* and the other word forms of selected review words.

Antonyms

Ask students to identify the antonym of *warm,* the word *cool.*

Research and Writing

Ask students to write "Tips for Staying Warm in Cold Weather." Have students research the topic. The research may include interviewing outdoor sports experts, doctors, nutritionists, ski clothing sales people, or anyone having an idea about how best to guard against the cold and keep warm.

413 *gone*

Other Word Forms, Writing Sentences

❖ Have students brainstorm for common other word forms of *gone: go* (105), *went* (143), *goes, going*. Have students write the other word forms in sentences. Then have students rearrange the words in each sentence and delete capitals and punctuation. Partners then exchange and unscramble the sentences trying to match the word order of the original sentences.

❖ Ask students to write the antonym of *gone,* the word *come* (123).

414 *finally*

Word Analysis, Writing Sentences

❖ Have students write *finally* and another word form of *fine* (400), *finely*. Then have students write the words in sentences to differentiate these often-confused words. Review *then* (53) and *than* (73), *are* (15) and *our* (109).

Suffix Practice, Vocabulary Skills

❖ Have students write *final*. Then add the *ly* suffix to make *finally*. Have students find and write words with the *ly* suffix, such as *warmly* (*warm* 412), *strongly* (*strong* 381), *completely* (*complete* 365), *nearly* (*near* 243). Next have students write *final* and add the *ize* suffix to it to make *finalize*. Then have students add *ize* to *special* (361) and *real* (*really* 313). Discuss the meanings of the words with the *ize* suffix. Then have students write the words with the *ly* and *ize* suffixes in sentences.

415 *summer*

Other Word Forms, Word Analysis, Hypothesizing

❖ Have students brainstorm for common other word forms of *summer: summery, summertime*. Have students contrast *summery* and *summary*. Have students answer this question: What do you think might happen if summertime weather disappeared forever from your region?

Antonyms

❖ Ask students to identify the antonym of *summer,* the word *winter* and predict its spelling.

Book Tie-In, Writing a Letter

❖ Use *The Sierra Club Summer Book* (Linda Allison, Little, 1989) for abundant activities on how to spend a summer day. Follow up with students writing an imaginary letter to a friend telling about what they did on a summer day.

Book Tie-In, Writing a List, Making Predictions

❖ Ask students which holiday is celebrated on a midsummer July day in the United States. Then introduce a fact-filled Fourth of July wordbook, *Doodle Dandy!: The Complete Book of Independence Day Words* (Lynda Graham-Barber, Bradbury, 1992). Prior to reading, have students list words they think may be featured in the book.

416 *understand*

Other Word Forms, Prefix Practice, Writing Sentences

❖ Have students brainstorm for common other word forms of *understand: understands, understanding, understood, understandable*. Have students write the *mis* prefix before *understand,* and discuss how the prefix changes the meaning. Have students write the other word forms in sentences.

Research and Writing, Public Speaking

❖ Explain to students that a good way to understand something better is to prepare to teach it to someone. Have students research a current controversial topic, tell about both sides to the controversy in writing, and then present the information orally to help the class understand the issues.

Dictation and Writing ❖ Dictate these partial sentences for students to write and complete:
I don't understand why _____ .
My mother can't understand _____ .
I understand things best at school when _____ .

417 *moon*

Other Word Forms, Vocabulary Skills, Writing Sentences ❖ Have students brainstorm for common other word forms of *moon: moons, moonbeams, moonlight, moonlit*. Discuss unfamiliar words. Have students write the other word forms in sentences. Then have students play Go to the Moon (see *Spelling Sourcebook 1*, page 90, a variation of Race Track Spelling) using the other word forms of *moon* and selected review words and their other word forms.

Book Tie-In, Writing Legends ❖ Have students study legends of the *moon* beginning with *Legends of the Sun and Moon* (Eric and Tessa Hadley, Cambridge, 1983) and the picture book *Witch Hazel* (Alice Schertle, HarperCollins, 1991), an explanation for the moon's emergence into the sky. Ask students to write and illustrate their own moon legends.

Book Tie-In, Research and Writing ❖ Use *The Moon Seems to Change* (Franklyn Branley, Harper, 1987) about our ever-changing understanding of the moon. Have students write a sequel story featuring more recently-discovered information about the moon. Students may wish to use the *Reader's Guide* for gathering sources for this information.

Book Tie-In, Hypothesizing ❖ Use *To the Moon and Back: A Collection of Poems* (Nancy Larrick, Selector, Dial, 1991). Then ask students to write why they think Larrick chose this title for her book.

418 *animals*

Book Tie-In, Creating a Book, Reading ❖ Use *Animals Should Definitely Not Wear Clothing* (Judi Barrett, Atheneum, 1970). Read aloud the first 3–4 pages. Then have students use the book as a model for their own class-made book (see page 138, Creating Classroom Books). When the book is complete, have a student read the rest of Barrett's book to the class and the students' book.

Book Tie-In, Writing a Book Jacket ❖ Introduce a fine collection of poetry for all ages on the topic of animals, *A Zooful of Animals* (William Cole, Houghton, 1992). Follow up with students writing a book jacket that would entice readers.

419 *mind*

Multiple Meanings, Writing a List ❖ Brainstorm for meanings of *mind.* Then have students check a dictionary for verification. Review the different meanings of *fine* (400) and *blue* (407). Then have students create a list of words that can be used in more than one way.

Other Word Forms, Vocabulary Skills, Writing Questions and Answers, Hypothesizing ❖ Have students brainstorm for common other word forms of *mind: minds, minded, minding, mindful*. Discuss unfamiliar words. Have students write this question and the answer: What should you do if you went to the grocery store and you could find no one there minding the store?

Homophone Usage ❖ Introduce the homophone of *mind*, the word *mined*. Have students write the homophones in sentences to differentiate them.

Reasoning Skills, Writing Riddles and Brain Teasers ❖ Have students use their mind by reading *Lightning Inside You: And Other Native American Riddles* (John Bierhorst, Editor, Morrow, 1992), which offers thought-provoking projects that build insights into Native American culture. Also use *Merlin Book of Logic Puzzles* (Margaret Edmiston, Sterling, 1992) and *Mind Twisters* (Godfrey Hall, Random, 1992). Then follow up with students finding and writing a riddle or brain teaser for the class to try to solve.

Book Tie-In, Writing Descriptions ❖ Use the picture book *Cakes and Miracles: A Purim Tale* (Barbara Goldin, Viking, 1991), in which a blind boy creates pictures in his mind. Follow up with students writing descriptions of the mind pictures they can create.

Idiomatic Usage, Writing Explanations ❖ Have students explain in writing what they think it means to say these expressions (then discuss):

to change your mind	to lose your mind
to have something on your mind	to mind your own business
to have something in mind	to mind your p's and q's
to give someone a piece of your mind	Out of sight, out of mind.

420 *outside*

Antonyms ❖ Ask students to write the antonym of *outside,* the word *inside* (321).

Dictation and Writing ❖ Dictate these partial sentences for students to write and complete:

When it's cold outside, I _____ .

In the summer on a hot day outside, I _____ .

Book Tie-In, Making Predictions, Writing Reasons ❖ Use *Outstanding Outsides* (Hana Machotka, Morrow, 1993), a scientific picture book that introduces "outsides," such as snake scales and hedgehog spines. Have students try to identify the "outsides" before revealing the answers. Ask students to write their guesses and provide reasons for their choices.

421 *power*

Other Word Forms, Vocabulary Skills, Writing Sentences ❖ Have students brainstorm for common other word forms of *power: powers, powered, powering, powerful, powerfully, powerless.* Discuss unfamiliar words. Have students write the other word forms in sentences.

Book Tie-In, Reasearch and Writing ❖ Use *Wind Power* (Mike Cross, Gloucester, 1985) for a look at this interesting source of power. Ask students to find and write other power sources. Answers may include solar, water, geothermal, nuclear, atomic, natural gas, and oil.

Research and Writing, Public Speaking ❖ Have students research one of the following topics, tell about their findings in writing, and then present the information orally to the class:

a powerful political leader of the past and how the leader used the power in a positive way

a powerful political leader of the past and how the leader used the power in a negative way

a currently powerful political leader and what you'd like to see the leader do with the power

422 *problem*

Book Tie-In,
Writing Explanations

Use *What, Me Worry?: How to Hang In When Your Problems Stress You Out* (Alice Fleming, Scribner, 1992) for commonsense solutions to everyday problems of youngsters and young adults. The book's anecdotes of problems faced and solved by famous people can be a catalyst for students writing about their problems and explaining their solutions.

Dictation and Writing,
Hypothesizing

Dictate this partial sentence for students to write and complete:
The biggest problem in the United States (or Canada) is _____ .

423 *longer*

Antonyms, Writing Words

Ask students to identify the antonym of *longer,* the word *shorter.*
Then have students write the antonyms of *meaner (kinder—kind* 214), *lower (higher—high* 224), *darker (lighter—light* 227), *older (younger—young* 256), *earlier (later* 288), *taller (shorter—short* 304), *hotter (colder—cold* 312), *slower (faster—fast* 376).

Creating a Word Puzzle,
Antonyms

Have students create a crossword puzzle using the antonym of the game word as the clue. (Use graph paper or the blackline master grid on page 108 of **Spelling Sourcebook 1**.)

424 *winter*

Other Word Forms, Vocabulary
Skills, Writing Sentences

Have students brainstorm for common other word forms of *winter: winters, wintered, wintering, wintry.* Discuss unfamiliar words. Have students write the other word forms in sentences.

Antonyms

Ask students to write the antonym of *winter,* the word *summer* (415).

Book Tie-In, Writing a Journal

Use *An Indian Winter* (Russell Freedman, Holiday, 1992), a journal and text describing Maximillian's winter of 1833–1834 with the Hidatsa and Mandan peoples in what is now North Dakota. Then have students write a journal entry for one of the people that describes a problem faced during that winter.

Book Tie-In,
Research and Writing

Use *Where Do They Go? Insects in Winter* (Millicent Selsam, Macmillan, 1982) to investigate how 12 species of insects cope with winter. Ask students to select another animal species' winter habits to research and write about.

Writing Names of Cities,
Comparing and Contrasting,
Research and Writing

Provide students with two small slips of paper. Have students write the name of a city outside their state or province on each slip. Place the papers in a container, and have each student draw one slip. Next, have them compare and contrast the winter of the city written on the drawn paper with that of their own city. Have students research the information and report the results in writing.

425 *deep*

Other Word Forms,
Vocabulary Skills,
Writing Questions and Answers

Have students brainstorm for common other word forms of *deep: deeper, deepest, deeply, deepen, deepens, deepened, deepening.* Discuss unfamiliar words. Have students write the other word forms in sentences that ask a question. Then have students exchange papers and answer the questions using the same word forms of *deep* in the responses.

Book Tie-In, Making a Poster ❖ Use *Window on the Deep: The Adventures of Underwater Explorer Sylvia Earle* (Andrea Conley, Watts, 1991) for a pictorial introduction to scuba diving and life in the deep ocean, and *Sharks and Other Creatures of the Deep* (Philip Steele, Dorling, 1991), a compendium of information about the unusual inhabitants deep in the oceans. Follow up by asking students to create a poster featuring life in the deep.

Antonyms ❖ Ask students to identify the antonym of *deep*, the word *shallow* and predict its spelling.

Sound-Symbol Awareness, Sorting Words ❖ Have students write *deep* and listen to the long *e* sound. Then have students collect more words with long *e* to note the most frequent spellings for the long *e* (most common: *ee* [*see*], *e* [*me*], *ea* [*eat*], *e*-consonant-*e* [*these*]). Create a list of long *e* words. Have students write the words in categories sorted by the spelling for the long *e*. Have one category for "other" to accommodate less common spellings.

426 *heavy*

Other Word Forms, Spelling Rules, Suffix Practice, Plural Practice, Writing Sentences ❖ Have students brainstorm for common other word forms of *heavy: heavier, heaviest, heavily, heaviness*. Discuss unfamiliar words. Review the spelling rule for adding suffixes to words ending in consonant-*y* (see *Spelling Sourcebook 1*, page 85). Have students apply the rule by adding appropriate suffixes to *ready* (357) and *early* (324). Then have students create plurals of *body* (285), *city* (273), *story* (237), *study* (234), and *country* (228). Have students write sentences using the words they made.

Antonyms ❖ Ask students to write the antonym of *heavy*, the word *light* (227).

Writing Similes ❖ Use *A Surfeit of Similes* (Norton Juster, Morrow, 1989), which introduces similes through humorous conversations. Then ask students to write similes using the frame: "as heavy as ____ ." Continue making similes with a review of *little* (92), *large* (185), *hard* (242), *hot* (368), *fast* (376), *round* (401), and *deep* (425).

427 *carefully*

Other Word Forms, Writing Sentences ❖ Have students brainstorm for common other word forms of *carefully: care, cared, caring, careless, carelessness, carelessly, careful, carefulness*. Have students write the other word forms in sentences. Then have students rearrange the words in each sentence and delete capitals and punctuation. Partners then exchange and unscramble the sentences trying to match the word order of the original sentences.

Suffix Practice, Writing Words ❖ Have students write *care* and then add *ful* (suffix meaning "full of") and the *ly* suffix to make *carefully*. Have them repeat the pattern with *help* (137), *thought* (179), *rest* (351), *power* (421), *peace, joy,* and *success*. Then have students play Connect the Dots (see *Spelling Sourcebook 1*, page 87) using words with the *ful* and *ly* suffixes.

428 *follow*

Other Word Forms,
Writing Questions and Answers,
Hypothesizing

Have students brainstorm for common other word forms of *follow: follows, followed, following, follower.* Have students write this question and the answer: What would you do if you thought someone was following you and your friend while you were shopping at the mall? Then discuss students' answers and agree on appropriate behaviors.

Book Tie-In, Writing Stories

Use *Follow Me* (Nancy Tafuri, Greenwillow, 1990), a young child's wordless picture story about a sea lion who follows a crab on an exploring trip. Have students write a text for the story appropriate for young readers. They may then share the results with young children.

Visual Skill-Building,
Writing Words, Writing Sentences

Play the Word Look-Alike game. Ask students to circle the words in each row that are like the underlined word. Then they turn the paper over, picture the underlined word, and write it.

<u>follow</u>	yellow	fellow	mellow	follow	dollar	follow
<u>mind</u>	find	mined	dine	mend	mind	mint
<u>moon</u>	moan	noon	moon	moon	room	mood
<u>warm</u>	worm	warm	arms	want	warn	warm
<u>past</u>	post	mast	last	pest	passed	past

Next, have students write the underlined words in sentences.

429 *beautiful*

Other Word Forms, Vocabulary
Skills, Writing Sentences

Have students brainstorm for common other word forms of *beautiful: beautifully, beauty, beautify, beautifies, beautified, beautifying.* Discuss unfamiliar words. Have students write the other word forms in sentences.

Book Tie-In, Writing Speculations

Use *Miss Rumphius* (Barbara Cooney, Viking, 1982), in which Miss Rumphius promises her grandfather that she will make the world a more beautiful place. Ask students to write one thing they would do if they had made the same promise.

Book Tie-In,
Comparing and Contrasting

Use *Vasilissa the Beautiful* (Elizabeth Winthrop, Adapter, HarperCollins, 1991), a Russian fairy tale reminiscent of "Cinderella" and "Hansel and Gretel." Following the reading, have students compare and contrast this tale with another that has similarities.

Antonyms, Writing Stories

Ask students to identify the antonym of *beautiful,* the word *ugly.* Have students find two versions of "The Ugly Duckling," read them, and then write their own version.

Synonyms, Writing a List

Ask students to list synonyms for *beautiful,* such as *pretty, attractive, lovely, wonderful, gorgeous.*

430 *everyone*

Dictation and Writing,
Hypothesizing

Dictate these partial sentences for students to write and complete:
  I want everyone to _____ .
  The one thing everyone wants changed is _____ .
  Almost everyone likes to eat _____ .

Analogies, Writing Sentences ❖ Review analogies. Then have students write these analogies and complete them with words of frequencies 400–430:

> no thing : nothing :: every one : _____ (everyone)
> can : can't :: ugly : _____ (beautiful)
> power : powerfully :: care : _____ (carefully)
> warm : summer :: cool : _____ (winter)
> passed : past :: rode : _____ (road or rowed)

Then have students write the answer words in sentences.

431 *leave*

Other Word Forms, Spelling Rules, Suffix Practice, Writing Words, Visual Skill-Building ❖ Have students brainstorm for common other word forms of *leave: leaves, left* (169), *leaving.* Review the spelling rule for adding suffixes to words ending in silent *e* (see **Spelling Sourcebook 1**, page 85). Review adding the *ing* to *notice* (379), *complete* (365), *become* (336), *close* (328), *move* (290), *give* (159), *name* (155), *take* (135), *come* (123), *write* (108), *make* (72), *have* (25). Have students write their *ing* words in the boxes of a grid (use graph paper or the blackline grid on page 108 of **Spelling Sourcebook 1**). Then have students outline each word written in the grid to accentuate its shape.

Idiomatic Usage, Writing Explanations ❖ Have students explain in writing what they think it means to say these expressions (then discuss):

> leave no stone unturned
> to leave someone holding the bag
> to leave well enough alone
> to leave something or someone out
> Take it or leave it.
> to take leave of your senses

432 *everything*

Antonyms ❖ Ask students to write the antonym of *everything,* the word *nothing* (329).

Compound Words ❖ Have students write *every* and *thing.* Then have them write compounds that use one of these words, such as *everybody, everywhere, nothing* (329), *something* (178).

433 *game*

Multiple Meanings, Writing Sentences ❖ Brainstorm for meanings of *game.* Then have students check a dictionary for verification. Review words that can be used in different ways, such as *left* (169), *might* (173), *sound* (175), *saw* (177), *state* (371), *stand* (387), *class* (391), *fine* (400), *blue* (407), *mind* (419). Have students write the words in sentences to illustrate their different meanings.

Other Word Forms, Vocabulary Skills, Writing Sentences ❖ Have students brainstorm for common other word forms of *game: games, gaming, gamely, gamy.* Discuss unfamiliar words. Have students write the other word forms in sentences. Then have students list their favorite games to play or watch.

Book Tie-In, Reasoning Skills, Creating a Book ❖ Challenge students to play the thinking games they'll find in *Mathemagic* (Raymond Blum, Sterling, 1991) and *Ghostly Games* (John Speirs, Random, 1991). Have students create a class-made book of thinking games using these or other sources for entries (see page 138, Creating Classroom Books).

434   *system*

Book Tie-In, Research and Writing

Introduce students to our solar system with *The Children's Space Atlas: A Voyage of Discovery for Young Astronauts* (Robin Kerrod, Millbrook, 1992). Then have students choose one planet to research. Have them summarize their findings in writing. Sources may include the books *Mercury* and *Venus* (Seymour Simon, Morrow, 1992).

Vocabulary Development

Have students find and write instances for which we use the word *system*. Choices may include circulatory system, weather system, stereo system, watering system, nervous system.

435   *bring*

Other Word Forms, Writing Questions and Answers, Hypothesizing

Have students brainstorm for common other word forms of *bring: brings, brought* (327), *bringing*. Have students write this question and the answer: What do you think might happen if the principal brought nine new students into your class today?

Idiomatic Usage, Writing Explanations

Have students explain in writing what they think it means to say these expressions (then discuss):

to bring home the bacon   to bring up the rear
to bring something about   to bring the house down
to bring something to a close   to bring something up

Book Tie-In, Research and Writing, Making a Poster

Use *Bringing Back the Animals* (Teresa Kennedy, Amethyst, 1991) for information about 12 endangered animals, each pictured in a double-page spread. Have students choose one of the animals featured and research current information on its endangered status. They may then create a poster featuring information about the endangered animal with ideas of what must be done to save it.

436   *watch*

Other Word Forms, Writing Sentences, Multiple Meanings, Spelling Rules

Have students brainstorm for common other word forms of *watch: watches, watched, watching, watcher*. Have students write the other word forms in sentences. Discuss the different meanings of *watch* and *watches* (noun and verb). Review the spelling rule for making *watch* into *watches* (see **Spelling Sourcebook 1**, page 85).

Book Tie-In, Making a Chart

Use *The TV Kid* (Betsy Byars, Viking, 1976), the tale of a boy who watches so much TV that he can no longer distinguish reality from fantasy. Follow up by asking students to make a personal chart of the amount of TV they watch for one week.

437   *shell*

Sound-Symbol Awareness, Writing Words

Have students write *shell* and underline the *sh*. Point out that *sh* always makes the sound the students hear at the beginning of *shell*. However, there are other spellings for *sh*. Ask students to brainstorm for these. Choices may include *sure* (251), *spacious* (space 320), *special* (361), *machine, addition, nation, pressure, ocean*. Have students write the words and underline the letters making the *sh* sound.

Contractions, Word Analysis, Writing Sentences

Have students write *she will*. Then have them write its contraction *she'll*. Contrast *she'll* with *shell*. Have students write the two words in sentences.

438 *dry*

Other Word Forms,
Spelling Rules, Suffix Practice

Have students brainstorm for common other word forms of *dry: drier, driest, dries, dried, drying.* Review the spelling rule for adding suffixes to words ending in consonant-*y* (see ***Spelling Sourcebook 1***, page 85). Have students apply the rule by adding appropriate suffixes to *try* (254), *fry, cry, pry, shy.* Have students write sentences using the words they made.

Antonyms

Ask students to identify the antonym of *dry,* the word *wet.*

Book Tie-In, Choral Reading,
Research and Writing

Use *Bringing the Rain to Kapiti Plain* (Verna Aardema, Dial, 1981), which tells in rhyme how rain was brought to Kapiti Plain to end the severe drought. Enjoy the cumulative story chorally with students. Then have students locate on a map places where water is often scarce. Have students find out ways people in these areas conserve water.

439 *within*

Compound Words, Writing Words

Have students play Compound Bingo (see ***Spelling Sourcebook 1***, page 87) with *within* and selected compounds.

Visual Skill-Building,
Writing Words

Have students write *within.* Then have them write words inside *within* (*wit, it, with, thin, in*). Expand the words-in-words activity to selected review words and words students wish to use from other subject areas.

440 *floor*

Other Word Forms, Vocabulary
Skills, Writing Sentences

Have students brainstorm for common other word forms of *floor: floors, floored, flooring, floorboard.* Discuss unfamiliar words. Have students write the other word forms in sentences. Then have students rearrange the words in each sentence and delete capitals and punctuation. Partners then exchange and unscramble the sentences trying to match the word order of the original sentences.

Sound-Symbol Awareness,
Writing Words

Have students write *floor* and underline the *oo.* Then ask them to list more words with *oo* to conclude that *oo* makes various sounds in words. Among the words they may list are *good* (106), *school* (194), *door* (292), and *moon* (417).

441 *ice*

Other Word Forms, Vocabulary
Skills, Spelling Rules, Writing
Questions and Answers

Have students brainstorm for common other word forms of *ice: ices, iced, icing, icy, iceberg.* Discuss unfamiliar words. Review the spelling rule for adding suffixes to words ending in silent *e* (see ***Spelling Sourcebook 1***, page 85). Have students write this question and the answer: What is your favorite cake and icing?

Book Tie-In, Writing a List,
Making Predictions,
Making a Chart

Use *Scoop After Scoop: A History of Ice Cream* (Stephen Krensky, Macmillan, 1986). Ask students to list ice cream flavors, write predictions of people's favorites, and then conduct a survey of the favorite kinds. Have students chart the survey results and compare them with their predictions.

Book Tie-In, Writing a Journal

Use *Desert of Ice: Life and Work in Antarctica* (John Hackwell, Scribner, 1991), a brief book about this ice-cold continent. Hackwell was a member of a research expedition to Antarctica. Have students follow up by writing a journal entry as if written by Hackwell on the journey.

442 *ship*

Other Word Forms,
Writing Questions and Answers,
Hypothesizing

Have students brainstorm for common other word forms of *ship: ships, shipped, shipping, shipment, shipshape, shipyard.* Have students write this question and the answer: What might be happening now if a shipment of boxes containing five hundred baby chicks had been delivered to your school early this morning?

Spelling Rules, Suffix Practice,
Writing Sentences

Review the spelling rule for doubling the final consonant before adding suffixes (see **Spelling Sourcebook 1**, page 85). Have students apply the rule by adding suffixes to *ship, stop* (396), *run* (306), *top* (269), *big* (158), *shop.* Have students write sentences using the words they made.

Book Tie-In, Writing Stories

Use *Sheep on a Ship* (Nancy Shaw, Houghton, 1989) as a model for a sequel tale of the sheep on the ship.

Book Tie-In, Writing a List,
Writing Definitions

For students interested in sailing, use *The Visual Dictionary of Ships and Sailing* (Roger Tritton, Dorling, 1991), which includes information and photographs of different kinds of boats, ropes and knots, navigation, and sails. Follow up with students making a list of sailing terms with definitions appropriate for a newcomer to the topic.

443 *themselves*

Dictation and Writing,
Hypothesizing

Dictate this partial sentence for students to write and complete:
    Some people keep to themselves because _____ .

Analogies, Writing Sentences

Review analogies (see 430). Then have students write these analogies and complete them with words of frequencies 400–443:
    our : ourselves :: them : ____ (themselves)
    plant : tree :: boat : ____ (ship)
    following : follow :: bringing : ____ (bring)
    light : heavy :: ugly : ____ (beautiful)
    mind : mined :: blew : ____ (blue)

Have students write the answer words in sentences.

Plural Practice

Write *self* on the chalkboard. Then have students write its plural *selves.* Have students find *elf* and *elves* inside *self* and *selves.*

444 *begin*

Spelling Rules, Other Word
Forms, Writing Sentences

Review the rule for doubling the final consonant before adding suffixes (see *ship* 442). Ask students to write why *begin* does or does not follow this rule. Then have students brainstorm for common other word forms of *begin: begins, began, begun, beginning, beginner.* Have students write the other word forms in sentences.

Book Tie-In

Use *And in the Beginning* (Sheron Williams, Atheneum, 1992) for a Swahili folktale that intersperses dialect. Have students identify examples of the dialect and then find other tales that make use of dialect.

Antonyms

Ask students to write the antonym of *begin,* the word *end* (170). Have students write *ending, ends, ended* and their antonyms.

Book Tie-In, Creating a Book ❖ Use *Alligators to Zooplankton: A Dictionary of Water Babies* (Les Kaufman, Watts, 1991), unusual stories about how life begins in the water. Use the alphabetical book as a model for students to create dictionaries on a topic of their choice, such as "Arrowhead to Zuni: A Dictionary of Native Americans."

445 *fact*

Other Word Forms, Vocabulary Skills ❖ Have students write *fact* and its common other word forms *fact: facts, factual, factually*. Then they underline *act, acts, actual, actually*. Discuss unfamiliar words.

Book Tie-In, Research and Writing ❖ Use *Animal Fact/Animal Fable* (Seymour Simon, Crown, 1992), an unusual animal information book that states an opinion or fable about an animal followed by the fact. After the reading, ask students to research and write more fact and fable statements to challenge classmates to distinguish.

446 *third*

Dictation and Writing ❖ Dictate these partial sentences for students to write and complete:
I want to be first instead of third when _____ .
I'd like to be third instead of first when _____ .

Writing Words ❖ Have students play the All-Play Spelling Bee, a spelling bee in which students are never eliminated from play (see ***Spelling Sourcebook 1***, page 86), using *third* and selected review words and their other word forms.

447 *quite*

Word Analysis, Writing Sentences ❖ Have students write the look-alike words *quite, quiet,* and *quit*. Then have students write the words in sentences to differentiate them. Then review *our* (109)/*are* (15) and *then* (53)/*than* (73), *picture* (232)/*pitcher, weather/whether* (399), *she'll/shell* (437). Have students write these often-confused words in sentences.

Sound-Symbol Awareness, Writing Words ❖ Point out to students the high reliability of the *qu* spelling pattern. Have students find and write more words in which *q* is followed by *u*, such as *quiet, quick, question, square, equal, quake*.

448 *carry*

Multiple Meanings, Writing Sentences ❖ Brainstorm for meanings of *carry*. Then have students check a dictionary for verification. Review words that can be used in different ways, such as *over* (82), *long* (91), *just* (97), *back* (103), *watch* (436). Have students use the words in sentences to illustrate their different meanings.

Other Word Forms, Vocabulary Skills, Spelling Rules, Suffix Practice, Writing Sentences ❖ Have students brainstorm for common other word forms of *carry: carries, carried, carrying, carrier, carriage*. Discuss unfamiliar words. Review the spelling rule for adding suffixes to words ending in consonant-*y* (see ***Spelling Sourcebook 1***, page 85). Have students apply the rule by adding suffixes to *study* (234), *marry, empty, hurry*. Have students write sentences using the words they made.

*Idiomatic Usage,
Writing Explanations*

Have students explain in writing what they think it means to say these expressions (then discuss):

can't carry a tune	to get carried away
to carry your own weight	to carry something out
cash-and-carry	to carry on

449 *distance*

*Other Word Forms, Vocabulary
Skills, Writing Sentences*

Have students brainstorm for common other word forms of *distance: distant, distantly, distances, distanced, distancing.* Discuss unfamiliar words. Have students write the other word forms in sentences.

*Writing a List, Sequencing,
Writing Abbreviations*

Ask students to list words that denote measures of distance (or length), such as *inch, mile, meter.* Then make a cumulative list of words on the chalkboard. Then they sequence the words from the smallest increments to the largest. Next, have students find and write the abbreviations of the words.

450 *although*

Writing Words, Word Analysis

Dictate these words to students and have them check their spellings, if necessary: *also* (119), *always* (183), *almost* (216), *already* (411), *altogether, almighty.* Then have them write what each of these words has in common (*al*). Contrast the spelling of these words with the spelling of *all right.*

451 *sat*

*Other Word Forms,
Writing Questions and Answers*

Have students brainstorm for common other word forms of *sat: sit, sits, sitting, sitter.* Have students write this question and the answer: If you needed a sitter for one week while your parents were away, whom would you choose? Why?

Suffix Practice, Writing Words

Have students list words that double the final consonant before a suffix that begins with a vowel. Then have them write those words with the appropriate suffixes. Next, have students list words that have a changed past-tense spelling instead of the *ed* ending. Have them write the word and its past tense (*sit–sat*). Choices may include *made* (81), *thought* (179), *came* (122), *went* (143), *found* (152), *saw* (177), *knew* (252), *told* (255), *heard* (262), *done* (294), *ran* (*run* 306), *brought* (327), *became* (334), *grew* (*grow* 337), *built* (360), *stood* (373), *felt* (377), *kept* (378), *held* (410).

452 *possible*

*Other Word Forms,
Vocabulary Skills, Spelling Rules,
Writing Sentences*

Have students brainstorm for common other word forms of *possible: possibly, possibilities.* Discuss unfamiliar words. Review the spelling rule for adding suffixes to words ending in silent *e* (see **Spelling Sourcebook 1**, page 85). Have students write the other word forms in sentences.

Prefix Practice, Writing Sentences

Have students add the prefix *im* to *possible.* Discuss the addition of *im* to *moveable* (*move* 290), *proper, practical, patient,* and *polite.* Discuss how the prefix changes the meaning. Have students write the words with the prefixes in sentences.

Research and Writing,
Hypothesizing, Public Speaking

Have students research one of the following topics, tell about their findings in writing, and then present the information orally to the class:

something that most people thought was impossible years ago, but was achieved

something that most people think is impossible today, but you think is possible and will be achieved

453 *heart*

Multiple Meanings,
Writing Sentences

Brainstorm for meanings of *heart.* Then have students check a dictionary for verification. Review words that can be used in different ways, such as *place* (131), *take* (135), *still* (153), *line* (161), *play* (274), *run* (306), *watch* (436), *carry* (448). Have students write the words in sentences to illustrate their different meanings.

Compound Words,
Vocabulary Skills

Have students find and write compound words that use *heart,* such as *heartache, heartbeat, heartsick, heartthrob, heartstricken, heartbroken, heartbreak, heartburn.* Make a cumulative list on the chalkboard. Discuss unfamiliar words.

Homophone Usage

Introduce the homophone of *heart,* the word *hart* (male deer).

Idiomatic Usage,
Writing Explanations

Have students explain in writing what they think it means to say these expressions (then discuss):

to have a broken heart	a heart-to-heart talk
to follow your heart	to take heart
to get to the heart of the matter	to know something by heart
to eat your heart out	to lose heart
to have a heart of stone	to steal someone's heart
	(See literature entry below.)

Book Tie-In,
Writing a Story Ending

Use *The Man Who Kept His Heart in a Bucket* (Sonia Levitin, Dial, 1991), a fantasy tale in which a man fears his heart may be broken unless he carries it with him in a bucket. The story begins when a maiden steals his heart. Have students write a story ending before it is read.

Making Valentines

Use *213 Valentines* (Barbara Cohen, Holt, 1991), in which a fourth grader schemes to get valentines from celebrities. Follow up with the class creating heart-shaped valentines sent from the stars.

454 *real*

Other Word Forms, Vocabulary
Skills, Writing Questions and
Answers, Hypothesizing

Have students review common other word forms of *real: really* (313), *realize, reality.* Discuss unfamiliar words. Have students write this question and the answer: What might you have said or done for your parent to reply, "Come back to reality!"

Homophone Usage,
Writing Sentences

Introduce the homophone of *real,* the word *reel.* Have students check a dictionary for the meanings of *reel.* Then have students write the homophones in sentences to differentiate them. Next, have students play Mystery Words, an activity for reinforcing homophones in context (see ***Spelling Sourcebook 1,*** page 89).

Book Tie-In,
Writing a Book Jacket

❖ Use *Almost the Real Thing: Simulation in Your High-Tech World* (Gloria Skurzynski, Bradbury, 1991) for an intriguing explanation of close-to-real devices, including wind tunnels, crash dummies, and weightlessness simulators. Have students write a book jacket that would entice readers.

Antonyms, Writing Explanations

❖ Ask students to identify an antonym of *real*, the word *make-believe*. Then have students explain in writing how they know if a story they are reading is real or make-believe. Then they give an example of a real tale and one that is not.

455 *simple*

Other Word Forms,
Vocabulary Skills, Spelling Rules,
Writing Questions and Answers

❖ Have students brainstorm for common other word forms of *simple: simpler, simplest, simply, simplicity, simplistic, simplify, simplifies, simplified, simplifying*. Discuss unfamiliar words. Review the spelling rule for adding suffixes to words ending in silent *e* (see **Spelling Sourcebook 1**, page 85). Have students write this question and the answer: What might a writer do to simplify a story?

Book Tie-In,
Writing Explanations

❖ Use *Simple Machines and How They Work* (Harvey Weiss, Harper, 1983) to explore simple machines and explain their functions. Ask students to identify something they use that employs a simple machine and explain how it works.

Antonyms,
Creating a Word Puzzle

❖ Ask students to identify an antonym of *simple*, the word *difficult*. Review selected antonyms and their partners. Then have students make a crossword or word search puzzle using antonym pairs: They use one antonym partner in the puzzle and write the other partner as a clue (see Letter Grid Games, **Spelling Sourcebook 1**, page 88).

456 *snow*

Other Word Forms,
Writing Questions and Answers,
Hypothesizing

❖ Have students brainstorm for common other word forms of *snow: snows, snowed, snowing, snowy, snowier, snowiest, snowfall*. Have students write this question and the answer: What might happen if it started snowing fluffy white kernels of popcorn and didn't stop for three weeks?

Book Tie-In, Writing a List

❖ Use *A Very Young Skier* (Jill Krementz, Dial, 1990), a photo essay of Stephanie Cimino, a ski racer who lives in Sun Valley, Idaho. Have students list other recreational opportunities winter snow provides.

Research and Writing,
Public Speaking

❖ Have students research one of the following topics, tell about their findings in writing, and then present the information orally to the class:

where the most annual snowfall is recorded and where no snowfall has ever been recorded

how ski resorts make snow for skiers when the weather has not provided enough for skiing

what weather conditions produce snow

457 *rain*

Other Word Forms,
Compound Words, Vocabulary
Skills, Writing Sentences

❖ Have students brainstorm for common other word forms of *rain: rains, rained, raining, rainy, rainier, rainiest*. Then have students find and write compound words that use *rain*, such as *rainbow, rainfall, rainwear, raincoat, rainstorm, raindrop, rainwater*. Discuss unfamiliar words. Have students write selected words in sentences.

Homophone Usage ❖ Introduce the homophones of *rain, rein* and *reign*. Have students write the homophones in sentences to differentiate them. Introduce the homophones *deer* and *dear*. Then note with students which homophones are used in *reindeer*.

Idiomatic Usage, Writing Explanations ❖ Have students explain in writing what they think it means to say these expressions (then discuss):

as right as rain	rain or shine
When it rains it pours.	to save something for a rainy day
to come in out of the rain	to take a rain check
raining cats and dogs	to rain buckets

Book Tie-In, Writing Descriptions ❖ For poetry with a rainy-day theme, use *Rainy Day Rhymes* (Gail Radley, Selector, Houghton, 1992). Have students listen for words and descriptive phrases that describe the rain. Then have them write an original description of their rainy-day experience.

Book Tie-In, Comparing and Contrasting ❖ Use *The Rain Player* (David Wisniewski, Clarion, 1991), an original tale combining Mayan history and sports excitement when the god of rain is challenged to end the drought. Have students compare and contrast this tale to *Bringing the Rain to Kapiti Plain* (Verna Aardema, Dial, 1981), a Nandi tale of ending a drought. Suggest the use of a Venn diagram.

Book Tie-In, Writing Rhymes ❖ Use *It's Going to Rain* (Ada Litchfield, Atheneum, 1980), a rhyming tale that incorporates names: "It's going to rain," said Simon Paine. "How do you know," said Chester Snow. Ask students to write more verses using their own names or the names of their friends.

458 *suddenly*

Suffix Practice, Writing Sentences ❖ Have students write *sudden* and then add the *ly* suffix. Have them write the following words with the *ly* suffix: *usual* (278), *certain* (353), *complete* (365), *beautiful* (429), *possible* (452), *real* (454), *simple* (455). Have students use a dictionary to check uncertain spellings. Then have them write the words they made in sentences.

Dictation and Writing ❖ Dictate these partial sentences for students to write and complete:

When I suddenly saw the full moon, I was sure _____ .
I was already home from school when I suddenly remembered _____ .
Suddenly, in the dark across the room, I saw _____ .

459 *easy*

Antonyms, Synonyms ❖ Ask students to write a synonym and an antonym for *easy, simple* (455) and *hard* (242).

Idiomatic Usage, Writing Explanations ❖ Have students explain in writing what they think it means to say these expressions (then discuss):

as easy as pie	to take it easy
easier said than done	on easy street
easy come, easy go	Easy does it.

Writing Comparatives, Spelling Rules ❖ Have students write *heavy* (426) and its comparative and superlative forms (*heavier, heaviest*). Then have students follow the model with *easy, windy* (*wind* 341), *ready* (357), *early* (324), *sunny* (*sun* 257). Ask students to write in their own words the spelling rule for adding suffixes to words that end in consonant-*y* (see ***Spelling Sourcebook 1***, page 85).

Remember . . .

Develop spelling accountability as students write—see *Spelling Sourcebook 1,* Article 8, page 33. Spelling mastery is achieved ONLY when students can spell and use words consistently correctly in writing.

460 *leaves*

Multiple Meanings, Writing a List, Writing Sentences

❖ Brainstorm for meanings of *leaves*. Then have students check a dictionary for verification. Have students list words that can be used in more than one way and write the words in sentences to illustrate their different meanings.

Research and Writing, Public Speaking

❖ Have students research one of the following topics, tell about their findings in writing, and then present the information orally to the class:

> how and why leaves change color in autumn
> kinds of deciduous trees and how they differ from evergreen trees

Or have students create an art project using leaves. Then write how they created it and present the art and how-to information orally to the class.

461 *lay*

Book Tie-In, Writing a List, Making Predictions

❖ Use *Chickens Aren't the Only Ones* (Ruth Heller, Putnam, 1981), which discusses animals that lay eggs. Before the reading, ask students to list animals they know that lay eggs. After the reading, have students review their list and add animals that were omitted.

Visual Skill-Building, Writing Words, Writing Sentences

❖ Play the Word Look-Alike game. Ask students to circle the words in each row that are like the underlined word. Then they turn the paper over, picture the underlined word, and write it.

<u>lay</u>	bay	day	lay	lap	lay	hay	pay
<u>leaves</u>	loaves	loves	eaves	leaves	leans	leads	leaves
<u>rain</u>	rein	main	ruin	stain	rains	rain	airs

Next, have students write the underlined words in sentences.

462 *size*

Other Word Forms, Vocabulary Skills, Spelling Rules, Writing Questions and Answers, Hypothesizing

❖ Have students brainstorm for common other word forms of *size: sizes, sized, sizing, sizable*. Discuss unfamiliar words. Review the spelling rule for adding suffixes to words ending in silent *e* (see *Spelling Sourcebook 1*, page 85). Have students write this question and the answer: How might school be different if students were assigned to grades by physical sizes?

Homophone Usage

❖ Introduce the homophone of *size*, the word *sighs*. Have students write the homophones in sentences to differentiate them.

Art, Writing to Persuade

❖ Have students design a billboard to announce newly available sizes for a familiar product (travel size, family size, elephant size, microscopic size). Remind students that the ad must sell the product.

463 *wild*

Multiple Meanings, Writing Sentences

❖ Brainstorm for meanings of *wild*. Then have students check a dictionary for verification. Review words that can be used in different ways, such as *down* (84), *country* (228), *second* (235), *story* (237), *point* (272), *order* (309), *mean* (349), *mind* (419), *heart* (453). Have students write the words in sentences to illustrate their different meanings.

Other Word Forms, Vocabulary Skills, Writing Questions and Answers, Hypothesizing

Have students brainstorm for common other word forms of *wild: wilder, wildest, wilderness, wildly, wildlife.* Discuss unfamiliar words. Have students write this question and the answer: What might happen if the wildest horse from the rodeo was loose on your school playground running wildly about?

Book Tie-In, Writing a News Story, Writing Reasons

Have students write *wildlife.* Then introduce *Places of Refuge: Our National Wildlife Refuge System* (Dorothy Hinshaw Patent, Clarion, 1992), which explains the need to protect species. Have students follow up by writing a news story about one species that they think needs protection telling how and why the species needs urgent help.

Book Tie-In, Writing Descriptions

Use *Songs of the Wild West* (Alan Axelrod, Simon, 1991), which includes songs, period paintings, myths, and lively details of America's wild frontier. Then have students describe an old Wild West character, real or make-believe.

Antonyms

Ask students to identify an antonym of *wild,* the word *tame.*

464   *weather*

Book Tie-In, Reading, Writing Descriptions

Have students select weather poems to read orally to the class from *Weather Report* (Jane Yolen, Selector, Wordsong, 1993). Have students find and write words and phrases from the poems, or have them write original ones that best describe weather conditions typical of their area.

Book Tie-In, Creating a Book

Use *A January Fog Will Freeze a Hog and Other Weather Folklore* (Hubert Davis, Crown, 1977) as an introduction to collecting weather folklore for a class-made book (see page 138, Creating Classroom Books).

Book Tie-In, Making Predictions

For motivational lessons on weather forecasting, use *The Weather Sky* (Bruce McMillan, Farrar, 1991) and *The Sierra Club Book of Weatherwisdom* (Vicki McVey, Sierra, 1991). Have students write weather forecasts over time and then compute the accuracy of the predictions.

Homophone Usage

Weather and *whether* (399) are often pronounced as homophones. Have students write sentences to differentiate them.

465   *miss*

Other Word Forms, Multiple Meanings, Writing Sentences

Have students brainstorm for common other word forms of *miss: misses, missing, missed.* Have students write two sentences that use *missing* to reflect different meanings.

Book Tie-In, Writing Speculations

Use *Will We Miss Them? Endangered Species* (Alexandra Wright, Charlesbridge, 1992) to familiarize students with endangered animals. Have students follow up by writing what purpose they think the author had for choosing this topic for her book.

Capitalization, Writing Abbreviations, Book Tie-In, Writing Stories

Have students write *Miss.* Point out the capital *M* and that *Miss* requires no period. Then have students find and write titles, such as *Mr., Mrs., Ms., Rev., Col., Dr., Sr.* Point out the capital letter that begins each title and the period required at the end. Then have students write about their make-believe experience when Miss Nelson's substitute, Miss Viola Swamp, is their teacher for a day (*Miss Nelson Is Missing*, Harry Allard, Houghton, 1977).

466   *pattern*

Multiple Meanings

Brainstorm for multiple uses of *pattern* (*dress pattern, weather pattern, behavior pattern, traffic pattern, quilt pattern*). Review multiple uses of *system* (434).

Analogies, Writing Words, Creating a Word Puzzle

Review analogies (see 430, 443). Then have students write these analogies and complete them with words of frequencies 444–464:

pattern : patterns :: leaf : _____ (leaves)
unable : able :: impossible : _____ (possible)
said : say :: begun : _____ (begin)
their : there :: reel : _____ (real)
one : three :: first : _____ (third)
quite : quiet :: whether : _____ (weather)

Have students write the answer words in a word search puzzle for a friend to complete. Provide students with graph paper or use the blackline master grid on page 108 of *Spelling Sourcebook 1*.

467   *sky*

Spelling Rules, Plural Practice, Writing Words

Review the plural rule that applies to *country* (228), *city* (273), and *body* (285) (see *Spelling Sourcebook 1*, page 85). Have students write the plural of *sky*. Then have them find and write more nouns that follow this spelling pattern.

Idiomatic Usage, Writing Explanations

Have students explain in writing what they think it means to say these expressions (then discuss):

pie in the sky   to reach for the sky
sky high   out of the clear, blue sky
The sky's the limit.   That's a lot of blue sky.

Book Tie-In, Research and Writing, Creating a Book

Use *Rainbows, Mirages and Sundogs: The Sky as a Source of Wonder* (Roy Gallant, Macmillan, 1987), which answers everyday questions about the sky: Why is the sky blue? Why do stars twinkle? Have students follow up by writing the answers to selected questions in their own words for a class book (see page 138, Creating Classroom Books).

Book Tie-In, Writing Descriptions

Use *Skydiving* (Norman Barrett, Watts, 1988), which highlights the basics of a thrilling sport. Follow up with students writing a description of the feelings they think may be felt by a skydiver during a dive.

468   *walked*

Other Word Forms, Writing Sentences

Have students brainstorm for common other word forms of *walked*: *walk, walks, walking, walker*. Have students write the other word forms in sentences. Then have students rearrange the words in each sentence and delete capitals and punctuation. Partners then exchange and unscramble the sentences trying to match the word order of the original sentences.

Book Tie-In, Writing a Journal

Use *Mirette on the High Wire* (Emily Arnold McCully, Putnam, 1992), which tells about a high-wire walker who has lost his nerve and Mirette, who longs to learn the art of wire walking. Have students follow up the reading by writing journal entries as if written by Mirette and the high-wire walker.

Making Predictions, Research and Writing

Have students predict where they might find information on a "Tennessee walking horse." Then have them find and write about these horses.

Synonyms, Vocabulary Skills, Writing Descriptions ❖ Have students write *walk*. Then write synonyms for *walk* that more specifically describe the kind of *walk*, such as *amble, lumber, meander, plod, prance, saunter, shuffle, stagger, stroll, strut, swagger, totter, trek, trudge*. Discuss unfamiliar words. Have students write a description of a story character or real person using one of the synonyms.

469 *main*

Book Tie-In, Research and Writing, Art ❖ Discuss change with students: How has our city changed in the last few years? Use the wordless book, *The Story of a Main Street* (John Goodall, Macmillan, 1987), which chronicles the historical changes of a town's main street. Help students to research how a main street in your neighborhood or city has changed. Ask students to describe their findings in words and pictures.

Homophone Usage ❖ Introduce the homophones of *main*, the words *mane* and *Maine*. Have students write the homophones in sentences to differentiate them.

Multiple Meanings, Writing Sentences ❖ Brainstorm for meanings of *main*. Then have students check a dictionary for verification. Review words that can be used in different ways, such as *play* (274), *turn* (289), *face* (291), *cut* (293), *mind* (419), *game* (433), *leaves* (460). Have students write the words in sentences to illustrate their different meanings.

Sound Symbol Awareness, Sorting Words ❖ Have students write *main* and listen to the long *a* sound. Then have students collect more words with long *a* to note the most frequent spellings for long *a* (most common: *ay* [*play*], *ai* [*train*], *a*-consonant-*e* [*same*]). Create a list of long *a* words. Have students write the words in categories sorted by the spelling for the long *a*. Have one category for "other" to accommodate less common spellings.

470 *someone*

Compound Words, Writing Words ❖ Have students write *someone* and underline the two word parts of the compound. Then have students brainstorm for more compound words and play Compound Bingo (see **Spelling Sourcebook 1**, page 87) using the compounds.

Dictation and Writing ❖ Dictate these partial sentences for students to write and complete:
  If someone is late for school in the morning _____ .
  I really like someone who _____ .
  Someone who lives in the country can _____ .

471 *center*

Other Word Forms, Writing Questions and Answers, Generalizing ❖ Have students brainstorm for common other word forms of *center: centers, centered, centering, central, centrally*. Discuss unfamiliar words. Have students write an answer to this question: What can you say about all the shopping centers you have visited?

Visual Skill-Building, Homophone Usage, Vocabulary Skills ❖ Have students write *center*. Then write words they find inside *center* (*cent, enter*). Have students identify the homophones for *cent* and write the words on the chalkboard (*sent, scent*). Discuss the meanings of the three homophones. Then have students write the homophones in sentences to differentiate them.

472 *field*

Other Word Forms, Vocabulary Skills, Writing Sentences ❖ Have students brainstorm for common other word forms of *field: fields, fielded, fielding, fielder.* Discuss unfamiliar words. Have students write the other word forms in sentences.

Book Tie-In, Drawing Conclusions ❖ Use *Pumpkins: A Story for a Field* (Mary L. Ray, Harcourt, 1992), which tells about an innovative and humorous scheme to save a favorite field from development. Follow up with students identifying and writing the conclusion the author wants the reader to make (the importance of conservation of open space).

Book Tie-In, Making a Time Line ❖ *McCrephy's Field* (Christopher and Lynne Myers, Houghton, 1991) tells the story of how a field changes over 50 years. Have students create a time line for the field.

Multiple Meanings ❖ Brainstorm for meanings of *field.* Then have students check a dictionary for verification. Review words that can be used in different ways, such as *short* (304), *run* (306), *book* (307), *order* (309), *hold* (370), *class* (391), *wild* (463). Have students use the words in oral sentences to illustrate their different meanings.

473 *stay*

Other Word Forms, Homophone Usage ❖ Have students brainstorm for common other word forms of *stay: stays, stayed, staying.* Have students identify the homophone of *stayed* (*staid*) and use the homophones in sentences to differentiate them.

Other Word Forms, Writing Words ❖ Have students play All in the Family (see **Spelling Sourcebook 1**, page 86) using the other word forms of *stay* and the other word forms of selected review words.

Sorting Words, Sound-Symbol Awareness ❖ Have students play Word Sorts (see **Spelling Sourcebook 1**, page 92) using these words: *stay, space* (320), *state* (371), *lay* (461), *play* (274), *day* (114), *rain* (457), *they* (19), *place* (131), *great* (146), *main* (469), *game* (433), *change* (264). Then review the most common spellings for long *a: ai, ay, a*-consonant-*e* and two common exceptions, *they* and *great.*

474 *itself*

Dictation and Writing ❖ Dictate these partial sentences for students to write and complete:
A fire will go out by itself if _____ .
An animal that can take care of itself in the wild is _____ .

Compound Words, Writing Words ❖ Have students find and write more compound words that use *selves* or *self,* such as *himself* (277), *themselves* (443), *yourself, herself, myself.*

475 *boat*

Other Word Forms, Writing Sentences ❖ Have students brainstorm for common other word forms of *boat: boats, boated, boating, boater.* Have students write the other word forms in sentences.

Book Tie-In, Writing a Bibliography ❖ Use *The Magic Boat* (Demi, Holt, 1990), a Chinese folktale. Follow up by asking students to collect folklore from many different countries and cultures. Create a class bibliography of these with short descriptions of the stories. Have students locate the countries on a map.

Book Tie-In, Making Judgments ❖ Use *Boat* (Eric Kentley, Knopf, 1992) for interesting instruction about boats. Following the reading, have students write what they think the most important ideas were in the book.

Writing a List ❖ Have students list kinds of boats, such as a canoe, ferry, kayak, sailboat, tugboat, steamboat, rowboat, raft, dory, freighter, pedal boat. Have students check uncertain spellings using a dictionary.

476 *question*

Other Word Forms, Vocabulary Skills, Writing Questions and Answers, Making Inferences ❖ Have students brainstorm for common other word forms of *question: questions, questioned, questioning, questioner, questioningly, questionable, questionnaire.* Discuss unfamiliar words. Have students write this question and the answer: What might the situation be if your parent looks at you questioningly?

Book Tie-In, Research and Writing ❖ Use *New Questions and Answers About Dinosaurs* (Seymour Simon, Morrow, 1990), which uses a question and answer format. Follow up by asking students to choose a topic to research and present in the same question-and-answer format.

Antonyms ❖ Ask students to write the antonym of *question,* the word *answer* (265).

Writing Questions and Answers ❖ Have students write questions for their classmates to try to answer. Have them make a separate answer sheet. Choose a topic, such as movies:

Question 1: Which movie has won the most awards?
Answer 1: *Ben-Hur* won eleven Oscars.

Give students a chance to write answers to the questions. Then have them compare answers with the ones on the answer sheet.

477 *wide*

Other Word Forms, Writing Sentences ❖ Have students brainstorm for common other word forms of *wide: wider, widest, widely, width, wideness, widen, widened.* Have students write the other word forms in sentences. Then have students rearrange the words in each sentence and delete capitals and punctuation Partners then exchange and unscramble the sentences trying to match the word order of the original sentences.

Antonyms ❖ Ask students to identify an antonym of *wide,* the word *narrow.*

Sound -Symbol Awareness ❖ Have students write *wide* and listen to the long *i* sound. Then have students collect more words with long *i* to note the most frequent spellings for long *i* (most common: *y* [*my*], *igh* [*right*], *ind* [*kind*], *i*-consonant-*e* [*smile*]). Create a list of long *i* words. Have students write the words in categories sorted by the spelling for the long *i*. Have one category for "other" to accommodate less common spellings.

478 *least*

Antonyms ❖ Ask students to write an antonym of *least,* the word *most* (99).

Idiomatic Usage, Writing Explanations ❖ Have students explain in writing what they think it means to say these expressions (then discuss):

to say the least   not in the least
at least   to take the path of least resistance
last but not least   when least expected

Sound-Symbol Awareness,
Vocabulary Skills,
Writing Sentences

❖ Have students write *least*. Then ask them to follow these directions to make new and review words and to give answers to the questions:

Change *least* to make *list* (372).
Change *least* to make *last* (166).
Change *least* to make *beast, yeast, feast*.
Change *least* to make *east*. (What city is east of you?)
Change *least* to make *leash*. (When might you use a leash?)
Change *least* to make *league*. (What are two meanings of league?)

Discuss unfamiliar words. Then have students write a sentence for each word they made.

479 *tiny*

Writing Comparatives,
Spelling Rules

❖ Have students write *tiny*. Then have them change *tiny* to *tinier* and *tiniest*. Review the appropriate suffix rule on page 85 of **Spelling Sourcebook 1**. Have students brainstorm for more words that follow this spelling rule.

Comparing and Contrasting,
Book Tie-In, Writing Stories

❖ Ask students to compare and contrast versions of Hans Christian Andersen's original *Thumbelina* (Alison Claire Darke, Doubleday, 1991; James Riordan, Putnam, 1991; Amy Ehrlich, Dial, 1979; Lisbeth Zwerger, Picture Book, 1986). Then have students write a version of their own. Ask students to collect other classic stories about miniature characters, such as *Tom Thumb*.

Book Tie-In,
Research and Writing

❖ Use *Miniature Horses* (Dorothy Hinshaw Patent, Cobblehill, 1991), an informative color essay on the history, breeding, training, and care of these tiny horses. Follow up with students researching and writing about miniature breeds of dogs.

480 *hour*

Homophone Usage

❖ Introduce the homophone of *hour*, the word *our* (109). Note *are* (15), often confused with *our*. Have students write the words in sentences to differentiate them.

Writing Words, Writing
Abbreviations, Sequencing,
Alphabetical Order

❖ Ask students to create a collection of words that denote time, such as *hour, minute, year* (225). Have students sequence the increments from small to large. Then have students write the words with their abbreviations in alphabetical order.

Dictation and Writing

❖ Dictate these partial sentences for students to write and complete:

One hour from now, _____ .
It usually takes an hour or more to _____ .

Research and Writing, Writing
Explanations, Hypothesizing

❖ Have students find out and explain in writing what *hourly wage* means. Then help them to find out what the current minimum hourly wage is. Ask students to hypothesize in writing what might happen if this minimum were doubled tomorrow. . . or cut in half. Ask, Why is there a law for minimum hourly wages?

481 *happened*

Other Word Forms,
Writing Questions and Answers

❖ Have students brainstorm for common other word forms of *happened: happen, happens, happening, happenings*. Have students write the other word forms in sentences that ask a question. Then they exchange papers and answer the questions using the same word forms in their replies.

Writing Questions and Answers, Research and Writing, Hypothesizing

❖ Have students write the questions below and then research and write the answers:

What happens on March 25 in Greece, July 4 in the United States, and October 1 in Nigeria? (The people celebrate Independence Day.)

What happens to the calendar on leap year? (An extra day is added in February.)

What happened to President Abe Lincoln at Ford's Theater on April 14, 1865, during the play, *An American Cousin?* (Lincoln was shot.)

What might happen if manholes were any shape but round?

(The cover could fall through the hole when the cover is taken off by workers if its shape was anything but round.)

482 *foot*

Multiple Meanings, Writing Sentences

❖ Brainstorm for meanings of *foot*. Then have students check a dictionary for verification. Review words that can be used in different ways, such as *ground* (311), *table* (314), *course* (317), *space* (320), *main* (469), *field* (472). Have students write *foot* in sentences to illustrate different meanings.

Other Word Forms, Vocabulary Skills, Writing Sentences

❖ Have students brainstorm for common other word forms of *foot: foots, footed, footing, footings, footage, feet.* Discuss unfamiliar words. Have students write the other word forms in sentences.

Plural Practice

❖ Review irregular plurals (see ***Spelling Sourcebook 1***, page 85). Write *foot* and *feet* on the chalkboard. Have students find and write more examples of irregular plurals. Choices may include *child/children* (200), *goose/geese, man* (111)/*men* (148), *woman/women, mouse/mice, ox/oxen, tooth/teeth.*

Compound Words, Vocabulary Skills

❖ Have students find and write compound words that use *foot,* such as *football, footbridge, foothill, footlights, footnote, footpath, footprint, footrest, footsteps, footstool, footwear, footwork.* Make a cumulative class list on the chalkboard. Discuss unfamiliar words.

Idiomatic Usage, Writing Explanations

❖ Have students explain in writing what they think it means to say these expressions (then discuss):

to foot the bill	to put your foot down
to get off on the wrong foot	to wait on someone hand and foot
to get your foot in the door	to put your foot in your mouth
on foot	(See literature entry below.)
to put your best foot forward	

Book Tie-In, Making a Poster, Art

❖ Use *Put Your Foot in Your Mouth and Other Silly Sayings* (James Cox, Random House, 1980). Follow up with students making a poster of a favorite silly saying with a literal illustration.

Book Tie-In, Research and Writing, Summarizing

❖ Use *Bigfoot and Other Legendary Creatures* (Paul R. Walker, Harcourt, 1992) to introduce students to the famous Bigfoot and to examine evidence that the creature exists. Follow up with students using the *Reader's Guide* to research and summarize any new "sightings."

483 *care*

Other Word Forms, Spelling Rules, Suffix Practice, Writing Questions and Answers, Making Inferences

Have students brainstorm for common other word forms of *care: cares, caring, caringly, careless, carelessly, carelessness, careful, carefully, carefulness.* Review the spelling rule for adding suffixes to words ending in silent *e* (see **Spelling Sourcebook 1**, page 85). Have students write this question and the answer: What might be happening if your friend reminds you not to be so careless?

Book Tie-In, Writing a List

Use *Taking Care of Your Dog* (Joyce Pope, Watts, 1987). Follow up by asking students to list things to remember for a friend who has a new pet dog. Pope has other books in this series, including care for gerbils, guinea pigs, rabbits, and hamsters.

Book Tie-In, Writing Descriptions

Use *One World* (Michael Foreman, Arcade, 1991) to stress the importance of taking care of our planet. Ask students to describe in writing a personal contribution they make to care for the environment.

484 *low*

Other Word Forms, Vocabulary Skills, Writing Questions and Answers, Making Judgments

Have students brainstorm for common other word forms of *low: lows, lower, lowest, lowers, lowered, lowering, lowly.* Discuss unfamiliar words. Have students write this question and the answer: Is it fair to lower a student's grade on an assignment if nine easy words are misspelled? Why or why not?

Antonyms

Ask students to write the antonym of *low,* the word *high* (224).

Research and Writing, Art, Public Speaking

Have students research one of the following topics, tell about their findings in writing, and then present the information orally to the class using a self-made visual aid:

the lowest temperatures ever recorded in your city and state

the places having the lowest and the highest elevation in the United States (highest: Mt. McKinley , 20,320 ft.; lowest: Death Valley, 282 ft. below sea level)

the meaning and the weather consequences of a low pressure and high pressure front

485 *else*

Word Analysis, Writing Words

Have students write *else* and note that *else* both begins and ends with the same letter. See if students can think of words from A–Z that begin and end with the same letter. For example, *area* (384), *bib, comic, did* (83), *else, fluff, going, health* . . . Have students use a dictionary for help.

486 *gold*

Other Word Forms, Vocabulary Skills, Writing Sentences

Have students brainstorm for common other word forms of *gold: golden, gilt, gilded.* Discuss unfamiliar words. Have students write the other word forms in sentences.

Idiomatic Usage, Writing Explanations

Have students explain in writing what they think it means to say these expressions (then discuss):

All that glitters is not gold.   to have a heart of gold
as good as gold   worth its weight in gold

Multiple Meanings, *Writing Sentences*	❖ Brainstorm for meanings of *gold*. Then have students check a dictionary for verification. Review words that can be used in different ways, such as *draw* (338), *less* (340), *letter* (344), *mean* (349), *felt* (377), *game* (433). Have students write the words in sentences to illustrate their different meanings.

487 *build*

Other Word Forms, *Writing Questions and Answers,* *Making Decisions*	❖ Have students brainstorm for common other word forms of *build: builds, builder, building, built, buildings.* Have students write this question and the answer: When the builder asks you what you'd like to have built in your classroom to make it a better place to learn, what might you reply?
Book Tie-In, Research	❖ Use *Corals: The Sea's Great Builders* (The Cousteau Society, Simon, 1992), which provides vivid photographs that can be a catalyst to research on how the corals build massive reefs.
Book Tie-In, Writing Directions	❖ Use *Animals Build Amazing Homes* (Hedda Nussbaum, Random, 1979) for easy-to-read information on how 15 different animals build their homes. Ask students to follow up with a written set of tongue-in-cheek animals' directions for building various shelters.

488 *glass*

Multiple Meanings, *Writing Sentences*	❖ Brainstorm for meanings of *glass*. Then have students check a dictionary for verification. Review words that can be used in different ways, such as *rest* (351), *fire* (356), *hold* (370), *state* (371), *mind* (419). Have students write the words in sentences to illustrate their different meanings.
Other Word Forms, *Vocabulary Skills, Plural Practice,* *Writing Sentences*	❖ Have students brainstorm for common other word forms of *glass: glasses, glassful, glassware, glassy.* Discuss unfamiliar words. Note with students the rule for plurals with words that end in *ss* (see ***Spelling Sourcebook 1***, page 85). Have students write the other word forms in sentences.
Book Tie-In, Writing a List	❖ Use *Glass* (Susan Cackett, Gloucester, 1988) as a resource on how glass is made. Then ask students to list things made of glass, such as a window, Cinderella's shoe, and a canning jar.
Word Analysis, Writing Words	❖ Have students write *glass* and other words with *ss: across* (247), *less* (340), *class* (391), *possible* (452), *miss* (465), *business, guess, unless.* Then have students play Password (see ***Spelling Sourcebook 1***, page 89) using the words with *ss*.

489 *rock*

Multiple Meanings, *Writing Words*	❖ Brainstorm for meanings of *rock*. Then have students check a dictionary for verification. Review words that can be used in different ways, such as *matter* (386), *stand* (387), *class* (391), *leaves* (460). Then have students brainstorm for more words that have more than one meaning. Have students use words with different meanings to play Spelling Baseball (see ***Spelling Sourcebook 1***, page 91).
Other Word Forms, Vocabulary *Skills, Writing Questions and* *Answers, Hypothesizing*	❖ Have students brainstorm for common other word forms of *rock: rocks, rocked, rocking, rocky, rockier, rockiest, rocker, rockery.* Discuss unfamiliar words. Have students write this question and the answer: What might have happened to make you tell your parent you had a rocky day at school?

Book Tie-In, Writing Rhymes, Choral Reading ❖ Use the silly rhyming story *"There Are Rocks in My Socks!" Said the Ox to the Fox* (Patricia Thomas, Lothrop, 1979) as a model for students to write their own nonsensical rhyming tales. Have students read their rhymes chorally.

Writing Speculations, Book Tie-In ❖ Ask students to think creatively and list all the possible uses of rocks. Then read *Rocks in My Pockets* (Marc Harshman and Bonnie Collins, Cobblehill, 1991) to reveal a use that students may not have anticipated. (The Woods family put rocks in their pockets to keep the wind from blowing them off their mountaintop farm.)

Book Tie-In, Writing a Summary ❖ For easy-to-demonstrate experiments with rocks, use *Adventures With Rocks and Minerals: Geology Experiments for Young People* (Lloyd Barrow, Enslow, 1991). Have students write summaries of the experiments demonstrated in class.

490 *tall*

Writing Comparatives, Spelling Rules ❖ Have students write *tall, taller, tallest*. Review the spelling rules for adding these suffixes to words (see **Spelling Sourcebook 1**, page 85). Have students apply the rules to *red* (298), *hot* (368), *dry* (438), *easy* (459).

Book Tie-In, Writing Tall Tales ❖ Use *The Baron on the Island of Cheese* (Adrian Mitchell, Philomel, 1986) to introduce tall tales. Have students write their own tall tales on long, narrow paper to compile into a tall book of tall tales.

Antonyms ❖ Ask students to write the antonym of *tall,* the word *short* (304).

491 *alone*

Dictation and Writing ❖ Dictate these partial sentences for students to write and complete:
I remember that one time when I was alone, ____ .
One animal you should leave alone is ____ .

Word Analysis, Writing Words ❖ Have students find and write *a*____ words, such as *alone, around* (120), *again* (141), *ago* (322).

492 *bottom*

Antonyms ❖ Ask students to write the antonym of *bottom,* the word *top* (269).

Idiomatic Usage, Writing Explanations ❖ Have students explain in writing what they think it means to say these expressions (then discuss):

to bottom out	to hit bottom
from the bottom of your heart	to learn something from the bottom up
from top to bottom	the bottom of the barrel
to get to the bottom of something	the bottom line

493 *check*

Multiple Meanings, Writing Sentences ❖ Brainstorm for meanings of *check*. Then have students check a dictionary for verification. Review words that can be used in different ways, such as *fine* (400), *blue* (407), *watch* (436). Have students write the words in sentences to illustrate their different meanings.

Other Word Forms, Vocabulary Skills, Writing Sentences ❖ Have students brainstorm for common other word forms of *check: checks, checked, checking, checker.* Discuss unfamiliar words. Have students write the other word forms in sentences. Then have students exchange papers. Next, students rewrite the sentences changing the tense of each.

494 *reading*

Other Word Forms, Homograph Usage, Writing Sentences

Have students brainstorm for common other word forms of *reading: read, reads, reader.* Have students note the different pronunciations and meanings of the homograph *read.* Then have them write sentences using both meanings.

Book Tie-In, Writing a Book Report

Use *How to Write Your Best Book Report* (Elizabeth James and Carol Barkin, Lothrop, 1986). After students have read a library book, they may use the book's suggestions to write a book report.

495 *fall*

Multiple Meanings, Writing Sentences

Brainstorm for meanings of *fall.* Then have students check a dictionary for verification. Review words that can be used in different ways, such as *heart* (453), *leaves* (460), *wild* (463), *miss* (465). Have students write the words in sentences to illustrate their different meanings.

Other Word Forms, Word Analysis, Writing Words

Have students brainstorm for common other word forms of *fall: falls, fallen, falling, fell.* Note with students that the past tense of *fall* does not end with *ed,* but has the changed spelling *fell.* Have students find and write more words that follow this spelling pattern, such as *said* (43) and *made* (81).

Antonyms

Ask students to identify the antonym of one meaning of *fall,* the word *spring,* and predict its spelling.

Idiomatic Usage, Writing Explanations

Have students explain in writing what they think it means to say these expressions (then discuss):

to fall apart at the seams	to fall asleep
to fall flat on your face	to fall behind
to fall in line	to fall in love
to have a falling out	to break someone's fall

Book Tie-In, Writing a List, Career Awareness

Fear of falling from high places is common. Read *The Saint and the Circus* (Roberto Piumini, Tambourine, 1991), which features a tottering tightrope walker. Have students list careers in which the fear of falling must be overcome (high-rise window washers, crane workers, chimney sweeps, roofers, bridge maintenance workers, tree toppers).

Book Tie-In, Writing Descriptions

Use *Exploring Autumn: A Season of Science Activities, Puzzlers, and Games* (Sandra Markle, Atheneum, 1991) for fall fun. Have students follow up by describing a fall, or autumn, activity they like.

496 *poor*

Multiple Meanings, Writing Sentences

Brainstorm for meanings of *poor.* Then have students check a dictionary for verification. Review words that can be used in different ways, such as *foot* (482), *gold* (486), *glass* (488), *rock* (489). Have students write the words in sentences to illustrate their different meanings.

Antonyms

Ask students to identify the antonym of *poor,* the word *rich,* and predict its spelling.

Word Analysis, Sorting Words ❖	Have students write *poor* and underline the *oo.* Then have them write and listen to the *oo* in *good* (106), *too* (112), *look* (117), *school* (194), *food* (198), *took* (210), *soon* (236), *room* (266), *door* (292), *book* (307), *moon* (417), *floor* (440), *foot* (482). Students then sort the words by the sound of the *oo,* taking into consideration natural differences in pronunciation. Help students conclude that *oo* spells a variety of sounds in words.

497   *map*

Other Word Forms, Writing Questions and Answers, Hypothesizing ❖	Have students brainstorm for common other word forms of *map: maps, mapped, mapping.* Have students write this question and the answer: For what purpose do you think maps are used most often by adults?
Spelling Rules, Suffix Practice, Writing Sentences ❖	Review the spelling rule for doubling the final consonant before adding suffixes (see ***Spelling Sourcebook 1***, page 85). Have students apply the rule by adding suffixes to the following words; they must decide which should double the final consonant and which should not: *boat* (475), *rain* (457), *begin* (444), *ship* (442), *order* (309), *cut* (293), *turn* (289), *let* (230), *want* (193), *get* (101), *will* (46). Have students write sentences using the words with suffixes.
Book Tie-In, Making Maps ❖	Use *Maps: Getting From Here to There* (Harvey Weiss, Houghton, 1991) for an illustrated introduction to map making. Follow up with students making maps of the continents. For a guided tour of the continents, use *Geography* (Lionel Bender, Simon, 1992).

498   *friend*

Other Word Forms, Vocabulary Skills, Writing Sentences ❖	Have students brainstorm for common other word forms of *friend: friends, friendship, friendly, friendless, friendlier, friendliest.* Discuss unfamiliar words. Have students write the other word forms in sentences. Then have students rearrange the words in each sentence and delete capitals and punctuation. Partners then exchange and unscramble the sentences trying to match the word order of the original sentences.
Book Tie-In, Writing a Story ❖	Use *Somebody Loves You, Mr. Hatch* (Eileen Spinelli, Bradbury, 1991), a story of the importance of friendship in everyone's life. Ask students to write about a time that they did something special for a friend or a friend did something special for them.
Writing Explanations, Creating a Book ❖	Ask students to write a personal confirmation of the saying, "A friend in need is a friend indeed." Compile the results into a class-made book (see page 138, Creating Classroom Books).
Antonyms ❖	Ask students to identify the antonym of *friend,* the word *enemy,* and predict its spelling.
Synonyms ❖	Ask students to list synonyms for *friend,* such as *pal, companion, comrade, chum, partner, ally.*

499   *language*

Book Tie-In, Creating a Book, Exploring Languages ❖	Use *First Words: Premiers Mots, Primeras Palabras, Erste Worte, Prime Parole* (Ivan and Jane Chermayeff, Abrams, 1990), a five-language picture book to serve as a model for students to create a parallel book in languages of their choice.

Book Tie-In, Following Directions ❖ For an introduction to Chinese writing, use *Long Is a Dragon: Chinese Writing for Children* (Peggy Goldstein, China, 1991). Have students follow the directions to write and read Chinese words.

Book Tie-In, Writing Questions and Answers ❖ To improve students' abilities to write more effectively, use *What's Your Story?: A Young Person's Guide to Writing Fiction* (Marion Bauer, Clarion, 1992). Then have students write questions (with answers) that a teacher might ask the class about this book.

500 *job*

Synonyms, Book Tie-In, Writing Want Ads, Career Awareness ❖ Brainstorm for *job* synonyms (*vocation, work, occupation*). Then use *All in a Day's Work: Twelve Americans Talk About Their Jobs* (Neil Johnson, Joy Street/Little, 1989). The challenges and rewards of various jobs are highlighted. Follow up the reading with students writing classified want ads for each of these jobs and others.

Research and Writing, Career Awareness ❖ Have students research one of the following topics, tell about their findings in writing, and then present the information orally to the class using a self-made chart as a visual aid:

  jobs of people who work in a hospital

  the jobs that friends and classmates do to help at home

  the different jobs involved in building a house

501 *music*

Other Word Forms, Vocabulary Skills, Writing Sentences ❖ Have students brainstorm for common other word forms of *music: musician, musicians, musical, musically*. Discuss unfamiliar words. Have students write the other word forms in sentences.

Word Analysis, Writing Sentences ❖ Have students compare and contrast the words *musician* and *magician*. Expand the lesson to *are* (15) and *our* (109), *then* (53) and *than* (73), *air* (160) and *error*, *once* (206) and *ounce*, *thought* (179) and *though* (330), *quite* (447) and *quiet* and *quit*. Have students write the often-confused words in sentences.

Book Tie-In, Writing Myths ❖ How did music come to earth? An Aztec myth provides the answer in *All of You Was Singing* (Richard Lewis, Atheneum, 1991). Ask students to create their own myths to provide another answer to the question.

Book Tie-In, Writing a List ❖ Use *The Philharmonic Gets Dressed* (Karla Kuskin, Harper, 1982), a clever picture book showing how the members of the Philharmonic prepare for a performance. Have students write the names of the instruments pictured in the book.

502 *buy*

Other Word Forms, Writing Questions and Answers, Hypothesizing ❖ Have students brainstorm for common other word forms of *buy: buys, bought, buying, buyer*. Have students write this question and the answer: What do you think might happen if you bought a puppy with your own money and took the new pet home as a surprise?

Homophone Usage ❖ Ask students to write the homophone of *buy*, the word *by* (27). Introduce *bye*. Have students write sentences to differentiate the words.

Antonyms ❖ Ask students to identify the antonym of *buy*, the word *sell*. Then discuss the homophone of *sell*, the word *cell*.

Idiomatic Usage, ❖ Have students explain in writing what they think it means to say these
Writing Explanations expressions (then discuss):

to buy a pig in a poke   to buy something sight unseen
to buy something for a song   to buy on credit

Book Tie-In, Making Judgments ❖ Use *Smart Spending: A Consumer's Guide* (Lois Schmitt, Macmillan, 1989),
brief case studies of young teen spenders. Following the reading, have students
write the consumer ideas that were the most important ones for them.

503 *window*

Book Tie-In, ❖ Use *Window* (Jeannie Baker, Greenwillow, 1991), a wordless book that
Drawing Conclusions examines the world over time through a window. Follow up the reading by
asking students to identify and write the point the author is making—that the
wilderness is being overtaken by civilization.

Analogies, Writing Words, ❖ Review analogies (see 430, 443, 466). Then have students write these analogies
Writing Sentences and complete them with words of frequencies 483–503:

wood : table :: glass : ____ (window)
kept : keep :: built : ____ (build)
light : heavy :: top : ____ (bottom)
hour : our :: by : ____ (buy)
60 minutes : hour :: autumn : ____ (fall)

Have students write the answer words in sentences.

504 *mark*

Multiple Meanings, ❖ Brainstorm for meanings of *mark.* Then have students check a dictionary for
Writing Sentences verification. Review words that can be used in different ways, such as *can* (38),
time (69), *down* (84), *long* (91). Have students write the words in sentences to
illustrate their different meanings.

Other Word Forms, Vocabulary ❖ Have students brainstorm for common other word forms of *mark: marks,*
Skills, Writing Questions and *marked, marking.* Discuss unfamiliar words. Have students write this question
Answers, Hypothesizing, and the answer: When the principal tells all students that they must have
Writing Reasons everything they bring to school marked for identification, how might you mark
your things and why?

Sound-Symbol Awareness, ❖ Have students write *mark.* Then ask them to follow these directions to make
Writing Sentences new and review words:

Change *mark* to make *dark* (402), *bark, shark, park, stark, lark.*
Change *mark* to make *mask.*
Change *mark* to make *market.* (Have students write *supermarket.*)
Change *mark* to make the name of a planet. (Mars)

Then have students write a sentence for each word they made.

505 *heat*

Other Word Forms, ❖ Have students brainstorm for common other word forms of *heat: heats, heated,*
Writing Questions and Answers, *heating, heater.* Have students write these questions and the answers:
Comparing and Contrasting,
Writing Speculations How are homes today heated differently than in times past? Why?

How might homes in the future be heated differently than today's homes?
Why?

Prefix Practice, Vocabulary Skills, Writing Questions and Answers

Have students add the *pre* and *re* prefixes to *heat*. Then have them add the *re* prefix to *reading* (494), *check* (493), *build* (487), *state* (371). Have students write these questions and the answers:

Why might you preheat an oven?
How might you reheat food?
What books are worth rereading?
Why should you recheck your paper for spelling?
Why might it be necessary to rebuild a building?
Why might someone ask you to restate your question?

Book Tie-In, Accessing Knowledge, Informational Writing

Use *Hot and Cold* (Irving Adler, Harper, 1975). Before the reading have students write what they know about how heat is measured and produced. Then explore this information in the book. Next, have students rewrite their initial pieces adding information they learned.

506 *grew*

Homophone Usage, Other Word Forms, Writing Questions and Answers, Writing Speculations

Have students brainstorm for common other word forms of *grew: grow, grows, grown, growing, growth.* Discuss the homophones *grown* and *groan.* Have students write this question and the answer: When you're full grown, how tall do you think you'll be and what makes you think that?

Dictation and Writing

Dictate these partial sentences for students to write and complete:

The beautiful plant grew so high that _____ .
As it grew later, my friend and I _____ .
When the winter weather grew cold, _____ .

507 *listen*

Other Word Forms, Writing Questions and Answers

Have students brainstorm for common other word forms of *listen: listens, listening, listened, listener.* Have them write the other word forms in sentences that ask a question. Then have students exchange papers and answer the questions using the same word forms of *listen* in the responses.

Reading, Storytelling, Writing Stories

Have selected students read a story from *Stories From the Days of Christopher Columbus: A Multicultural Collection for Young Readers* (Richard Young and Judy Young, August, 1992), which retells tales that might have been listened to at the end of the day by sailors on Columbus's voyage. Then have students tell the tale to the class. Follow up with students writing a tale they have been told but have never seen in print or have not read for a long time.

Word Analysis, Writing Words

Have students write *listen* and underline the letter they do not hear when the word is said (*t*). Then have them find and write more words with silent consonants, such as *walked* (468), *although* (450), *answer* (265).

508 *ask*

Other Word Forms, Writing Sentences

Have students brainstorm for common other word forms of *ask: asks, asked, asking.* Have students write the other word forms in sentences.

Book Tie-In, Creating a Book

Use *Ask Dale Murphy* (Dale Murphy and Chris Patton, Algonquin, 1987), a question-and-answer book for baseball fans. Use the book as a model for a student-made question-and-answer book on a topic students know about (see page 138, Creating Classroom Books).

Dictation and Writing,
Writing Speculations

Dictate these partial sentences for students to write and complete:

I must answer no if someone asks me _____ .

Of course, I would say yes if a person asked me _____ .

509   *single*

Other Word Forms, Vocabulary
Skills, Writing Questions and
Answers, Spelling Rules

Have students brainstorm for common other word forms of *single: singly, singular, singularly, singles, singled*. Discuss unfamiliar words. Have students write this question and the answer: What can you say about spelling rules for making singular nouns plural? (See **Spelling Sourcebook 1**, page 85.)

510   *clear*

Other Word Forms, Vocabulary
Skills, Writing Questions and
Answers, Hypothesizing

Have students brainstorm for common other word forms of *clear: clears, cleared, clearing, clearer, clearest, clearly, clearness, clearance*. Discuss unfamiliar words. Have students write this question and the answer: Why do stores have clearance sales?

Idiomatic Usage,
Writing Explanations

Have students explain in writing what they think it means to say these expressions (then discuss):

Clear out.	as clear as mud
to clear something up	Clear the air.
in the clear	to clear the table
to steer clear of something	The coast is clear.

Multiple Meanings,
Writing Sentences

Have students find and write meanings of *clear* using a dictionary for verification. Then have students write *clear* in sentences to illustrate its different meanings.

511   *energy*

Other Word Forms, Vocabulary
Skills, Writing Sentences

Have students brainstorm for common other word forms of *energy: energize, energetic*. Discuss unfamiliar words. Have students write the other word forms in sentences.

Book Tie-In, Writing a Summary

Use *The Science Book of Energy* (Neil Ardley, Gulliver, 1992), for fun and easy experiments on energy. Have students write summaries of the experiments demonstrated.

Book Tie-In, Research and
Writing, Public Speaking

Use *Solar Power* (Robin McKie, Gloucester, 1985), which tells about the many possibilities of this power source. Ask students to research other energy sources, such as wind, oil, natural gas, geothermal power, water, and nuclear power and report in writing and orally on their advantages and disadvantages.

512   *week*

Other Word Forms,
Writing Questions and Answers

Have students brainstorm for common other word forms of *week: weeks, weekly, weekend, weekends*. Have students write these questions and the answers:

What happens weekly at your school?

What happens weekly at home?

What would you like to happen weekly that takes place less often?

Homophone Usage

Ask students to identify the homophone of *week*, the word *weak*. Have students write sentences to differentiate them.

513 *explain*

Prefix Practice, Writing Words ❖ Have students write *explain* and underline the *ex*. Then find and write more words that begin with *ex*. Choices may include *example* (261), *experience*, *experiment*, *exactly*, *extra*.

Other Word Forms, Word Analysis ❖ Have students brainstorm for common other word forms of *explain: explains, explained, explaining, explanation, explanatory*. Discuss unfamiliar words. Ask students to write the other word forms and underline the forms spelled with *plain* and those spelled with *plan*. Then note the difference in pronunciation between the words with the two different spellings.

Writing Explanations ❖ Ask students to write about a disagreement they had with someone. Have them explain why they were correct and the other person was wrong.

514 *lost*

Other Word Forms, Word Analysis, Writing Sentences ❖ Have students brainstorm for common other word forms of *lost: lose, loses, losing, loser, loss, losses*. Write *lose* and *loose* on the chalkboard and have students contrast the spellings and meanings. Have students write the other word forms of *lost* in sentences. Then have students rearrange the words in each sentence and delete capitals and punctuation. Partners then exchange and unscramble the sentences trying to match the word order of the original sentences.

Book Tie-In, Writing Explanations ❖ Use *Billy's Beetle* (Mick Inkpen, Harcourt, 1992), a silly picture book about Billy's lost beetle, which appears throughout the illustrations on his would-be rescuers. Have students follow up by explaining how something they lost was discovered to be close by all along.

Book Tie-In, Research, Writing Speculations ❖ Use *Lost Cities* (Roy Gallant, Watts, 1985) for a historical account of the rediscovery of ancient cities, such as Crete and Pompeii. With information from the book and further research, have students speculate in writing how and why the cities were lost.

Antonyms ❖ Ask students to write the antonym of *lost*, the word *found* (152).

515 *spring*

Multiple Meanings, Writing Sentences, Art ❖ Brainstorm for meanings of *spring*. Then have students check a dictionary for verification. Have students illustrate the different meanings of *spring* on art paper.

Other Word Forms, Vocabulary Skills, Writing Questions and Answers ❖ Have students brainstorm for common other word forms of *spring: springs, sprang, sprung, springing, springtime*. Discuss unfamiliar words. Have students write this question and the answer: What would you like to do when the first signs of springtime have sprung?

Book Tie-In, Creating a Book ❖ Use *Exploring Spring: A Season of Science Activities, Puzzles, and Games* (Sandra Markle, Atheneum, 1990), a book of interesting season-related information and projects for intermediate students. Use this book as a model for a student-made book about another season (see page 138, Creating Classroom Books).

Idiomatic Usage,
Writing Explanations

Have students explain in writing what they think it means to say these expressions (then discuss):

no spring chicken   to spring something on someone
to spring for something   Spring has sprung.

Antonyms

Ask students to write the antonym of one meaning of *spring,* the word *fall* (495).

516   *travel*

Book Tie-In, Developing a Guide

Use *First Travel Guide to the Moon: What to Pack, How to Go, and What to See When You Get There* (Rhoda Blumberg, Four Winds, 1980). Then ask students to create their own travel guide to somewhere real or make-believe.

Other Word Forms,
British Spellings

Have students brainstorm for common other word forms of *travel: travels, traveled, traveling, traveler.* Note the British spellings *travelled, travelling,* and *traveller.* Have students write the other word forms in sentences.

517   *wrote*

Other Word Forms, Homophone Usage, Writing Questions and Answers, Generalizations

Have students brainstorm for common other word forms of *wrote: write* (108), *writes, written, writing, writer.* Have students write a homophone for *write* (*right* 116, *rite*) and *wrote* (*rote*). Discuss unfamiliar words. Have students write this question and the answer: What can you say about all the books that your favorite writer has written?

Word Analysis, Vocabulary Skills

Have students find and write words that begin with *wr.* Choices may include *write* (108), *wrist, wrong, wrestle, wring, wrap.* Discuss unfamiliar words. Have students note the beginning sound of each word (*r*) and the letters they see (*wr*).

518   *farm*

Other Word Forms, Writing Questions and Answers, Comparing and Contrasting

Have students brainstorm for common other word forms of *farm: farms, farmed, farming, farmer, farmers, farmhouse, farmyard.* Have students write this question and the answer: How do you think a farmer's job has changed between farming today and in the past?

Book Tie-In,
Writing an Interview

Use *You Call That a Farm?: Raising Otters, Leeches, Weeds, and Other Unusual Things* (Sam Epstein and Beryl Epstein, Farrar, 1991), which examines farms and their unique products: parrots for zoos, catfish to eat, shrimp for testing poison, alligators for leather. Follow the reading by having students write a make-believe magazine interview with one of the farmers whose products are featured in the book.

519   *circle*

Other Word Forms,
Spelling Rules, Vocabulary Skills,
Writing Sentences

Have students brainstorm for common other word forms of *circle: circles, circled, circling, circular.* Review the spelling rule for adding suffixes to words ending in silent *e* (see **Spelling Sourcebook 1**, page 85). Discuss unfamiliar words. Have students write the other word forms in sentences.

Word Analysis, Writing Words

Have students write *circle* and underline the two *c* letters. Note the different sound made by each *c.* Use the word *check* (493) to point out the *ck* and *ch* spelling patterns. Than have students find and write words with *c* that would illustrate these four examples, such as *could* (70), *children* (200), *city* (273), *rock* (489).

Remember . . .

Develop spelling accountability as students write—see ***Spelling Sourcebook 1,*** Article 8, page 33. Spelling mastery is achieved ONLY when students can spell and use words consistently correctly in writing.

520 *whose*

Homophone Usage ❖ Ask students to identify the homophone of *whose*, the word *who's*. Have students write sentences to differentiate them.

Writing Sentences, Homophone Usage ❖ Have students fill in the blanks in these sentences with the right words:

_____ (Whose, Who's) _____ (already, all ready) to go?

_____ (Whose, Who's) turn is it _____ (to, two, too) read?

_____ (It's, Its) time for the animals to eat _____ (there, their) food.

_____ (Whose, Who's) friend is at _____ (our, hour, are) door?

521 *correct*

Other Word Forms, Prefix Practice, Vocabulary Skills, Writing Questions and Answers ❖ Have students brainstorm for common other word forms of *correct: corrects, corrected, correcting, correction, correctional, correctly, correctness, corrective.* Have students write *correct* with the *in* prefix. Discuss unfamiliar words. Have students write these questions and the answers:

Why do some people use corrective eye wear?

How would you feel if your hair was cut incorrectly?

Why is it important to spell every word correctly on a job application?

522 *bed*

Other Word Forms, Hypothesizing, Spelling Rules, Writing Sentences ❖ Have students brainstorm for common other word forms of *bed: beds, bedded, bedding, bedroom, bedtime.* Ask students to write what they might find in the bedding department of a large store. Ask students to write why the *d* is doubled in *bedding*. Have them write the other word forms in sentences.

Idiomatic Usage, Writing Explanations ❖ Have students explain in writing what they think it means to say these expressions (then discuss):

Early to bed, early to rise, makes a man healthy, wealthy, and wise.

to get up on the wrong side of the bed

to go to bed with the chickens

to put something to bed

523 *measure*

Other Word Forms, Vocabulary Skills, Spelling Rules, Writing Questions and Answers ❖ Have students brainstorm for common other word forms of *measure: measures, measured, measuring, measurement.* Discuss unfamiliar words. Review the spelling rule for adding suffixes to words ending in silent *e* (see ***Spelling Sourcebook 1***, page 85). Have students write these questions and the answers:

What kind of measurement would you use for measuring flour for a cake? . . . the depth of the snow after a snowstorm? . . . the heat on a summer day? . . . your weight? . . . the school day? . . . your age?

Book Tie-In, Creating a Graph ❖ Use *Measurements* (Caroline Arnold, Watts, 1984) for an explanation of measuring, including size, distance, speed, time, and temperature. Follow up the reading by having students measure each other's height and create a graph of the measurements.

524 *straight*

Other Word Forms, Writing Questions and Answers, Multiple Meanings ❖ Have students brainstorm for common other word forms of *straight: straighter, straightest, straighten, straightens, straightened, straightening, straightener.* Have students write these questions and the answers:

> What are you doing if you are straightening your bedroom at home? . . . straightening curly hair? . . . straightening your papers?

Homophone Usage ❖ Ask students to identify the homophone of *straight,* the word *strait.* Discuss the meaning of *strait.* Have students write sentences to differentiate them.

Idiomatic Usage, Writing Explanations ❖ Have students explain in writing what they think it means to say these expressions (then discuss):

to get something straight	straight from the horse's mouth
to keep a straight face	to vote a straight ticket
to set someone straight	Straighten up!

Antonyms ❖ Ask students to identify an antonym of *straight,* the word *crooked,* and predict its spelling.

525 *base*

Other Word Forms, Vocabulary Skills, Writing Questions and Answers ❖ Have students brainstorm for common other word forms of *base: bases, based, basing, basic, basics, basement, basements.* Discuss unfamiliar words. Have students write these questions and the answers: What is the basic ingredient of bread? . . . a tossed salad? . . . a sundae? . . . lemonade?

Idiomatic Usage, Writing Explanations ❖ Have students explain in writing what they think it means to say these expressions (then discuss):

> to touch base with someone
> to base your opinion on something
> off base

Book Tie-In ❖ For baseball enthusiasts, introduce the series *Southside Sluggers Baseball Mysteries* (by either Daniel Greenburg or Steven Otfinoski, Simon, 1992), which feature a baseball team and its ongoing challenges.

526 *mountain*

Other Word Forms, Vocabulary Skills, Writing Sentences ❖ Have students brainstorm for common other word forms of *mountain: mountains, mountaineer, mountaineering, mountainside, mountainous.* Discuss unfamiliar words. Have students write the other word forms in sentences.

Book Tie-In, Making a Chart ❖ Use *Mountains* (Keith Lyle, Silver, 1987) for a survey of the earth's mountains. Follow up with students creating a chart of the world's tallest mountains and their comparative heights.

Book Tie-In, Writing Explanations ❖ For information on avalanches, use *Avalanche* (Stephen Kramer, Carolrhoda, 1992). Then have students write the cause and prevention of this mountain phenomenon.

527 *caught*

Multiple Meanings,
Writing Sentences
Brainstorm for meanings of *caught*. Then have students check a dictionary for verification. Review words that can be used in different ways, such as *sound* (175), *show* (184), *feet* (201), *side* (203), *kind* (214), *clear* (510), *spring* (515). Have students write the words in sentences to illustrate their different meanings.

Other Word Forms, Vocabulary
Skills, Writing Sentences
Have students brainstorm for common other word forms of *caught: catch, catches, catching, catcher.* Discuss unfamiliar words. Have students write the other word forms in sentences. Then have students rearrange the words in each sentence and delete capitals and punctuation. Partners then exchange and unscramble the sentences trying to match the word order of the original sentences.

Homophone Usage
Ask students to identify the homophone of *caught*, the word *cot*. Have students write sentences to differentiate them.

528 *hair*

Other Word Forms, Vocabulary
Skills, Writing Sentences
Have students brainstorm for common other word forms of *hair: hairs, hairy, hairier, hairiest, hairless.* Discuss unfamiliar words. Have students write the other word forms in sentences.

Homophone Usage
Ask students to identify the homophone of *hair,* the word *hare.* Have students write sentences to differentiate them.

Idiomatic Usage,
Writing Explanations
Have students explain in writing what they think it means to say these expressions (then discuss):

to give someone gray hair	neither hide nor hair
to get in someone's hair	to split hairs
to let your hair down	to tear your hair out
to make someone's hair stand on end	

Book Tie-In,
Writing Speculations, Art
Use *Cornrows* (Camille Yarbrough, Putnam, 1979) to initiate a discussion of hairstyles, past and present. Ask students to write and illustrate their predictions for hairstyles of the future.

Word Analysis, Homophone Usage
On the chalkboard write *hair* and *heir,* a homophone for *air.* Contrast the letters of *hair* and *heir.* Discuss the meaning of *heir.* Then discuss *error.*

529 *bird*

Idiomatic Usage,
Writing Explanations
Have students explain in writing what they think it means to say these expressions (then discuss):

A bird in the hand is worth two in the bush.	for the birds
a little bird told me	to kill two birds with one stone
as free as a bird	The early bird gets the worm.
Birds of a feather flock together.	a bird's eye view
	to eat like a bird

Book Tie-In,
Making Comparisons
Use *Birds of Antarctica: The Adélie Penguin* and *The Wandering Albatross* (Jennifer Owings Dewey, Little, 1989), two informative picture books. Have students write a comparison of these unusual birds, which are alike in many fascinating ways.

Compound Words, Writing Words ❖ Have students write compound words that use *bird.* Choices may include *birdbath, birdhouse, birdseed, birdcage, birdcall, birdbrain.* Expand the lesson to *side* (202), *light* (227), *rain* (457).

Book Tie-In, ❖ Use *John James Audubon* (Joseph Castner, Abrams, 1992). Following the *Writing Speculations* reading, have students write character traits of Audubon and tell how these traits contributed to his success in his art.

530   *wood*

Other Word Forms, ❖ Have students brainstorm for common other word forms of *wood: woods,* *Vocabulary Skills,* *wooden, wooded, woodiness, woody.* Discuss unfamiliar words. Have students *Writing Questions and Answers* write this question and the answer: What kind of wildlife might live in a wooded area?

Homophone Usage ❖ Ask students to write the homophone of *wood,* the word *would* (59). Have students write sentences to differentiate them.

Book Tie-In, Writing Descriptions ❖ Use *The Magic Wood* (Henry Treece, HarperCollins, 1992), a story-poem highlighting the eerie forest landscape typical of a Halloween imagination. Ask students to follow up by describing something they imagine being inside the wood's darkness.

Book Tie-In, ❖ Use *Orphan: The Story of a Baby Woodchuck* (Faith McNulty, Scholastic, *Informational Writing* 1992), in which the author cares for a woodchuck imparting information about woodchucks. Follow up by asking students to write an important idea they learned about woodchucks.

531   *color*

Other Word Forms, Vocabulary ❖ Have students brainstorm for common other word forms of *color: colors,* *Skills, Writing Questions and* *colored, coloring, colorful, colorfully, colorless, coloration.* Discuss unfamiliar *Answers, Contrasting* words. Note the Brittish spelling *colour.* Have students write this question and the answer: How would a colorful classroom differ from a colorless one?

Book Tie-In, ❖ Use *Roses Red, Violets Blue: Why Flowers Have Colors* (Sylvia Johnson, *Writing Explanations* Lerner, 1991) for a readable, scientific explanation of color, which includes vibrant photographs. Follow up the reading by having students write an explanation for why "ultraviolet colors" are invisible to the human eye.

Book Tie-In, Writing Poetry, ❖ Use *Hailstones and Halibut Bones* (Mary O'Neill, Doubleday, 1961), a classic *Oral Reading* collection of poems about various colors. Have students identify their favorite color and write an original poem about that color. This model could be used:

    COLOR NAME: adj., adj., adj.,

    _____ ing, _____ ing, _____ ing,

    adj., adj., adj.,

    COLOR!

Have students read their poem orally.

532 *war*

Other Word Forms, Vocabulary Skills, Prefix Practice, Writing Questions and Answers, Hypothesizing

Have students brainstorm for common other word forms of *war: wars, warred, warring, warlike, warrior, warfare.* Discuss unfamiliar words. Introduce the prefix *anti,* which means "against." Have students write and discuss *antiwar* and *antibody* (*body* 285). Then have students write these questions and the answers:

What might create warfare within a country among its own people?
What is the purpose of an antiwar march?
When might you use an antibody?

Book Tie-In, Research and Writing

Use *Don't You Know There's a War On?* (James Stevenson, Morrow, 1992), a powerful tale of a child during World War II. Following the reading have students research and explain why World War II was fought.

Antonyms

Ask students to identify the antonym of *war,* the word *peace,* and predict its spelling.

533 *fly*

Book Tie-In, Writing Descriptions

Introduce *fly* with *Old Black Fly* (Jim Aylesworth, Holt, 1992), humorous, alphabetical couplets about a villainous housefly, which features the refrain, "Shoo fly! Shoo fly! Shooo!" Have students describe in writing their personal experience being annoyed by a pesty fly.

Idiomatic Usage, Writing Explanations

Have students explain in writing what they think it means to say these expressions (then discuss):

as the crow flies	to fly the coop
to do something on the fly	fly-by-night
a fly in the ointment	to make the fur fly
to fly off the handle	Go fly a kite! (See literature entry below.)

Multiple Meanings

Brainstorm for meanings of *fly.* Then have students check a dictionary for verification.

Other Word Forms, Vocabulary Skills, Spelling Rules, Writing Questions and Answers, Hypothesizing

Have students brainstorm for common other word forms of *fly: flies, flew, flown, flying, flier, flight.* Discuss unfamiliar words. Review the spelling rule for adding suffixes to words ending in consonant-*y* (see **Spelling Sourcebook 1**, page 85). Have students write this question and the answer: What information might the flier posted on the school office bulletin board be announcing?

Writing a List, Word Origins

Have students list kinds of flies and flying insects, such as *housefly, mosquito, gnat, firefly, fruit fly, horsefly, dragonfly, butterfly.* Point out that *mosquito* is a word of Spanish origin, so *i* spells the long *e* sound. Other examples of the *i* spelling the long *e* sound in a Spanish word are *patio, siesta, fiesta, sierra,* and *lariat.*

Book Tie-In, Developing a Guide

Use *Kite Flying Is for Me* (Tom Moran, Lerner, 1984), an introduction to making and flying kites. Follow up by making a class guide to kite flying in your area. Include good places to fly and buy kites.

534 *yourself*

Compound Words, Writing Words ❖ Have students find and write more compound words that use *selves* or *self,* such as *himself* (277), *themselves* (443), *itself* (474), *herself, myself, ourselves.* Then expand the lesson by asking students to list more compound words. Play Compound Bingo (see ***Spelling Sourcebook 1,*** page 87) using the compounds.

535 *seem*

Other Word Forms, ❖ Have students brainstorm for common other word forms of *seem: seems,*
Writing Sentences   *seemed, seeming, seemingly.* Have students write the other word forms in sentences.

Book Tie-In, ❖ Use *Nature's Tricksters: Animals and Plants That Aren't What They Seem*
Writing a Book Jacket   (Mary Batten, Sierra, 1992). Follow up with students writing text for a book jacket to entice readers.

Homophone Usage ❖ Ask students to identify the homophone of *seem,* the word *seam.* Have students write sentences to differentiate them.

Dictation and Writing ❖ Dictate these partial sentences for students to write and complete:
   If my friend seems to be sad, perhaps I could _____ .
   I never seem to remember _____ .

536 *thus*

Word Usage ❖ Provide examples of appropriate use of *thus* in writing. Then have students write a sentence using *thus.*

Sound-Symbol Awareness, ❖ Have students write *thus.* Then ask them to follow these directions to make
Writing Sentences   new and review words:
   Change *thus* to make *us* (168), *bus.*
   Change *thus* to make *this* (22).
   Change *thus* to make *these* (58).
   Change *thus* to make *those* (182).
   Change *thus* to make *thumb.* (Have students find and write more words that
      end in silent *b,* such as *numb, tomb, lamb.*)
Have students write a sentence for each word they made.

537 *square*

Other Word Forms, ❖ Have students brainstorm for common other word forms of *square: squares,*
Vocabulary Skills, Spelling Rules,   *squared, squaring, squarest, squareness.* Then write how a carpenter uses an
Writing Speculations   instrument called a square, what might take place at a city square, and if they think a square deal is fair.

Antonyms, Art, Vocabulary Skills ❖ Ask students to identify the antonym of *square,* the word *round* (401). Then have them find and write the names of more shapes. Choices may include *rectangle, triangle, oval.* Next, have students draw the shapes and label them.

538   *moment*

Other Word Forms, Vocabulary Skills, Writing Questions and Answers, Hypothesizing

Have students brainstorm for common other word forms of *moment: moments, momentary, momentarily, momentous, momentum.* Discuss unfamiliar words. Have students write these questions and the answers:

What was your most momentous occasion?

What factors might contribute to a political candidate's gaining momentum?

Writing a Definition

Have students write how long a moment is.

539   *teacher*

Other Word Forms, Writing Sentences

Have students brainstorm for common other word forms of *teacher: teach, teaches, taught, teaching.* Have students write the other word forms in sentences.

Book Tie-In, Career Awareness, Creating a Book

Use *Teachers: A to Z* (Jean Johnson, Walker, 1987) for a unique, inside look at the teaching profession. Use this book as a model for students to create their own book of a profession of their choice (see page 138, Creating Classroom Books).

Book Tie-In, Writing Reasons, Evaluating

Use *Christa McAuliffe: Teacher in Space* (Corinne Naden and Rose Blue, Millbrook, 1991), a biography of the outstanding teacher whose work was cut short by the *Challenger* explosion. Then have students write what makes a teacher an outstanding one.

Career Awareness, Writing a List

Have students list career opportunities in which they would work within a school setting, such as *teacher, principal, librarian, school nurse, speech therapist, custodian, food servicer, secretary.* Then hold a class discussion to list the skills and interests necessary for each job.

540   *happy*

Other Word Forms, Spelling Rules, Writing Questions and Answers

Have students brainstorm for common other word forms of *happy: happier, happiest, happiness, happily.* Review the spelling rule for adding suffixes to words ending in consonant-*y* (see ***Spelling Sourcebook 1***, page 85). Have students write the other word forms in sentences that ask a question. Then have students exchange papers and answer the questions using the same word forms of *happy* in the responses.

Idiomatic Usage, Writing Explanations

Have students explain in writing what they think it means to say these expressions (then discuss):

happy-go-lucky   to strike a happy medium

as happy as a clam   as happy as a lark

Antonyms

Ask students to write the antonym of *happy,* the word *sad.*

Synonyms, Vocabulary Skills, Writing Sentences, Creating a Word Puzzle

Have students write *happy.* Then have them write synonyms for *happy* that are specific, such as *blissful, cheerful, delighted, ecstatic, elated, content, merry, exultant, glad, gleeful, jolly, jovial, joyful, jubilant, lighthearted, overjoyed, thrilled, tickled.* Discuss unfamiliar words. Have students create a word-search puzzle using happy and its synonyms (provide graph paper or use the blackline master on page 109 of ***Spelling Sourcebook 1***). Then students exchange and complete the puzzles.

541 *bright*

Multiple Meanings, Writing Sentences ❖ Brainstorm for meanings of *bright*. Then have students check a dictionary for verification. Review words that can be used in different ways, such as *second* (235), *story* (237), *paper* (241), *hard* (242), *main* (469), *wood* (530). Have students write the words in sentences to illustrate their different meanings.

Other Word Forms, Vocabulary Skills, Writing Questions and Answers, Writing Speculations ❖ Have students brainstorm for common other word forms of *bright: brighter, brightest, brightly, brightness, brighten, brightens, brightened, brightening, brightener.* Discuss unfamiliar words. Have students write this question and the answer: If someone brightened your day, what might the person have done?

Book Tie-In, Writing Explanations ❖ Ask students what it means to say, "Look on the bright side." Then use *Good Times on Grandfather Mountain* (Jacqueline Briggs Martin, Orchard, 1992) to illustrate the idiom. Ask students to explain in writing how people looked on the bright side when something unfortunate happened.

Antonyms ❖ Ask students to identify an antonym of *bright,* the word *dull,* and predict its spelling.

Sound-Symbol Awareness, Sorting Words ❖ Have students write *bright* and listen to the long *i* sound. Then have students collect more words with long *i* to note the most frequent spellings for long *i* (most common: *y* [*my*], *ight* [*right*], *ind* [*kind*], *i*-consonant-*e* [*smile*]). Create a list of long *i* words. Have students write the words in categories sorted by the spelling for the long *i*. Have one category for "other" to accommodate less common spellings.

542 *sent*

Other Word Forms, Writing Sentences ❖ Have students brainstorm for common other word forms of *sent: send, sends, sending, sender.* Have students write the other word forms in sentences.

Homophone Usage ❖ Ask students to identify the homophones of *sent,* the words *cent* and *scent.* Have students write sentences to differentiate them.

Book Tie-In, Writing Riddles, Oral Reading ❖ Use *Hey, Hay!: A Wagonful of Funny Homonym Riddles* (Marvin Terban, Clarion, 1991) as a catalyst for students to write their own silly riddles using homonyms—homophones and homographs. Have students read their best riddle to the class and have the class respond by writing their solution to the riddle.

543 *present*

Homograph Usage ❖ Discuss the two pronunciations and different meanings of this homograph. Ask students to write sentences to differentiate the words.

Other Word Forms, Vocabulary Skills, Writing Questions and Answers ❖ Have students brainstorm for common other word forms of *present: presents, presented, presenting, presence, presentable, presentation, presently.* Discuss unfamiliar words. Have students write these questions and the answers:
  How might you make your presence known at school in a positive way?
  Who are presently the Canadian Prime Minister and the U.S. President?

Book Tie-In, Writing Stories ❖ Use *The Golden Locket* (Carol Greene, Harcourt, 1992), an adaptation of an Indian folktale that begins with Miss Teaberry's finding a locket and making a present of it to a girl down the road. The girl responds with a present . . . Miss Teaberry presents the present to another . . . who responds with a present . . . and so goes the story. Also use *The Present* (Michael Emberley, Little, 1991), in which Arne has trouble deciding which present to give his nephew. Then have students write about an experience giving or receiving a present.

Book Tie-In, Following Written Directions, Writing a Summary, Public Speaking ❖ Use *Make Gifts!* (Kim Solga, North Light, 1991), which inspires readers to create presents, such as jewelry, handmade paper, and pop-up cards, by following step-by-step directions. Have students create a present and summarize in writing how they did it. Then they may share their project orally.

Antonyms ❖ Ask students to identify the antonym of one meaning of *present,* the word *absent,* and predict its spelling.

544 *plan*

Other Word Forms, Spelling Rules, Suffix Practice, Writing Sentences ❖ Have students brainstorm for common other word forms of *plan: plans, planned, planning, planner.* Review the spelling rule for doubling the final consonant before adding suffixes (see **Spelling Sourcebook 1**, page 85). Have students apply the rule to the following words; they must decide which should double the final consonant and which should not: *correct* (521), *clear* (510), *map* (497), *build* (487), *begin* (444), *shell* (437), *stop* (396), *sad* (323), *point* (272). Have students write sentences using the words with suffixes.

Writing Words, Word Analysis ❖ Have students write *plan* and *plane.* Discuss how the addition of the *e* changes the vowel sound. Then have students find and write more words that follow this pattern, such as *mad/made* (81), *can* (38)/*cane, fin/fine* (400) and *not* (30)/*note.*

545 *rather*

Dictation and Writing ❖ Dictate these partial sentences for students to write and complete:
I would rather not _____ .
When it's rather hot outside I _____ .

Visual Skill-Building, Writing Words, Writing Sentences ❖ Play the Word Look-Alike game. Ask students to circle the words in each row that are like the underlined word. Then they turn the paper over, picture the underlined word, and write it.

<u>rather</u>	matter	other	rather	gather	father	mother
<u>bright</u>	might	bright	fight	bring	brought	bright
<u>whose</u>	hose	where	house	whom	whose	who's
<u>wrote</u>	wrote	write	rote	wrong	white	whole

Next, have students write the underlined words in sentences.

546 *length*

Other Word Forms, Writing Sentences ❖ Have students brainstorm for common other word forms of *length: long, longer, longest, longish.* Have students write the other word forms in sentences. Then have students exchange papers. Next, students rewrite the sentences, changing the verb tense in each.

Antonyms ❖ Ask students to identify an antonym of *length,* the word *width,* and predict its spelling.

Writing Words ❖ Have students play Connect the Dots (see ***Spelling Sourcebook 1***, page 87) using *length* and selected review words.

Visual Skill-Building, ❖ Provide students with graph paper (or use the blackline master on page 109 of
Writing Words ***Spelling Sourcebook 1***). Have students write the letters of *length* in the boxes and outline the word's shape. Expand the lesson to selected review words.

547 *speed*

Other Word Forms, ❖ Have students brainstorm for common other word forms of *speed: speeds,*
Writing Sentences *sped, speeded, speeding, speedy, speedier, speediest, speeder.* Have students write the other word forms in sentences.

Research, Writing a Summary ❖ Introduce students to speed records. Use the biography of the Olympic Gold Medal speed skater, *Eric Heiden: Winner in Gold* (Nathan Aaseng, Lerner, 1980); *The Cheetah: Nature's Fastest Racer* (Randall Eaton, Dodd, 1981); and *Michael Andretti at Indianapolis* (Michael Andretti and Robert Carver and Douglas Carver, Simon, 1992). Then have students research other speed records and summarize them in writing.

Writing Stories ❖ Have students play Finish the Story (see ***Spelling Sourcebook 1***, page 88) using *speed* and selected review words.

548 *machine*

Other Word Forms, ❖ Have students brainstorm for common other word forms of *machine: machines,*
Vocabulary Skills, Spelling Rules, *machinery, machinist.* Discuss unfamiliar words. Review the spelling rule for
Writing Questions and Answers adding suffixes to words ending in silent *e* (see ***Spelling Sourcebook 1***, page 85). Have students write this question and the answer: What machines do you use daily?

Book Tie-In, Art, ❖ Use *Simple Machines* (Anne Horvatic, Dutton, 1989) for a straightforward
Writing Explanations explanation of how machines work, such as a wheelbarrow. Then have students make pictures of simple machines, with an explanation of how the machine helps them and others.

Book Tie-In, Research and ❖ Use *Robert Goddard* (Karin Farley, Silver, 1993), a biography of the pioneer
Writing, Evaluating, rocket scientist who fulfilled his childhood dream of building a flying machine.
Creating a Book Have students research and list inventors and their mechanical inventions. Have them evaluate how the inventions contributed to society and impacted their own life. Compile the results into a class-made book (see page 138, Creating Classroom Books).

549 *information*

Other Word Forms, Vocabulary ❖ Have students brainstorm for common other word forms of *information:*
Skills, Writing Sentences *inform, informs, informed, informing, informer.* Discuss unfamiliar words. Have students write the other word forms in sentences. Then have students rearrange the words in each sentence and delete capitals and punctuation. Partners then exchange and unscramble the sentences trying to match the word order of the original sentences.

Research and Writing,
Public Speaking

Have students research one of the following topics, tell about their findings in writing, and then present the information orally to the class:

the information most often requested on a job application

the information included in a city telephone directory, besides phone numbers and addresses of residents

what resources to use for information on vacation spots in a given city, synonyms for given words, nutritional contents of a packaged food, used bicycles for sale, and topics of interest in published magazines.

550 *except*

Other Word Forms, Vocabulary
Skills, Writing Questions and
Answers, Writing Explanations

Have students brainstorm for common other word forms of *except: excepts, excepted, excepting, exception, exceptions, exceptional, exceptionally.* Discuss unfamiliar words. Have students write the answers: What do you think is meant when your teacher says:

"Homework is due Friday. No exceptions."

"Your book report was exceptional."

"Class begins at eight for all students except our band members."

Homophone Usage, Dictation and
Writing, Book Tie-In

Except and *accept* are often pronounced as homophones. Have students write sentences to differentiate them. Then dictate these partial sentences for students to write and complete:

My homework machine works well, except _____ .

(Use Shel Silverstein's poem, "The Homework Machine" in *A Light in the Attic,* Harper, 1974)

I cannot accept your present because _____ .

551 *figure*

Multiple Meanings,
Writing Sentences

Brainstorm for meanings of *figure.* Then have students check a dictionary for verification. Review words that can be used in different ways, such as *change* (264), *point* (272), *play* (274), *ground* (311), *foot* (482), *glass* (488). Have students write the words in sentences to illustrate their different meanings.

Other Word Forms,
Vocabulary Skills, Spelling Rules,
Writing Sentences

Have students brainstorm for common other word forms of *figure: figures, figured, figuring, figurative, figuratively.* Discuss unfamiliar words. Review the spelling rule for adding suffixes to words ending in silent *e* (see **Spelling Sourcebook 1**, page 85). Have students write the other word forms in sentences.

Book Tie-In, Writing Riddles
and Brain Teasers

Ask students to "figure it out" with *Behind the King's Kitchen: A Roster of Rhyming Riddles* (William Smith and Carol Ra, Wordsong, 1992), which allows for a wide range of difficulty levels. Have students research riddles and brain teasers and then write a favorite to try to stump the class.

Figurative Language

Have students find and write examples of figurative language. Then have them write an original example.

552 *you're*

Homophone Usage, Dictation and Writing

You're and *your* (40) are often pronounced as homophones. Discuss the differences in meaning. Ask students to write sentences to differentiate the words. Review *there* (37), *they're,* and *their* (42); *to* (5), *two* (65), and *too* (112); *its* (76) and *it's* (253). Then dictate these sentences for students to write:

Your teacher will present two books to students that they're sure to like.
It's beautiful weather now except for a chance of light rain.
You're to give the dog its food in that square dish over there.
Their farm is much too large for only two people to work.

553 *free*

Multiple Meanings, Writing Sentences

Brainstorm for meanings of *free.* Then have students check a dictionary for verification. Review words that can be used in different ways, such as *table* (314), *course* (317), *space* (320), *draw* (338). Have students write the words in sentences to illustrate their different meanings.

Other Word Forms, Vocabulary Skills, Writing Sentences

Have students brainstorm for common other word forms of *free: frees, freed, freeing, freedom, freedoms, freely, freer, freest.* Discuss unfamiliar words. Have students write the other word forms in sentences.

Idiomatic Usage, Writing Explanations

Have students explain in writing what they think it means to say these expressions (then discuss):

as free as a bird   free and easy
free-for-all   to go scot-free
to feel free to do something to give someone free rein

Book Tie-In, Research and Writing, Writing Explanations

Use *Freedom* (Lois Cantwell, Watts, 1985) for an explanation of the concept of freedom. Follow up with students researching and writing about America's symbols of freedom. Book sources may include *The Statue of Liberty: America's Proud Lady* (Jim Haskins, Lerner, 1986) and *The Story of the Liberty Bell* (Natalie Miller, Childrens, 1965). Have students explain why the symbols stand for freedom.

554 *fell*

Other Word Forms, Vocabulary Skills, Writing Sentences

Have students review common other word forms of *fell: fall, falls, fallen, falling.* Discuss the meanings of *fall* and *falls.* Have students write the different meanings in sentences.

Sound-Symbol Awareness, Creating a Word Puzzle

Have students write *fell.* Then ask them to follow these directions to make new and review words:

Change *fell* to make *feel* (355).
Change *fell* to make *well* (132), *tell* (147).
Change *fell* to make *shell* (437), *bell, sell, yell.*
Change *fell* to make *felt* (377).
Change *fell* to make *full* (363).
Change *fell* to make *few* (181).

Have students create a Word Search Puzzle using these words and other words for a classmate to complete.

555 *suppose*

Other Word Forms, Vocabulary Skills, Spelling Rules, Suffix Practice, Writing Sentences

❖ Have students brainstorm for common other word forms of *suppose: supposes, supposed, supposing, supposedly.* Discuss unfamiliar words. Review the spelling rule for adding suffixes to words ending in silent *e* (see **Spelling Sourcebook 1**, page 85). Review suffix additions to *figure* (551), *machine* (548), *square* (537), *measure* (523), *care* (483), *size* (462), *possible* (452), *ice* (441), *complete* (365), *move* (290), *change* (264), *picture* (232). Have students write selected other word forms in sentences.

Word Analysis, Visual Skill-Building, Writing Words, Writing Sentences

❖ Have students list words with double letters. Then write *suppose* on the chalkboard, and draw an outline around it to accentuate its shape. Provide students with graph paper (or use the blackline master on page 109 of **Spelling Sourcebook 1**). Have students write words with double letters in the boxes and outline the shape of each word (see Letter Grid Games on page 88 of **Spelling Sourcebook 1**). Then have students make word shapes for review words, exchange papers with a partner, and see if the partner can fill in the boxes with the appropriate words. Next, have students write sentences using these words.

556 *natural*

Other Word Forms, Vocabulary Skills, Writing Sentences

❖ Have students brainstorm for common other word forms of *natural: nature, natures, naturally, naturalize.* Discuss unfamiliar words. Have students write the other word forms in sentences.

Book Tie-In, Developing a Brochure

❖ Use *Natural Wonders and Disasters* (Billy Goodman, Little, 1991) and *The Seven Natural Wonders of the World* (Celia King, Chronicle, 1991), which show and tell about the earth's natural wonders. Ask students to create a "natural wonders" brochure for tourists for their geographic area (see page 138, Creating Classroom Books).

Book Tie-In, Hypothesizing, Information Resources

❖ Use *Natural History from A to Z: A Terrestrial Sampler* (Tim Arnold, McElderry, 1991), an alphabetical exploration of mind-expanding tidbits of information. Have students follow up by hypothesizing in writing how and where Arnold was able to find the information that makes his book so fascinating.

557 *ocean*

Other Word Forms, Vocabulary Skills, Writing Sentences

❖ Have students brainstorm for common other word forms of *ocean: oceans, oceanic, oceanography.* Discuss unfamiliar words. Have students write the other word forms in sentences.

Book Tie-In, Creating a Book

❖ Use *Oceans* (Philip Whitfield, Viking, 1991) and *Mysteries and Marvels of Ocean Life* (Rick Morris, Usborne, 1983) to explore the idiosyncrasies of marine life. From this information and other sources, ask students to create a trivia book of interesting facts about ocean life (see page 138, Creating Classroom Books).

Book Tie-In, Writing Opinions

❖ Use *Make a Splash!* (Thompson Yardley, Millbrook, 1992) for puzzles and activities that relate to the ocean life chain. Engage students in the projects and then ask them to write a book review of the book.

Visual Skill-Building, Sound-Symbol Awareness

❖ Have students write *ocean.* Then they touch each letter with the point of their pencil and spell it. Have them note the sounds the *c* and the *ea* make in *ocean.*

558 *government*

Other Word Forms, Vocabulary Skills, Writing Questions and Answers, Research ❖ Have students brainstorm for common other word forms of *government: govern, governs, governed, governing, governor, governors, governable, governess*. Discuss unfamiliar words. Have students write these questions and the answers:

> Who is currently your state governor?
> How long has this governor governed?

Book Tie-In, Research and Writing ❖ Use *Shh! We're Writing the Constitution* (Jean Fritz, Putnam, 1987) to introduce students to the challenges facing the founders of America's government. Have students research and list countries of the world in which new governments are being formed.

Using a Dictionary Pronunciation Key ❖ Some words are misspelled because they are often mispronounced, such as *government*. Have students use a dictionary to check the correct pronunciation of *government*. Expand the lesson to *probably* (383), *February, library, athlete, arctic, recognize, sophomore, quantity, candidate, restaurant, hundred* (374), *surprise, pumpkin, finally* and other words often mispronounced.

559 *baby*

Book Tie-In, Writing a List, Vocabulary Skills ❖ Use *The Baby Zoo* (Bruce McMillan, Scholastic, 1992), an informative text with exciting pictures of baby zoo animals appropriate for intermediate grade learners. Ask students to add to the list of names of animal babies included in the book (bear/cub, sheep/lamb, kangaroo/joey).

Book Tie-In, Writing a Story Ending ❖ Use *The Rainbabies* (Laura Melmed, Lothrop, 1992), a fairy tale about a couple who desperately want a child and are presented with a "dozen shimmering drops of water, each holding a tiny baby" that delight them. But Mother Moonshower later comes to retrieve the babies. What then happens to the couple? Have students write the fairy tale ending before Melmed's happy ending is read.

Spelling Rules, Plural Practice, Writing Words ❖ Review the spelling rule for making plurals of words ending in consonant-*y* (see *Spelling Sourcebook 1*, page 85). Have students change *baby* to *babies*. Then have students follow this model with *fly* (533), *sky* (467), *city* (273), *country* (228), *cherry, bunny, lady*. Then have them find and write more words that follow this spelling pattern.

560 *grass*

Dictation and Writing ❖ Dictate these partial sentences for students to write and complete:

> Grass will probably stay green if _____ .
> Playing on grass is better than _____ .

Writing Similes ❖ Students may have heard the simile "as green as grass." Have students write more similes.

561 *plane*

Other Word Forms, Vocabulary Skills, Writing Sentences ❖ Have students brainstorm for common other word forms of *plane: planes, planed, planing*. Discuss unfamiliar words. Have students contrast *plane* with *plan* (544). Have them write the other word forms of *plane* and *plan* in sentences.

Book Tie-In, Following Written Directions, Writing Directions	❖ Use *The Paper Airplane Book* (Seymour Simon, Viking, 1971) for lessons on how to fold paper airplanes. The book also explains why various constructions result in different flying patterns. Have students fold paper into planes, fly the planes, and then write the directions for creating the plane that provides the best flying experience.
Homophone Usage	❖ Ask students to identify the homophone of *plane,* the word *plain.* Then have students review the spelling of *explain* (513).
Clipped Words	❖ Have students compile a list of clipped words, beginning with *plane/airplane.* Choices may include *math/mathematics, limo/limousine, teen/teenager, gym/gymnasium, bike/bicycle, fridge/refrigerator.*
Book Tie-In, Career Awareness, Evaluating	❖ Use *A Week in the Life of an Airline Pilot* (William Jaspersohn, Little, 1991), a narrative about a commercial pilot. Following the reading, have students write why they think they are or are not suited for the career of a pilot.

562 *street*

Book Tie-In, Writing Speculations, Public Speaking	❖ Use *Violence on America's Streets* (Gene Brown, Millbrook, 1992) for a discussion of crime and unsuccessful attempts toward solutions. Ask students to formulate a possible solution to one issue presented, write why it should work, and present the idea orally to the class.
Writing Abbreviations	❖ Write the abbreviation for *street* (*st.* or *St.*). Then have students list abbreviations for such things as units of measurement, days of the week, months, states, provinces, and parts of speech used in the dictionary.

563 *couldn't*

Contractions, Writing Words	❖ Have students write *couldn't* and the words from which it is made (*could, not*). Then have students find and write more contractions that use *not,* such as *can't* (380), *don't* (190), *isn't, won't, shouldn't, wouldn't, aren't, doesn't, wasn't, weren't, hasn't, haven't, hadn't, mustn't, didn't.*
Sorting Words	❖ Have students play Word Sorts (see **Spelling Sourcebook 1**, page 92) using these words: *couldn't, it's* (253), *they're, you're* (552), *don't* (190), *that's* (390), *can't* (380), *we're, haven't, didn't, she's.*

564 *reason*

Other Word Forms, Prefix Practice, Vocabulary Skills, Writing Sentences	❖ Have students brainstorm for common other word forms of *reason: reasons, reasoned, reasoning, reasonable, reasonably.* Then have students add the *un* prefix to *reasonable* and note how the prefix changes the meaning. Discuss unfamiliar words. Have students write the other word forms in sentences.
Book Tie-In, Reasoning, Writing Explanations	❖ Challenge students' abilities to reason with *World's Most Baffling Puzzles* (Charles Townsend, Sterling, 1991) and *Hidden Pictures* (Linda Bolton, Dial, 1993). Have students explain in writing how they reasoned their way to solutions.

Sound-Symbol Awareness, Writing Sentences

❖ Have students write *reason*. Then ask them to follow these directions to make new and review words and to answer the questions:

Change *reason* to make *son* (the opposite of *daughter*).
Change *reason* to make *season*. (What season is it now?)
Change *reason* to make *really* (313).
Change *reason* to make *raisin*. (How are raisins made?)

Then have students write a sentence for each word they made.

565 *difference*

Other Word Forms, Vocabulary Skills, Writing Questions and Answers, Hypothesizing, Comparing and Contrasting

❖ Have students brainstorm for common other word forms of *difference: differ, differs, differed, differing, different* (139), *differently, differentiate*. Discuss unfamiliar words. Have students write these questions and the answers:

How does a library differentiate books? Why?
How does today's weather differ from yesterday's?
How is a cat different from a dog as a pet?

Book Tie-In, Writing a Biography

❖ Use *People Who Make a Difference* (Brent Ashabranner, Cobblehill/Dutton, 1989), a collection of stories about ordinary people who are extraordinarily committed to making life better for themselves and others. Ask students to write a biographical sequel about someone they know who is making a difference.

Suffix Practice, Vocabulary Skills

❖ Have students write *different* (139) and *difference* and underline the *ence* suffix of *difference*. Review *important* (195) and *importance, present* (543) and *presence, distant* and *distance* (449) and have students note whether the suffix is spelled *ence* or *ance*. Discuss the meanings of the words with and without the suffix. Then have students change *silent, excellent, innocent, intelligent, elegant,* and *defiant* to nouns ending with *ence* or *ance*. Have students check a dictionary to verify spellings. Discuss unfamiliar words.

566 *maybe*

Word Analysis, Writing Sentences

❖ Have students write *maybe* and *may be*. Discuss the difference between the look-alike words. Review *always* (183) /*all ways, already* (411) /*all ready, shell* (437) /*she'll, quite* (447) /*quiet/quit, our* (109) /*are* (15), *then* (53) /*than* (73), *picture* (232) /*pitcher*. Have students write these often-confused words in sentences.

567 *history*

Other Word Forms, Vocabulary Skills, Writing Questions and Answers, Writing Reasons

❖ Have students brainstorm for common other word forms of *history: histories, historian, historic, historical, historically*. Discuss unfamiliar words. Have students write these questions and the answers:

For what reasons might a building be historical?
What recent event will be recorded in the future as a historic one? Why?

Magazine Tie-In, Outlining

❖ Use issues of *Cobblestone: The History Magazine for Young People*. The issues are thematic and include activities and information. Have students choose an article and outline its important information.

Book Tie-In,
Creating a Timeline
❖ Use *The Big Tree* (Bruce Hiscock, Holiday, 1991), which traces American history through the growth of a two-hundred-year-old New York maple tree. Readers receive a history and botany lesson simultaneously. Follow up with students constructing a timeline of American history.

Creating a Calendar, Research
❖ Ask students to choose the month of their birthday and create a calendar for that month. Ask them to research historic events that occurred during that month and note the events on their calendar.

568 *mouth*

Idiomatic Usage,
Writing Explanations
❖ Have students explain in writing what they think it means to say these expressions (then discuss):

to bad-mouth something	to live from hand to mouth
born with a silver spoon in your mouth	to put your foot in your mouth
	Put your money where your mouth is.
by word of mouth	to take the words right out of your mouth
to have a big mouth	to shoot off your mouth

Analogies, Writing Words,
Writing Sentences
❖ Review analogies (see 466, 503). Then have students write these analogies and complete them with words of frequencies 548–568 or their other word forms:

rooms : house :: teeth : _____ (mouth)
could not : couldn't :: you are : _____ (you're)
important : importance :: different : _____ (difference)
blue : sky :: green : _____ (grass)
there : they're :: accept : _____ (except)
foot : feet :: baby : _____ (babies)
United States : president :: state : _____ (governor)

Have students write the answer words in sentences.

569 *middle*

Idiomatic Usage,
Writing Explanations
❖ Have students explain in writing what they think it means to say these expressions (then discuss):

caught in the middle	to play both ends against the middle
in the middle of nowhere	smack dab in the middle

Book Tie-In,
Informational Writing,
Comparing and Contrasting
❖ For a lively introduction to the Middle Ages, use *Medieval People* and *Medieval Places* (Sarah Howarth, Millbrook, 1992). Ask students to write what they know about the Middle Ages before and after reading, to compare and contrast their knowledge.

570 *step*

Other Word Forms,
Spelling Rules, Suffix Practice
❖ Have students brainstorm for common other word forms of *step: steps, stepped, stepping.* Review the spelling rule for doubling the final consonant before adding suffixes (see *Spelling Sourcebook 1*, page 85). Have students apply the rule to the following words; they must decide which should double the final consonant and which should not: *reason* (564), *speed* (547), *plan* (544), *farm* (518), *map* (497), *build* (487), *stop* (396), *add* (335), *run* (306), *sun* (257), *end* (170), *get* (101), *find* (87), *can* (38). Ask students to write each word with its appropriate suffixes.

Idiomatic Usage,
Writing Explanations

Have students explain in writing what they think it means to say these expressions (then discuss):

to be out of step	to step on someone's toes
step by step	Step on it.
to step out of line	Step it up.
take steps to make something happen	

Sound-Symbol Awareness,
Writing Sentences

Have students write *step*. Then ask them to follow these directions to make new and review words and to answer the questions:

Change *step* to make *stop* (396).
Change *step* to make *strap*. (How might you use a strap?)
Change *step* to make *steep*. (How might you use a steep hill?)
Change *step* to make *stem*. (Where might you see a stem?)
Change *step* to make *stew*. (What might be in a stew?)
Change *step* to make *stay* (473).

Then have students write a sentence for each word they made.

571 *child*

Plural Practice, Writing Words

Review irregular plurals (see *Spelling Sourcebook 1*, page 85). Write *child* and *children* (200) on the chalkboard. Have students find and write more examples of irregular plurals, such as *foot* (482) /*feet, goose/geese, man* (111) /*men* (148), *woman/women, mouse/mice, ox/oxen, tooth/teeth.*

Research, Writing Reasons,
Creating a Reading List

Ask students to find out who are the most popular children's book authors for readers their age. Sources may include their own reading experiences, reading choices of their friends, and ideas from librarians and bookstore clerks. Have students list popular children's book authors, the most important books they've written, and a statement about each book telling why it is so popular. Then have students share their lists. Are there some books that students have not read that are popular among readers their age? Ask students to put these books on their reading list.

572 *strange*

Other Word Forms,
Vocabulary Skills, Spelling Rules,
Writing Sentences

Have students brainstorm for common other word forms of *strange: stranger, strangest, strangeness, strangely.* Discuss unfamiliar words. Ask students to write why the final silent *e* in *strange* is not dropped before the suffixes are added (see *Spelling Sourcebook 1*, page 85). Have students write the other word forms in sentences.

Book Tie-In, Creating a Book

Kids love strange facts! Some of the strangest, most interesting animal facts can be found in *Elephants Can Jump and Other Freaky Facts About Animals* (Barbara Seuling, Dutton, 1985), *Lies People Believe About Animals* (Susan Sussman, Whitman, 1987), and *Dawn to Dusk in the Galápagos: Flightless Birds, Swimming Lizards, and Other Fascinating Creatures* (Rita Gelman, Little, 1991). Ask students to create a "Strange But True" book about animals using these and other sources (see page 138, Creating Classroom Books).

Book Tie-In, Writing Stories

Use *Seven Strange and Ghostly Tales* (Brian Jacques, Philomel, 1991). Then have students write a strange and ghostly tale.

573 *wish*

Other Word Forms, Vocabulary Skills, Spelling Rules, Writing Questions and Answers

Have students brainstorm for common other word forms of *wish: wishes, wished, wishing, wishingly, wishful.* Discuss unfamiliar words. Review the rule for adding suffixes to words ending in *sh* (see ***Spelling Sourcebook 1***, page 85). Have students write this question and the answer: What is an example of wishful thinking?

Other Word Forms, Writing Words

Have students play All in the Family (see ***Spelling Sourcebook 1***, page 86) using the other word forms of *wish* and the other word forms of selected review words.

Dictation and Writing

Dictate this partial sentence for students to write and complete:
   If I had a wish machine that could make wishes come true, I'd _____ .

Creating a Greeting Card

Have students create a greeting card wishing someone an appropriate wish and then send or deliver it.

574 *soil*

Dictation and Writing

Dictate these partial sentences for students to write and complete:
   To get the soil ready for planting, it's important to _____ .
   When my shoes get soiled, I _____ .

Sound-Symbol Awareness, Writing Sentences

Have students write *soil.* Then ask them to follow these directions to make new words and answer the questions:
   Change *soil* to make *soiled.* (What is a synonym for *soiled*?)
   Change *soil* to make *spoil.* (What might a *spoiled* child do?)
   Change *soil* to make *oil.*
   Change *soil* to make *boil.*

Then have students write a sentence for each word they made.

575 *human*

Other Word Forms, Vocabulary Skills, Writing Sentences

Have students brainstorm for common other word forms of *human: humans, humanity, humanly, humanistic, humanitarian.* Discuss unfamiliar words. Have students write the other word forms in sentences.

Prefix Practice, Writing Words, Writing a Definition

Have students add the *in* prefix to *human* and *humane.* Discuss how it changes the meaning. Explain that the prefixes *in, im,* and *un* can mean "not." Then have them write one of these prefixes before *direct* (*direction* 619), *reasonable* (*reason* 564), *natural* (556), *planned* (*plan* 544), *happy* (540), *correct* (521), *explained* (*explain* 513), *clear* (510), *possible* (452) *movable* (*move* 290). Have students check a dictionary if they are uncertain about which prefix to use. Then have students explain in writing what each of the prefixed words means.

Book Tie-In, Writing Questions, Research and Writing

Use *Outside and Inside You* (Sandra Markle, Bradbury, 1991) for a look at the human body through pictures and easy-flowing text. Before reading the book, have students compile a list of questions they have about the body and how it works. After reading, students may research any questions left unanswered and write answers to them.

576   *trip*

Multiple Meanings,
Writing Sentences

Brainstorm for meanings of *trip*. Then have students check a dictionary for verification. Review words that can be used in different ways, such as *letter* (344), *mean* (349), *fire* (356), *state* (371), *free* (553). Have students write the words in sentences to illustrate their different meanings.

Other Word Forms,
Spelling Rules, Suffix Practice

Have students brainstorm for common other word forms of *trip: trips, tripped, tripping.* Review the spelling rule for doubling the final consonant before adding suffixes (see **Spelling Sourcebook 1**, page 85). Have students apply the rule to the following words; they must decide which should double the final consonant and which should not: *trap, tip, tap, plan* (544), *map* (497), *begin* (444), *stop* (396), *box* (388), *hot* (368), *rest* (351), *run* (306).

Writing Descriptions,
Writing Reasons

Have students describe in writing their dream trip. Have them tell who would go, where they'd go, what they'd do there, how they'd get there and back, and why it is their choice.

577   *woman*

Antonyms

Ask students to write the antonym of *woman,* the word *man* (111).

Plural Practice

Review irregular plurals (see **Spelling Sourcebook 1**, page 85). Have students write *woman* and *women.* Review *child* (571) /*children* (200), *foot* (482) /*feet* (201), *man* (111) /*men* (148).

Research and Writing, Public
Speaking, Writing a Question

Have students research one of the following topics, tell about their findings in writing, and then present the information orally to the class:

a woman who has won acclaim in the field of sports

a woman who has made an important contribution in public service

the first woman in space (Valentina Tereshkova, 1963)

Following the presentations to the class, have students write one question they'd like to ask each of the accomplished women.

578   *eye*

Other Word Forms, Vocabulary
Skills, Compound Words,
Writing an Eyewitness Account

Have students brainstorm for common other word forms of *eye: eyes, eyed, eyeing, eyeful.* Then have students brainstorm for compound words that use *eye,* such as *eyeball, eyelash, eyebrow, eyelid, eyedropper, eyesight, eyewitness.* Discuss unfamiliar words. Have students write an eyewitness account of a real or make-believe happening.

Homophone Usage

Ask students to write the homophones of *eye,* the words *I* (24) and *aye.* Discuss the meaning of *aye.*

Idiomatic Usage,
Writing Explanations

Have students explain in writing what they think it means to say these expressions (then discuss):

An eye for an eye, a tooth for a tooth.
the apple of your eye
to catch someone's eye
to have stars in your eyes
to have eyes bigger than your stomach
to have eyes in the back of your head

in the public eye
to pull the wool over
    someone's eyes
to see eye to eye
a sight for sore eyes
without batting an eye

Book Tie-In,
Creating Visual Puzzles

Use *Visual Magic* (David Thompson, Dial, 1991) and *Optical Illusions* (Laurence B. White and Ray Broekel, Watts, 1986) to explore images that fool the eyes and the scientific principles behind them. Follow up with students making their own illusionary puzzles to fool the eyes.

Palindromes, Writing Words,
Analyzing Words

A palindrome is a word, phrase, or sentence spelled the same forwards and backwards. *Eye* is a palindrome. Have students find and write more palindromes, such as *mom, dad, pop, noon, level, deed, peep, did, eve, Bob, Anna, Nan, radar, madam, tot, toot, kayak, repaper, rotator.* Palindrome sentences include *Step on no pets, Live not on evil, Was it a car or a cat I saw?*

579 *milk*

Visual Skill-Building,
Writing Words, Writing Sentences

Play the Word Look-Alike game. Ask students to circle the words in each row that are like the underlined word. Then they turn the paper over, picture the underlined word, and write it.

<u>milk</u>	mild	silk	milk	child	mill	wick
<u>strange</u>	change	strange	string	strange	strap	range
<u>through</u>	though	thought	enough	through	tough	threw
<u>mouth</u>	south	mouth	mouse	north	month	mouth

Next, have students write the underlined words in sentences.

Writing Words

Have students play the All-Play Spelling Bee (see **Spelling Sourcebook 1**, page 86) using *milk* and selected review words.

Remember . . .

Develop spelling accountability as students write—see **Spelling Sourcebook 1**, Article 8, page 33. Spelling mastery is achieved ONLY when students can spell and use words consistently correctly in writing.

580 *choose*

Other Word Forms,
Vocabulary Skills, Spelling Rules,
Writing Sentences

Have students brainstorm for common other word forms of *choose: chooses, chose, chosen, choosing, choice, choices, choosy, choosier, choosiest.* Discuss unfamiliar words. Review the spelling rule for adding suffixes to words ending in silent *e* (see **Spelling Sourcebook 1**, page 85). Have students write the other word forms in sentences.

Homophone Usage

Ask students to identify the homophone of *choose,* the word *chews.* Have students write sentences to differentiate them.

Writing Words, Word Properties,
Writing Reasons

Introduce the activity "Choose." Have students write the words in each row, then choose one word that does not belong, and write why it is different from the others.

corn	bread	milk	measure
foot	mouth	ear	eye
street	walk	road	highway
ocean	river	lake	middle
you're	it's	that's	he's

581   *north*

Other Word Forms, Vocabulary Skills, Writing Questions and Answers

❖ Have students brainstorm for common other word forms of *north: northern, northerly, northward.* Discuss unfamiliar words. Have students write the other word forms in sentences that ask a question. Then have students exchange papers and answer the questions using the same word forms of *north* in the responses.

Antonyms, Writing Words

❖ Ask students to identify the antonym of *north,* the word *south.* Expand the lesson by saying these words and asking students to write the opposite word: *man* (*woman* 577), *could* (*couldn't* 563), *unnatural* (*natural* 556), *crooked* (*straight* 524), *incorrect* (*correct* 521), *enemy* (*friend* 498).

582   *seven*

Book Tie-In, Dictation and Writing, Writing a List

❖ Use *The World by Sevens: A Kid's Book of Lists* (Louis Phillips, Watts, 1981), which has curiosities arranged in lists of seven facts each. Dictate these partial sentences for students to write and complete with lists of seven:

My seven best friends are
Seven foods I couldn't live without are
The seven most important days of the year are
Seven birds I've seen in this area are
The seven main ways to keep a baby happy are
The seven most beautiful colors are
Seven important historical events are
Seven machines you might find on a farm are
The seven largest cities in this region are

Writing Number Words, Homophone Usage

❖ Have students write the number words *one* (28), *two* (65), *three* (125), *four* (211), *five* (276), *six* (354), *seven* (582), *eight, nine, ten* (375). Then have them write *first* (74), *second* (235), *third* (446), *fourth, fifth, sixth, seventh, eighth, ninth, tenth.* Next, have them identify homophones among these words (*one, two, four, eight*) and write their homophone partners (*won, to* 5, *too* 112, *for* 12, *fore, ate*). Have students use the homophones in sentences to differentiate them.

583   *famous*

Synonyms, Vocabulary Skills

❖ Ask students to research and list synonyms for *famous,* such as *celebrated, eminent, famed, notable, prominent, renowned, well-known.* Discuss unfamiliar words.

Writing Opinions, Writing a List, Debating

❖ Create categories with the class and then have students list their choice for the most famous living person within each category. Categories may include popular music, world government, cinema, sports, television, business. Have students share their choices for the famous people, debate the choices, and conclude with one class list of the "most famous."

584 *late*

Other Word Forms,
Suffix Practice

Have students review common other word forms of *late: later* (288), *latest, lately, lateness*. Review the *ly* ending. Have students write the *ly* suffix after *natural* (556), *present* (543), *bright* (541), *week* (512), *friend* (498), *main* (469). Have students write these *ly* words and the other word forms of *late* in sentences.

Antonyms, Synonyms

Ask students to identify an antonym of *late*, the word *early*. Then have them write a synonym for *late*, the word *tardy*.

Word Analysis,
Creating a Word Puzzle

Have students note the final silent *e* in *late*. Then have them use *late* and other words with final silent *e* to create a crossword puzzle for a classmate to complete (see Letter Grid Games, *Spelling Sourcebook 1*, page 88).

585 *pay*

Other Word Forms, Vocabulary
Skills, Writing Sentences

Have students brainstorm for common other word forms of *pay: pays, paid, paying, payment, payments, payable*. Discuss unfamiliar words. Have students write the other word forms in sentences. Then have students rearrange the words in each sentence and delete capitals and punctuation. Partners then exchange and unscramble the sentences trying to match the word order of the original sentences.

Prefix Practice,
Writing a Definition

Have students add prefixes to *pay* and *paid*, such as *re, pre, under, over, un, post*. Then have them define the new words.

Idiomatic Usage,
Writing Explanations

Have students explain in writing what they think it means to say these expressions (then discuss):

Crime doesn't pay.	to pay through the nose
to hit pay dirt	to rob Peter to pay Paul
to pay as you go	Pay up.
to pay your dues	to pay an arm and a leg for something
to pay the piper	to pay someone a visit

Sound-Symbol Awareness,
Sorting Words

Have students write *pay* and listen to the long *a* sound. Then have students collect more words with long *a* to note the most frequent spellings for long *a* (most common: *ay* [*play*], *ai* [*train*], *a*-consonant-*e* [*same*]). Create a list of long *a* words. Have students write the words in categories sorted by the spelling for the long *a*. Have one category for "other" to accommodate less common spellings.

586 *sleep*

Other Word Forms,
Writing Speculations

Have students brainstorm for common other word forms of *sleep: sleeps, slept, sleeping, sleeper, sleepers, sleepy, sleepless, sleeplessness*. Have students write this question and the answer: How do you think you might feel and act following a sleepless night?

Book Tie-In, Writing a List

Use *Do Not Disturb: Mysteries of Animal Hibernation and Sleep* (Margery Facklam, Little, 1989), which introduces the mysterious biological process of a winter's sleep. Ask students to list animals that hibernate in winter.

Book Tie-In, Hypothesizing ❖ Use *While the Shepherd Slept* (Matt Novak, Orchard, 1991), a picture-book story of sheep who creep away to town to perform vaudeville on the town stage while their shepherd sleeps. Ask students to write why they think the shepherd is so sleepy. Then read the ending that tells why—he dances each night on the same stage his sheep perform on during the day!

Word Analysis, Writing Words ❖ Have students list *sleep* and other words with double letters. Then have students play Spelling Baseball (see *Spelling Sourcebook 1*, page 91) using the words.

587 *iron*

Other Word Forms, ❖ Have students brainstorm for common other word forms of *iron: irons, ironed,*
Writing Sentences *ironing.* Have students write the other word forms in sentences.

Multiple Meanings, ❖ Brainstorm for meanings of *iron.* Then have students check a dictionary for
Writing Sentences verification. Review words that can be used in different ways, such as *felt* (377), *matter* (386), *stand* (387), *class* (391), *bright* (541), *trip* (576). Have students write the words in sentences to illustrate their different meanings.

588 *trouble*

Other Word Forms, ❖ Have students brainstorm for common other word forms of *trouble: troubles,*
Vocabulary Skills, Spelling Rules, *troubled, troubling, troublesome, troublemaker.* Discuss unfamiliar words. Review
Research and Writing the spelling rule for adding suffixes to words ending in silent *e* (see *Spelling Sourcebook 1*, page 85). Have students recall stories to name a story character who
had a troublesome time
was a troublemaker
solved troubles for someone else
got into trouble
was untroubled by something that would have troubled you

Idiomatic Usage, ❖ Have students explain in writing what they think it means to say these
Writing Explanations expressions (then discuss):

to ask for trouble   to go to the trouble to do something
to borrow trouble   no trouble
to spell trouble   to look for trouble

Synonyms, Vocabulary Skills, ❖ Ask students to research and list synonyms for *trouble,* such as *dilemma,*
Writing Sentences *predicament, quandary, mishap, calamity, hardship, misfortune.* Discuss unfamiliar words and ask students to write them in sentences.

589 *store*

Multiple Meanings, ❖ Brainstorm for meanings of *store.* Then have students check a dictionary for
Writing Sentences verification. Review words that can be used in different ways, such as *fine* (400), *blue* (407), *mind* (419), *game* (433). Have students write the words in sentences to illustrate their different meanings.

Other Word Forms, ❖ Have students brainstorm for common other word forms of *store: stores,*
Vocabulary Skills, Spelling Rules, *stored, storing, storage, storehouse.* Discuss unfamiliar words. Review the
Writing Questions and Answers, spelling rule for adding suffixes to words ending in silent *e* (see *Spelling*
Hypothesizing *Sourcebook 1*, page 85). Have students write this question and the answer: If all the electricity went out, how might cold food storage become a problem and how might you solve it?

590 *beside*

Word Analysis, Writing Words

Have students list *be____* words beginning with *beside*. Choices may include *because* (127), *between* (154), *below* (176), *began* (215), *before* (332), *became* (334), *become* (336), *behind* (342), *begin* (444), *beyond, believe, beneath*.

Compound Words, Writing Words

Have students write *beside* and underline the two word parts. Then have students find and write compound words that use *side,* such as *sidewalk, dockside, sideways, inside, outside, sidestep, sideshow, sidesaddle, sideline*.

591 *oil*

Other Word Forms, Vocabulary Skills, Writing Sentences

Have students brainstorm for common other word forms of *oil: oils, oiled, oiling, oily*. Discuss unfamiliar words. Have students write the other word forms in sentences.

Book Tie-In, Research and Writing

Use *Spill!: The Story of the Exxon Valdez* (Terry Carr, Watts, 1991), which objectively explores the historical oil spill and the cleanup. Follow up with students using the *Reader's Guide* to research and describe in writing current oil spills and their impact on the environment.

Sound-Symbol Awareness, Writing Words

Point out that *oi* and *oy* usually spell the same sound in words. Have students find and write examples. Choices may include *oil, boy* (205), *point* (272), *voice* (382), *soil* (574), *join, noise, avoid, enjoy, employee*.

592 *modern*

Book Tie-In, Writing Reasons

The Father of Modern Science was Galileo. Have students explore the impact this man had on society in *Galileo* (Leonard Fisher, Macmillan, 1992). Then have them write an answer to this question: Why is Galileo called the Father of Modern Science?

Antonyms

Ask students to identify an antonym of *modern,* the word *ancient,* and predict its spelling.

Comparing and Contrasting, Writing Speculations

Have students compare and contrast ancient dinosaurs with modern animals with *Dinosaur Encore* (Patricia Mullins, HarperCollins, 1993). Then have students speculate what might happen if the dinosaurs featured in the book suddenly reappeared to live among modern animals.

593 *fun*

Other Word Forms, Spelling Rules, Writing Sentences

Have students brainstorm for common other word forms of *fun: funny, funnier, funniest*. Review the spelling rule for adding suffixes to words ending in consonant-*y* (see **Spelling Sourcebook 1**, page 85). Have students write the other word forms in sentences.

Book Tie-In, Writing Descriptions

Use *Chicken Man* (Michelle Edwards, Lothrop, 1991), a picture-book story about Rody, who makes his jobs in an Israeli kibbutz appear to be such great fun that others take them over. Have students follow up by writing about a task they have done that was fun instead of work.

Synonyms, Vocabulary Skills, Writing Sentences

Ask students to research and list synonyms for *fun*. Choices may include *entertaining, amusing, enjoyable*. Discuss the meanings of unfamiliar words and ask students to write them in sentences.

594 *catch*

Other Word Forms, Vocabulary Skills, Writing Sentences

❖ Have students review common other word forms of *catch: catches, caught* (527), *catching, catcher.* Discuss unfamiliar words. Have students write the other word forms in sentences.

Idiomatic Usage, Writing Explanations

❖ Have students explain in writing what they think it means to say these expressions (then discuss):

to catch cold	to catch someone red-handed
to catch fire	caught short
to catch on	to catch your breath
to catch some z's	to catch someone off guard

595 *business*

Book Tie-In, Research and Writing

❖ Use *Dial-A-Croc* (Mike Dumbleton, Orchard, 1991), which introduces fictional Vanessa, an eager entrepreneur. Have students follow up by researching and describing in writing unusual real-life businesses that were started by creative entrepreneurs.

Spelling Rules, Plural Practice, Writing Words

❖ Review the spelling rule for making *business* plural (see **Spelling Sourcebook 1**, page 85). Have students write the plurals of *wish* (573), *grass* (560), *glass* (488), *watch* (436), *class* (391), *box* (388), *tax, church, lunch, dish, guess.*

596 *reach*

Other Word Forms, Writing Questions and Answers

❖ Have students brainstorm for common other word forms of *reach: reaches, reached, reaching.* Have students write the other word forms in sentences that ask a question. Then have students exchange papers and answer the questions using the same word forms of *reach* in the responses.

Sound-Symbol Awareness, Sorting Words

❖ Have students write *reach* and listen to the long *e* sound. Then have students collect more words with long *e* to note the most frequent spellings for the long *e* (most common: *ee* [*see*], *e* [*me*], *ea* [*eat*], *e*-consonant-*e* [*these*]). Create a list of long *e* words. Have students write the words in categories sorted by the spelling for the long *e*. Have one category for "other" to accommodate less common spellings.

Sound-Symbol Awareness, Vocabulary Skills

❖ Have students write *reach.* Then have them write words by changing the beginning letter(s). Choices may include *beach, bleach, breach, peach, teach.* Then have them make words by changing the ending letter(s). Choices may include *read* (165), *really* (313), *ready* (357), *real* (454), *reason* (564), *reap, rear.* Discuss unfamiliar words.

597 *lot*

Multiple Meanings, Writing Sentences

❖ Brainstorm for meanings of *lot.* Then have students check a dictionary for verification. Review words that can be used in different ways, such as *watch* (436), *carry* (448), *heart* (453), *leaves* (460), *store* (589). Have students write the words in sentences to illustrate their different meanings.

Word Analysis, Writing Sentences

❖ Have students write *a lot.* Point out that two words make up the phrase *a lot.* Write *allot* on the chalkboard and discuss its meaning. Review *always* (183) */all ways, already* (411) */all ready, shell* (437) */she'll, quite* (447) */quiet/quit, our* (109) */are* (15), *then* (53) */than* (73), *picture* (232) */pitcher, maybe* (566) */ may be.* Have students write these often-confused words in sentences.

Idiomatic Usage, Writing Explanations

❖ Have students explain in writing what they think it means to say these expressions (then discuss):

to cover a lot of ground	to have a lot on your mind
to have a lot going for you	leaves a lot to be desired
to have a lot of promise	to think a lot of someone

Dictation and Writing

❖ Dictate these partial sentences for students to write and complete:

My friends and I would be in a lot of trouble if _____ .

One place to get a lot of information about famous people is _____ .

A lot of government money is needed for _____ .

598 *won't*

Contractions, Writing Words

❖ Have students write *won't* and the words that make up the contraction (*will not*). Expand the lesson by asking students to find and write more contractions. Then have students write the words that make up each one.

Writing Contractions, Writing Abbreviations

❖ Have students play Race Track Spelling (see **Spelling Sourcebook 1**, page 90) using short-cut words—contractions and abbreviations.

599 *case*

Multiple Meanings, Writing Sentences

❖ Brainstorm for meanings of *case*. Then have students check a dictionary for verification. Review words that can be used in different ways, such as *wild* (463), *miss* (465), *field* (472), *foot* (482). Have students write the words in sentences to illustrate their different meanings.

Idiomatic Usage, Writing Explanations

❖ Have students explain in writing what they think it means to say these expressions (then discuss):

just in case	in any case
to be on someone's case	to make a federal case out of something

600 *speak*

Other Word Forms, Vocabulary Skills, Writing Sentences

❖ Have students brainstorm for common other word forms of *speak: speaks, spoke, spoken, speaking, speaker, speakers.* Discuss two meanings for *spoke.* Have students write the other word forms in sentences.

Idiomatic Usage, Writing Explanations

❖ Have students explain in writing what they think it means to say these expressions (then discuss):

Actions speak louder than words.	to speak your mind
nothing to speak of	to speak out of turn
so to speak	to speak up (See literature entry below.)

Book Tie-In, Making a Check List, Public Speaking

❖ Use *You Can Speak Up in Class* (Sara Gilbert, Morrow, 1991) to help those students who have a fear of speaking publicly. Share with students that this fear is common even among adults. Have students follow up the reading by creating a checklist of preparations to make prior to giving a public talk. Then have students prepare and deliver a brief talk to the class.

601 *shape*

Other Word Forms, Vocabulary Skills, Spelling Rules, Hypothesizing, Writing Reasons

Have students brainstorm for common other word forms of *shape: shapes, shaped, shaping, shapely.* Discuss unfamiliar words. Review the spelling rule for adding suffixes to words ending in silent *e* (see *Spelling Sourcebook 1*, page 85). Have students write this question and the answer: What current event may play a role in shaping the future of someone your age? Why?

Sound-Symbol Awareness, Writing Words

Note with students that the letters *sh* always spell the sound they hear at the beginning of *shape.* However, other letters also spell this sound. Have students find and write examples. Choices may include *ch* (*machine* 548), *ti* (*information* 549), *ci* (*special* 361), *ce* (*ocean* 557), *s* (*sure* 251), *si* (*mission*).

602 *eight*

Homophone Usage

Ask students to write the homophone of *eight*, the word *ate*. Then have students write the number words 1–10 that are homophones.

Research and Writing, Making a Chart, Public Speaking

Have students research one of the following topics, tell about their findings in writing, and then present the information orally to the class using a self-made chart as a visual aid:

> the eight books checked out most often from your school library
> eight important bicycle (or boating, skiing, camping, etc.) safety rules
> the eight biggest news stories in the last year
> the eight greatest athletes (or presidents, teachers, desserts, etc.)

Word Analysis, Writing Words

Have students find and write more words with *ght*. Choices may include *thought* (179), *straight* (524) and *bright* (541).

603 *edge*

Other Word Forms, Vocabulary Skills, Spelling Rules, Writing Sentences

Have students brainstorm for common other word forms of *edge: edges, edged, edging, edger, edgy.* Discuss unfamiliar words. Review the spelling rule for adding suffixes to words ending in silent *e* (see *Spelling Sourcebook 1*, page 85). Have students write the other word forms in sentences.

Idiomatic Usage, Writing Explanations

Have students explain in writing what they think it means to say these expressions (then discuss):

> to edge someone out   to be on the cutting edge
> to be on edge   to get a word in edgewise

604 *soft*

Other Word Forms, Writing Sentences

Have students brainstorm for common other word forms of *soft: softer, softest, softly, softness.* Have students write the other word forms in sentences.

Book Tie-In, Hypothesizing

Have students brainstorm for soft things. Then introduce *Feathers* (Dorothy Hinshaw Patent, Cobblehill, 1992) to show students the purpose, structure, and use of feathers. Ask students to hypothesize in writing what they think might happen if all animal coverings were soft feathers.

Antonyms

Ask students to write the antonym of *soft,* the word *hard* (242).

Book Tie-In, Writing Similes

Students may have heard the simile "as soft as silk." Review similes. Use *A Surfeit of Similes* (Norton Juster, Morrow, 1989). Then have students write more similes with *soft* and *hard* (242).

605 *village*

Plural Practice, Writing a Definition ❖ Ask students to write the plural of *village* and a definition for *villager.*

Book Tie-In, Research and Writing ❖ Use *The Village of Blue Stone* (Stephen Trimble, Macmillan, 1990), which uses a story format to describe the Anasazi, who lived in elaborate villages in New Mexico in 1100 A.D. Have students research and write how we learned what we know today about these ancient peoples and their lifestyle.

606 *object*

Homograph Usage ❖ Discuss the two pronunciations and different meanings of this homograph. Ask students to write sentences to differentiate them.

Other Word Forms, Vocabulary Skills, Writing Questions and Answers, Making a Judgment ❖ Have students brainstorm for common other word forms of *object: objects, objected, objecting, objection, objectionable, objective.* Discuss unfamiliar words. Have students write this question and the answer: From what you know about school rules, what might be an example of objectionable behavior for a student?

Book Tie-In, Creating a Book, Writing Descriptions ❖ The alphabet book *Gretchen's ABC* (Gretchen Simpson, HarperCollins, 1991) is suitable for older children. The illustrations challenge the viewer to name a familiar object by looking at a close-up of a salient detail. Follow up with students creating their own close-up puzzles from magazine pictures and compiling them into a class-made book, *Name the Object* (see page 138, Creating Classroom Books).

607 *age*

Other Word Forms, Vocabulary Skills, Spelling Rules, Writing Sentences ❖ Have students brainstorm for common other word forms of *age: ages, aged, aging, ageless.* Discuss unfamiliar words. Review the spelling rule for adding suffixes to words ending in silent *e* (see **Spelling Sourcebook 1**, page 85). Have students write the other word forms in sentences.

Book Tie-In, Writing Speculations ❖ Use *When I Was Your Age* (Ken Adams, Barron's, 1991). Then have students imagine themselves as a grandfather sixty years in the future and write things they might tell their grandchildren about how things were "when I was your age."

608 *minute*

Homograph Usage, Word Origins ❖ Discuss the two pronunciations and different meanings of this homograph. Ask students to write sentences to differentiate them. Note with students that *minutes,* meaning "notes of a meeting," came from the Latin *minutus,* or "small." The minutes are a small, or condensed, version of the happenings at a meeting. *Minutus* is also the origin of *minute,* meaning "small."

609 *wall*

Book Tie-In, Research and Writing, Comparing and Contrasting ❖ Use *The Berlin Wall: How It Rose and Why It Fell* (Doris Epler, Millbrook, 1992). Then have students research the Great Wall of China. Ask students to compare and contrast the two walls in writing. Points of diversity include their purpose, size, age, and construction.

Book Tie-In, Developing a Brochure	Use *A Wall of Names: The Story of the Vietnam Veterans Memorial* (Judy Donnelly, Random, 1991), an easy-to-read history of the memorial. Then have students create a brochure for memorial visitors that provides the information necessary to appreciate the structure.

610 *meet*

Other Word Forms, Writing Sentences	Have students brainstorm for common other word forms of *meet: meets, met, meeting*. Have students write the other word forms in sentences. Then have students rearrange the words in each sentence and delete capitals and punctuation. Partners then exchange and unscramble the sentences trying to match the word order of the original sentences.
Idiomatic Usage, Writing Explanations	Have students explain in writing what they think it means to say these expressions (then discuss):

       to make ends meet   to meet someone halfway
       to meet your match   more than meets the eye

Homophone Usage	Ask students to identify a homophone of *meet,* the word *meat.* Have students write sentences to differentiate them. The homophone *mete* could also be discussed.
Research and Writing, Hypothesizing	Ask students to find out which national television series is the longest running (*Meet the Press*). Provide the word *meet* as a clue. Then have students find out the kind of program *Meet the Press* is and ask them to hypothesize in writing why it has been successful.

611 *record*

Homograph Usage, Writing Sentences	Review the homographs *object* (606) and *minute* (608). Have students check a dictionary for pronunciations and meanings of *record.* Ask students to write sentences to differentiate the homographs.
Book Tie-In, Homograph Usage, Writing Riddles	Use *The Dove Dove: Funny Homograph Riddles* (Marvin Terban, Ticknor, 1988). Review the homographs *use* (88), *does* (128), *read* (165), *live* (217), *close* (328), *wind* (341), *present* (543), *object* (606) *minute* (608). Then ask students to write their own homograph riddles.
Other Word Forms, Vocabulary Skills, Writing Sentences	Have students brainstorm for common other word forms of *record: records, recorded, recording, recorder.* Discuss unfamiliar words. Have students write the other word forms in sentences.
Research and Writing, Book Tie-In	Have students research animal records. One resource could be *Animal Records* (Annette Tison and Talus Taylor, Putnam, 1984). Have students find and record the biggest fish (whale shark), the biggest animal (blue whale), the biggest land mammal (African elephant), the biggest reptile (colossal saltwater crocodile), the smallest bird (hummingbird), the tallest animal (giraffe), the animal that can jump the highest (puma), the fastest land mammal (cheetah), the fastest animal (peregrine falcon), the longest-lived animal (tortoise).

612 *copy*

Multiple Meanings, Writing Sentences	Brainstorm for meanings of *copy.* Then have students check a dictionary for verification. Review words that can be used in different ways, such as *gold* (486), *glass* (488), *rock* (489), *check* (493). Have students write the words in sentences to illustrate their different meanings.

Other Word Forms,
Spelling Rules, Suffix Practice,
Plural Practice, Writing Words

❖ Have students brainstorm for common other word forms of *copy: copies, copied, copying, copier.* Review the spelling rule for adding suffixes and making plurals of words ending in consonant-*y* (see **Spelling Sourcebook 1**, page 85). Review *funny (fun* 593), *history* (567), *baby* (559), *happy* (540), *fly* (533), *tiny* (479), *sky* (467), *easy* (459), *rainy (rain* 457), *carry* (448), *dry* (438), *heavy* (426), *early* (324), *family* (287), *city* (273), *story* (237), *study* (234), *country* (228). Have students use these and other consonant-*y* words to play Password (see **Spelling Sourcebook 1**, page 89).

Prefix Practice, Writing Words

❖ Have students add the *re* prefix to *copy.* Expand the lesson to *record* (611), *store* (589), *pay* (585), *heat* (505), *build* (487), *wind* (341), *order* (309), *play* (274), *place* (131), *write* (108), *use* (88).

613 *forest*

Book Tie-In, Writing Descriptions

❖ Use *An Ancient Forest* (Guy Spencer, Troll, 1988) for an introduction to the majestic redwoods in northern California. This area is the only place these tallest-of-all trees grow. Have students follow up by writing words that best describe these rare trees.

Book Tie-In, Hypothesizing

❖ Use *The Rain Forest* (Billy Goodman, Little, 1992) and *Rain Forest* (Barbara Taylor, Dorling, 1992). Follow up with students hypothesizing about what might happen if the world were to lose its rain forests.

Research,
Career Awareness, Evaluating

❖ Have students research about forest rangers. Then have them write whether this career would or would not be a good one for them.

614 *especially*

Dictation and Writing

❖ Dictate these partial sentences for students to write and complete:
My teacher thinks it is especially important to _____ .
One mountain that is especially beautiful is _____ .
Once when we had especially cold weather, I _____ .

Analogies, Writing Words,
Writing Sentences

❖ Review analogies (see 503, 568). Then have students write these analogies and complete them with words of frequencies 594–614 or their other word forms:
sure : measure :: special : ____ (especially)
water : ocean :: tree : ____ (forest)
disagree : object :: tiny : ____ (minute)
won : one :: ate : ____ (eight)
spoke : speak :: caught : ____ (catch)
Have students write the answer words in sentences.

615 *necessary*

Synonyms, Vocabulary Skills,
Writing Sentences

❖ Ask students to research and list synonyms for *necessary.* Choices may include *essential, mandatory, indispensable, needed, compulsory, required.* Discuss meanings of unfamiliar words and ask students to write them in sentences.

Prefix Practice, Writing Words

❖ Have students write *necessary.* Add the *un* prefix to the word, and discuss how the prefix changes the meaning. Then have students find and write more words with the *un* prefix.

Other Word Forms,
Vocabulary Skills,
Writing Sentences, Writing a List

❖ Have students brainstorm for common other word forms of *necessary:*
necessarily, necessity, necessities. Discuss unfamiliar words. Have students
write the other word forms in sentences. Then have students list ten necessities
for a successful picnic.

616 *he's*

Contractions, Homophone Usage,
Writing Sentences

❖ Have students write other contractions that include *he* (*he'd, he'll*). Then have
students write the homophones for *he'll—heal* and *heel—*and write them in
sentences.

Antonyms, Writing Words

❖ Ask students to identify the antonym of *he's,* the word *she's.* Expand the lesson
by saying these words and asking students to write the opposite word:
unnecessary (*necessary* 615), *will* (*won't* 598), *ancient* (*modern* 592), *south*
(*north* 581), *man* (*woman* 577), *round* (*square* 537), *enemy* (*friend* 498),
answer (*question* 476).

617 *unit*

Word Origins, Prefix Practice,
Writing Words

❖ Write *unit* and underline *uni.* Explain that *uni* can be a prefix meaning "one."
Relate the prefix to the meaning of *unicorn, unify, unicycle, universe.* Introduce
another prefix meaning "one," *mon* or *mono.* Provide the examples *monarch*
and *monorail.* Other prefixes expressing number are *bi* "two," and *tri* "three."
Have students find and write examples of each. Choices may include *bicycle,*
biplane, bifocals, triangle, tricycle, tricolor.

618 *flat*

Other Word Forms,
Vocabulary Skills,
Writing Questions and Answers

❖ Have students brainstorm for common other word forms of *flat: flatter, flattest,*
flatly, flatten, flatness, flattening, flattener. Discuss unfamiliar words. Have
students write the other word forms in sentences that ask a question. Then have
students exchange papers and answer the questions using the same word forms
of *flat* in the responses.

Multiple Meanings,
Writing Words

❖ *Flat* has multiple meanings. Ask students to write answers to these questions
that use *flat* in different ways:

What kind of shoes are *flats?*
What happened to the soda if it went *flat?*
What is a *flat* rate for doing a job?
What is *flat* paint?
How are a *flat* and an apartment alike?
What is meant by a "*flat* no?'
Why should a singer avoid singing in a *flat* key?

Spelling Rules, Suffix Practice,
Writing Words

❖ Review the spelling rule for doubling the final consonant before adding
suffixes (see ***Spelling Sourcebook 1***, page 85). Have students apply the rule to
flat, fat, fit, trip (576), *plan* (544), *map* (497), *begin* (444), *ship* (442).

Then have students find and write more words that follow this spelling pattern.
Then have students play Connect the Dots (see ***Spelling Sourcebook 1***, page
87) using the words.

Book Tie-In, *Writing Explanations*	❖ Use *"The Earth Is Flat"—And Other Great Mistakes* (Laurence Pringle, Morrow, 1983) to explore all-time great mistakes including the one in the title. Have students write a textbook explanation of the flat-earth theory that might have been taught to students centuries ago. Then have them write a modern-day description of our planet's shape.

619 *direction*

Writing Directions	❖ Have students write directions for getting from one place to another. Choices may include:

> from their classroom to the office
> from their house to their school (use a street map)
> from their house to a friend's house (use a street map)
> from their city to another city (use a road map)

Writing Directions, Sequencing	❖ Have students write directions for how to do something. Ask them to list the specific steps sequentially. Choices may include:

> how to make a peanut butter sandwich
> how to operate a bike lock
> how to check out a book in the school library
> how to make a bed

620 *south*

Other Word Forms, Vocabulary *Skills, Writing Sentences*	❖ Have students brainstorm for common other word forms of *south: southern, southerly.* Discuss unfamiliar words. Have students write the other word forms in sentences.
Book Tie-In	❖ Use *Folk Stories of the South* (M. A. Jagendorf, Vanguard, 1973). Then have students try to pinpoint characteristics of southern tales.
Book Tie-In, Writing a List	❖ Use *A Southern Time Christmas* (Robert Bernardini, Pelican, 1991), a take-off on "The Night Before Christmas," in which the reader can gain insights into customs that are uniquely southern. Have students follow up by creating a list of customs unique to different parts of our country and to different cultures.
Antonyms	❖ Ask students to write the antonym of *south,* the word *north* (581).
Writing State Names *and Abbreviations*	❖ Have students write the names of the southern states and their post office abbreviations.
Sound-Symbol Awareness, *Writing Sentences*	❖ Have students write *south.* Then ask them to follow these directions to make new and review words:

> Change *south* to make *mouth* (568).
> Change *south* to make *sound* (175).
> Change *south* to make *southern.*
> Change one letter of *south* to make *youth.* (Ask students to define *youth.*)
> Change *south* to make *shout.*

Then have students write a sentence for each word they made.

621 *subject*

Homograph Usage, Writing Words
❖ Discuss the two pronunciations and different meanings of this homograph. Ask students to write sentences to differentiate them. Have students find and write more homographs. Choices may include *record* (611), *minute* (608), *object* (606), *present* (543).

Other Word Forms, Vocabulary Skills, Writing Sentences
❖ Have students brainstorm for common other word forms of *subject: subjects, subjected, subjecting, subjective, subjectively, subjectivity.* Discuss unfamiliar words. Have students write the other word forms in sentences.

Vocabulary Skills, Comparing and Contrasting
❖ Discuss the difference between *objective* and *subjective* actions. Have students write an explanation of the difference between an objective and a subjective decision.

Writing Explanations, Using References, Writing Questions and Answers
❖ Have students explain how an encyclopedia is organized. Then ask them to write what subject they would look for in an encyclopedia to answer these questions:

> What famous lighthouses are there on the west coast of the United States?
> Who were the first explorers to the North Pole?
> What is the climate of Greenland in the winter?
> How was New York's Statue of Liberty built?
> What is baseball's Hall of Fame?

Then have students write similar questions, exchange questions with a classmate, and write the subject they would look for in an encyclopedia to answer each question. Have students verify their answers by checking encyclopedias.

622 *skin*

Other Word Forms, Vocabulary Skills, Synonyms
❖ Have students brainstorm for common other word forms of *skin: skins, skinned, skinning, skinny, skinless.* Discuss unfamiliar words. Have students write synonyms for *skinny.* Choices may include *thin, lean, slender, slim.*

Idiomatic Usage, Writing Explanations
❖ Have students explain in writing what they think it means to say these expressions (then discuss):

> Beauty is only skin deep.   nothing but skin and bones
> by the skin of your teeth   to save someone's skin
> to get under someone's skin   to skin someone alive
> There's more than one way to skin a cat.

623 *wasn't*

Contractions, Writing Words
❖ Have students write *wasn't* and the words from which it is made (*was, not*). Then have students find and write more contractions that use *not.* Choices may include *don't* (190), *can't* (380), *couldn't* (563), *won't* (598), *isn't, shouldn't, wouldn't, aren't, doesn't, wasn't, weren't, hasn't, haven't, hadn't, mustn't, didn't.*

Writing Reasons
❖ Have students write reasons why they think our language includes contractions.

624 *I've*

Contractions, Writing Words
❖ Have students write *I've* and the words from which it is made (*I, have*). Then have students find and write more contractions that use *have.* Choices may include *you've, we've, they've, could've, would've, should've, might've.*

Dictation and Writing   ❖ Dictate these partial sentences for students to write and complete:

I've learned that it is necessary to _____ .
When I've enough money, _____ .

625 *yellow*

Book Tie-In,
Writing a Book Jacket   ❖ Use *The Magic of Color* (Hilda Simon, Lothrop, 1981), which includes an explanation of color, optical illusions with color, and discussions of color mixtures. Follow up with students writing a book jacket synopsis of the book that would entice readers.

Using References   ❖ Have students explore the yellow pages of a telephone directory. Then have them write the listing category they would consult to find out these things: the cost of a new tropical fish aquarium, a repair service for their hair dryer, where to get their too-small coat altered to fit, where they could rent horses to go riding, where to buy roller blades, how much it costs to rent a video movie, information about scuba diving lessons, where to buy or rent an outfit to wear to a masquerade party, where to get a picture framed.

Research, Writing Explanations,
Writing Reasons   ❖ Have students research and write what each of these items is or means:

the yellow brick road (an element in *The Wizard of Oz*)
the Yellow Rose of Texas (song)
to tie a yellow ribbon around a tree trunk (safety for American war hostages/song)
a flashing yellow traffic signal (slow/caution)
Yellowstone (national park)

Then have students give reasons why they think school buses are painted yellow, why the moon can look yellow in the night sky, and why some leaves turn shades of yellow or red in autumn. Can students list more "yellows"?

626 *party*

Multiple Meanings   ❖ Review words that can be used in different ways, such as *poor* (496), *mark* (504), *clear* (510), *spring* (515). Then have students brainstorm for meanings of *party*. Have students check a dictionary for verification.

Other Word Forms,
Vocabulary Skills, Spelling Rules,
Writing Sentences   ❖ Have students brainstorm for common other word forms of *party: parties, partied, partier, partying*. Discuss unfamiliar words. Review the spelling rule for adding suffixes and making plurals of words ending in consonant-*y* (see *Spelling Sourcebook 1*, page 85). Have students write the other word forms in sentences.

Book Tie-In, Alliteration,
Writing Sentences   ❖ Use the zany picture-book story of a grand party, *The Horrendous Hullabaloo* (Margaret Mahy, Viking, 1992). Follow up with students finding examples of alliteration in the text. Then have students create original sentences using alliteration about a real or make-believe party.

Making a Poster   ❖ Discuss common political parties. Have each student create a poster for a political party which includes symbols for the party, important party leaders, history, and beliefs.

Creating an Invitation   ❖ Have students create a party invitation that includes all pertinent information. Discuss the meaning of RSVP on a party invitation.

627 *force*

Multiple Meanings, Writing Sentences

Brainstorm for meanings of *force*. Then have students check a dictionary for verification. Review words that can be used in different ways, such as *caught* (527), *bright* (541), *figure* (551), *lot* (597), *copy* (612). Have students write the words in sentences to illustrate their different meanings.

Other Word Forms, Vocabulary Skills, Prefix Practice, Hypothesizing, Writing Questions and Answers

Have students brainstorm for common other word forms of *force: forces, forced, forcing, forceful, forcefulness, forcefully, forcible.* Have students add the *en* prefix to *force.* Discuss unfamiliar words. Have students write these questions and the answers:

   When might it be necessary for someone to use a forceful voice?
   What is the major purpose of a country's armed forces?
   How are traffic laws enforced?
   What does it mean to force bulbs?
   Why might someone have a forced smile?

Writing a Story Ending

Have students play Finish the Story (see **Spelling Sourcebook 1**, page 88) using *force* and selected review words.

628 *test*

Other Word Forms, Writing Sentences

Have students brainstorm for common other word forms of *test: tests, tested, testing, tester.* Have students write the other word forms in sentences.

Public Speaking, Creating and Taking a Test

Have each student deliver an oral report on a current newspaper article. Have the class listen, take notes, and ask questions. Then the student gives the class a written test of previously prepared questions, corrects the tests, and returns them to classmates with appropriate grades and comments.

629 *bad*

Idiomatic Usage, Writing Explanations

Have students explain in writing what they think it means to say these expressions (then discuss):

   to come to a bad end   to get off to a bad start
   to go bad   to go from bad to worse
   in bad faith   in bad taste
   not half bad   to throw good money after bad

Book Tie-In, Writing Riddles

Use *Hink Pink Book* (Marilyn Burns, Little, 1981) to teach students to write "hink pink riddles": What's an "undisciplined boy?" A "bad lad!"

Antonyms

Ask students to write the antonym of *bad,* the word *good* (106).

Book Tie-In, Writing a Solution to a Problem

Use *The Cook and the King* (Maria Brusca and Tona Wilson, Holt, 1993), folklore featuring a bad tempered king. Before reading the ending, have students write how the king's bad temper might be reformed. Florinda, the king's cook, triumphs in this challenge by story's end.

630 *temperature*

Book Tie-In, Research and Writing

Use *Too Hot, Too Cold, or Just Right: How Animals Control Their Temperatures* (Lisa Yount, Walker, 1982), which tells how over 30 different animals control their temperature. Ask students to find out what the average body temperature is for humans (about 98.6°F) and how our bodies maintain this constant temperature.

Recording Information, Making a Chart, Writing a Summary ❖ Have students note the outside high and low temperatures for several consecutive days. Have students chart the results and then summarize the chart in writing.

631 *pair*

Writing a List, Book Tie-In, Creating a Book ❖ Have students work in pairs to write a list of things that are likely to be found in pairs, such as socks. Next, use *Can You Match This? Jokes About Unlikely Pairs* (Ann and Rick Walton, Lerner, 1989) to inspire students' own "pair" jokes. Compile the results into a class-made book (see page 138, Creating Classroom Books).

Homophone Usage ❖ Ask students to identify the homophones of *pair—pear* and *pare*. Have students write sentences to differentiate them.

Sound-Symbol Awareness, Writing Words, Vocabulary Skills ❖ Have students write *pair*. Then have them write words by changing the beginning letter(s). Choices may include *air* (160), *chair, fair, flair, hair* (528), *stair*. Then ask students to identify a spelling pattern that rhymes with *air* (___*are*). Next, have students list words that are spelled with the *are* pattern. Choices may include *bare, care* (483), *dare, fare, glare, hare, mare, pare, rare, stare, ware*. A less likely rhyming spelling pattern is *ear*, as in *bear* and *tear*. Discuss unfamiliar words.

632 *ahead*

Antonyms ❖ Ask students to write the antonym of *ahead*, the word *behind* (342).

Idiomatic Usage, Writing Explanations ❖ Ask students to explain in writing what they think it means to say each of these expressions (then discuss):
> to be ahead of the game
> to get the go-ahead
> to be ahead of your time (See dictation activity below.)

Dictation and Writing, Hypothesizing ❖ Dictate these partial sentences for students to write and complete:
> Someone I know who is ahead of their time is _____ .
> To get ahead in school, it is necessary to _____ .
> There may be trouble ahead for _____ .

Word Analysis, Alphabetical Order ❖ Have students list *a____* words, such as *ahead, about* (48), *away* (140), *alone* (491). Then have students alphabetize their list.

633 *wrong*

Other Word Forms, Vocabulary Skills, Writing Questions and Answers, Making Judgments ❖ Have students brainstorm for common other word forms of *wrong: wrongs, wronged, wronging, wrongly*. Discuss unfamiliar words. Have students write these questions and the answers:
> From recent current events, what situation illustrates someone who was wronged?
> What historical situation illustrates people treated wrongly?

Book Tie-In, Writing Explanations, Making Comparisons ❖ To illustrate social wrongs, introduce students to *Tar Beach* (Faith Ringgold, Crown, 1991) which received the Coretta Scott King award and was a Caldecott Honor Book and *Roll of Thunder, Hear My Cry* (Mildred Taylor, Dial, 1976), the 1976 Newbery Award book. Following the readings, ask students to explain in writing how Cassie Lightfoot in Ringgolds's book and Cassie Logan in Taylor's book were alike.

Antonyms, Writing Words Ask students to write the antonym of *wrong*, the word *right* (116). Expand the lesson by saying these words and asking students to write the opposite word: *behind* (*ahead* 632), *was* (*wasn't* 623), *north* (*south* 620), *unnecessary* (*necessary* 615), *hard* (*soft* 604), *rich* (*poor* 496). Then have students write more antonym pairs.

634 *practice*

Other Word Forms, Vocabulary Skills, Spelling Rules, Suffix Practice Have students brainstorm for common other word forms of *practice: practices, practiced, practicing, practitioner.* Discuss unfamiliar words. Review the spelling rule for adding suffixes to words ending in silent *e* (see ***Spelling Sourcebook 1***, page 85). Have students write suffix additions to *age* (607), *suppose* (555), *measure* (523), *care* (483), *notice* (379), *change* (264), *use* (88). Then discuss the spellings *noticeable, changeable, and useable.*

Other Word Forms, Writing Words Have students play All in the Family (see ***Spelling Sourcebook 1***, page 86) using the other word forms of *practice* and the other word forms of selected review words.

635 *sand*

Multiple Meanings, Writing Sentences Brainstorm for meanings of *sand.* Then have students check a dictionary for verification. Review words that can be used in different ways, such as *free* (553), *trip* (576), *iron* (587), *store* (589). Have students write the words in sentences to illustrate their different meanings.

Other Word Forms, Vocabulary Skills, Writing Sentences Have students brainstorm for common other word forms of *sand: sands, sanded, sanding, sander, sandy, sandier, sandiest.* Discuss unfamiliar words. Have students write the other word forms in sentences.

Compound Words, Vocabulary Skills Have students brainstorm for compound words that use *sand.* Choices may include *sandbag, sandbank, sandblast, sandbox, sandglass, sandman, sandpaper, sandpiper, sandstone, sandstorm, sandcastle* (see literature entry below). Discuss unfamiliar words.

Book Tie-In, Research, Writing a Summary Use *The Art and Industry of Sandcastles* (Jan Adkins, Walker, 1982) for amazing information about sandcastles. Have students use the *Reader's Guide* to research recent sand-sculpture contests and summarize the information in writing.

636 *tail*

Homophone Usage Ask students to identify the homophone of *tail*, the word *tale.* Have students write sentences to differentiate them.

Book Tie-In, Writing Stories Use *Fox Tale* (Yossi Abolafia, Greenwillow, 1991), a classic trickster tale, in which Bear trades honey for Fox's tail. Have students research other trickster tales in preparation for writing their own tale of a trickster.

Storytelling, Developing a Checklist To develop oral storytelling skills, read and then have students retell *Tailypo!* (Jan Wahl, Holt, 1991) to each other. This version of the classic African-American ghost story is ideal for telling. Students can prepare to retell the story to other classes by developing a checklist for successful storytelling. Then have students share the checklist ideas to develop one checklist for the class.

637 *wait*

Other Word Forms,
Writing Dialogue

Have students brainstorm for common other word forms of *wait: waits, waited, waiting, waiter, waitress.* Have students write the other word forms in sentences that contain speakers' exact words. Review the use of quotation marks in dialogue before students begin.

Homophone Usage

Ask students to identify the homophone of *wait,* the word *weight.* Have students write sentences to differentiate them.

Sound-Symbol Awareness,
Sorting Words

Have students write *wait* and listen to the long *a* sound. Then have students collect more words with long *a* to note the most frequent spellings for long *a* (most common: *ay* [*play*], *ai* [*train*], *a*-consonant-*e* [*same*]). Create a list of long *a* words. Have students write the words in categories sorted by the spelling for the long *a*. Have one category for "other" to accommodate less common spellings.

Writing Definitions

Have students write two interpretations of the phrase "to *wait* on someone."

638 *difficult*

Other Word Forms,
Writing Sentences

Have students brainstorm for common other word forms of *difficult: difficulty, difficulties.* Have students write the other word forms in sentences.

Antonyms

Have students write an antonym of *difficult,* the word *easy* (459).

Writing Words, Word Properties,
Writing Reasons

Review the activity "Choose" (580). Have students write the words in each row, then choose one word that does not belong, and write why it is different from the others.

difficult	hard	different	tough
practice	wait	tail	case
sandbox	football	airplane	temperature
pair	meet	yellow	eight
I've	won't	don't	wasn't

639 *general*

Multiple Meanings,
Writing Sentences

Brainstorm for meanings of *general.* Then have students check a dictionary for verification. Review words that can be used in different ways, such as *lot* (597), *case* (599), *copy* (612), *party* (626). Have students write the words in sentences to illustrate their different meanings.

Other Word Forms, Vocabulary
Skills, Writing Questions and
Answers, Generalizing

Have students brainstorm for common other word forms of *general: generals, generally, generalize, generalizes, generalized, generalizing, generalization, generalities.* Discuss unfamiliar words. Have students write these questions and the answers:

What statement can you make about the weather that is generally true?
Why is your statement about the weather a generalization?

Book Tie-In,
Research and Writing

Have students research and write about General Colin Powell. Sources may include the in-depth text *Colin Powell* (Warren Brown, Chelsea, 1992) and the simply written biography *Colin Powell: Straight to the Top* (Corrine Naden and Rose Blue, Millbrook, 1991). Have students research current information about the general using the *Reader's Guide* and report their findings in writing.

Antonyms, Writing General and Specific Statements ❖ Ask students to identify an antonym of *general,* the word *specific.* Then have students write two statements—a general one and a specific one. Have them read their two statements aloud for the class to decide which is general and which is specific.

Remember . . .

Develop spelling accountability as students write—see *Spelling Sourcebook 1,* Article 8, page 33. Spelling mastery is achieved ONLY when students can spell and use words consistently correctly in writing.

640   *cover*

Other Word Forms, Vocabulary Skills, Writing Questions and Answers ❖ Have students brainstorm for common other word forms of *cover: covers, covered, covering, coverage, coveralls.* Discuss unfamiliar words. Have students write the other word forms in sentences that ask a question. Then have students exchange papers and answer the questions using the same word forms of *cover* in the responses.

Prefix Practice, Writing Sentences ❖ Have students write *cover.* Then have them write the word with the prefixes *un, re,* and *dis* and write the prefixed words in sentences.

Sound-Symbol Awareness, Writing Sentences ❖ Have students write *cover.* Then ask them to follow these directions to make new and review words and to answer the questions:

  Change *cover* to make *over* (82).
  Change *cover* to make *clover.* (Where might clover be?)
  Change *cover* to make *discover.*
  Change *cover* to make *cove.* (How would you define *cove?*)
  Change one letter of *cover* to make *hover.* (How would you define *hover?*)
  Change one letter of *cover* to make *mover* (move 290).

Then have students write a sentence for each word they made.

641   *material*

Multiple Meanings, Writing Sentences ❖ Brainstorm for meanings of *material.* Then have students check a dictionary for verification. Review words that can be used in different ways, such as *through* (102), *too* (112), *right* (116), *place* (131). Have students write the words in sentences to illustrate their different meanings.

Other Word Forms, Vocabulary Skills, Writing a Character Sketch ❖ Have students brainstorm for common other word forms of *material: materials, materialist, materialistic, materialism.* Discuss unfamiliar words. Have students write a character sketch of a person who is materialistic.

Writing a List ❖ For a timed-write activity (about five minutes), ask students to list kinds of material, or fabric, such as silk. Let students use a dictionary for a spelling reference. A point is earned for each material spelled correctly.

642 *isn't*

Contractions, Writing Words ❖ Have students write *isn't* and the words from which it is made (*is, not*). Then review contractions that use *not*. Choices may include *wasn't* (623), *won't* (598), *couldn't* (563), *can't* (380), *don't* (190), *isn't, shouldn't, wouldn't, aren't, doesn't, wasn't, weren't, hasn't, haven't, hadn't, mustn't, didn't*. Expand the lesson to any contraction. Then have students who need additional reinforcement with contractions play Race Track Spelling (see ***Spelling Sourcebook 1***, page 90) using contractions.

643 *thousand*

Dictation and Writing ❖ Dictate these partial sentences for students to write and complete:

Our teacher has told us a thousand times _____ .

If someone gave our school a thousand _____ .

There are at least one thousand _____ .

Analogies, Writing Words, Writing Sentences ❖ Review analogies (see 568, 614). Then have students write these analogies and complete them with words of frequencies 623–643 or their other word forms:

tale : tail :: weight : _____ (wait)

was : wasn't :: right : _____ (wrong)

8 : eight :: 1,000 : _____ (thousand)

rock : music :: cotton : _____ (material)

pal : friend :: quiz : _____ (test)

Have students write the answer words in sentences. Then have them write an analogy.

Writing Number Words, Creating a Word Puzzle ❖ Have students write number words. Then have them create a Word Search or Crossword Puzzle (use the blackline master grid on page 108 of ***Spelling Sourcebook 1***) using the number words. Have students exchange puzzles and solve them.

644 *sign*

Multiple Meanings, Writing Sentences ❖ Brainstorm for meanings of *sign*. Then have students check a dictionary for verification. Review words that can be used in different ways, such as *great* (146), *sound* (175), *second* (235), *change* (264). Have students write the words in sentences to illustrate their different meanings.

Other Word Forms, Vocabulary Skills, Writing Questions and Answers, Research and Writing, Book Tie-In ❖ Have students brainstorm for common other word forms of *sign: signs, signed, signing, signer, signature*. Discuss unfamiliar words. Have students write these questions and the answers:

Who signed the Declaration of Independence?

How does the signature of John Hancock reflect the personality of this patriot? (Have students read *Will You Sign Here, John Hancock?* by Jean Fritz, Putman, 1976).

Writing Speculations, Book Tie-In ❖ Ask students to write about the confusion that could develop if there were no signs in the world. Then introduce *The Signmaker's Assistant* (Tedd Arnold, Dial, 1992), in which the assistant prints mischievous signs . . . and as a result, the townspeople tear down all the signs in rebellion. Then pandemonium!

Book Tie-In,
Interpreting a Signed Message

❖ Use *The Handmade Alphabet* (Laura Rankin, Dial, 1991) and *Handtalk* (Mary Beth Ancona and Remy Charlip, Macmillan, 1974) for an introduction to finger spelling and sign language. With the help of the pictures, students can develop skills to send a signed message, and classmates can write the message they think was sent.

645 *guess*

Other Word Forms, Homophone
Usage, Writing Sentences

❖ Have students brainstorm for common other word forms of *guess: guesses, guessed, guessing, guesser.* Discuss the homophones *guessed* and *guest* and have students write the homophones in sentences.

Spelling Rules, Plural Practice

❖ Review the spelling rule for making *guess* plural (see *Spelling Sourcebook 1*, page 85). Have students write the plurals for *wish* (573), *grass* (560), *glass* (488), *watch* (436), *class* (391), *box* (388), *tax, church, lunch, dish, dress, witch, inch, speech, success, ditch, fox, match.*

Book Tie-In, Writing Descriptions

❖ Use *Guess Who My Favorite Person Is* (Byrd Baylor, Macmillan, 1985), a book that uses vivid word imagery. Have students write their own descriptive words to create a similar guessing game.

Word Analysis, Writing Words

❖ Write *g___ss* on the chalkboard. Ask students to add the vowels to make *guess.* Point out the silent *u.* Have students play this vowel fill-in game with words with tricky vowel spellings, such as *said* (43), *people* (79), *thought* (179), *early* (324), *beautiful* (429), *build* (487), *language* (499), *measure* (523), *especially* (614).

646 *forward*

Other Word Forms, Vocabulary
Skills, Writing Sentences

❖ Have students brainstorm for common other word forms of *forward: forwards, forwarded, forwarding.* Discuss unfamiliar words. Have students write the other word forms in sentences.

Antonyms

❖ Ask students to identify the antonym of *forward,* the word *backward.*

Homophone Usage, Research,
Writing a List

❖ Have students identify the homophone of *forward,* the word *foreword.* Discuss its meaning and have students explore and list what might be included in a book's foreword.

Writing Other Word Forms

❖ Have students play the All-Play Spelling Bee (see *Spelling Sourcebook 1*, page 86) using *forward,* its other word forms, and selected review words and their other word forms.

647 *huge*

Other Word Forms, Vocabulary
Skills, Writing Sentences

❖ Have students brainstorm for common other word forms of *huge: huger, hugest, hugely, hugeness.* Discuss unfamiliar words. Have students write the other word forms in sentences.

Book Tie-In, Making a Chart

❖ Have students explore oversized animals with *Whales: Giants of the Deep* (Dorothy Hinshaw Patent, Holiday, 1987), *Elephants* (John Wexo, Zoobooks-Wildlife Education, 1986), and *Giants of Land, Sea and Air* (David Peters, Knopf, 1986). Then have them draw and label a size-comparison chart featuring huge animals.

648 *ride*

Multiple Meanings, Writing Sentences

Brainstorm for meanings of *ride*. Then have students check a dictionary for verification. Review words that can be used in different ways, such as *turn* (289), *point* (272), *state* (371), *mean* (349). Have students write the words in sentences to illustrate their different meanings.

Other Word Forms, Spelling Rules, Writing Sentences, Homophone Usage

Have students brainstorm for common other word forms of *ride: rides, rode, riding, ridden, rider*. Review the spelling rule for adding suffixes to words ending in silent *e* (see **Spelling Sourcebook 1**, page 85). Have students write the other word forms in sentences. Ask students to identify the other word form of *ride* that is a homophone (*rode, road* 406, *rowed*) and a word that may sound like a homophone (*rider, writer*).

Book Tie-In, Writing Character Traits

Use *Paul Revere's Ride* (Henry Wadsworth Longfellow, Dutton, 1990), a superb picture book of the famous midnight ride. As a follow up, ask students to write character traits one might attribute to Paul Revere.

649 *region*

Other Word Forms, Vocabulary Skills

Have students brainstorm for common other word forms of *region: regions, regional*. Discuss unfamiliar words. Have students write the other word forms in sentences.

Writing Words, Sound-Symbol Awareness, Sorting Words

Have students write *region* and listen to the sound the *g* makes. The have them write *huge* (647), *guess* (645), *sign* (644), *general* (639), *wrong* (633), *edge* (603), *strange* (572), *government* (558), *figure* (551), *bright* (541). Have students find and write more words with *g*. Then have them sort all the words with *g* into sets with the same sound/symbol spelling pattern.

650 *nor*

Dictation and Writing

Dictate these partial sentences for students to write and complete:
　　Try never to be late for school nor for _____ .
　　Be sure not to miss your ball practice nor your _____ .

Then introduce the spelling of *neither* and ask students to write and complete:
　　Neither plants nor animals can _____ .

Sound-Symbol Awareness, Writing Sentences

Have students write *nor*. Then ask them to follow these directions to make new and review words and to answer the questions:
　　Change *nor* to make *or* (26).
　　Change *nor* to make *northern*. (What are the northern states?)
　　Change *nor* to make *normal*. (How do you define *normal?*)

Then have students write a sentence for each word they made.

651 *period*

Multiple Meanings, Writing an Explanation

Period has more than one meaning. Ask students to write answers to these questions that use *period* in different ways:
　　How can periods of time be measured?
　　When would a writer use an exclamation mark instead of a period?

Other Word Forms, Vocabulary Skills, Writing Descriptions

Have students brainstorm for common other word forms of *period: periods, periodical, periodically*. Discuss unfamiliar words. Have students write about something they do at school or home periodically.

652 *blood*

Other Word Forms,
Writing Words

Have students brainstorm for common other word forms of *blood: bloody, bloodier, bloodiest.* Have students find and write base words and their comparative and superlative forms that follow the same pattern. Choices may include *sand* (635), *sleep* (586), *grass* (560), *hair* (528), *rock* (489), *wind* (341).

Research and Writing

Have students research and write about different human blood types.

Book Tie-In, Research,
Comparing and Contrasting

Use *Warm-Blooded Animals* (Maurice Burton, Facts on File, 1985). Then ask students to research cold-blooded animals to compare and contrast in writing these two kinds of animals.

653 *rich*

Other Word Forms, Vocabulary
Skills, Multiple Meanings,
Writing Sentences

Have students brainstorm for common other word forms of *rich: richer, richest, richly, richness, riches.* Discuss unfamiliar words and the multiple meanings of *rich.* Have students write the words in sentences to illustrate their different meanings.

Antonyms, Writing Words

Ask students to write the antonym of one meaning of *rich,* the word *poor* (496). Expand the lesson by saying these words and asking students to write the opposite word: *backward* (*forward* 646), *is* (*isn't* 642), *right* (*wrong* 633), *enemy* (*friend* 498), *impossible* (*possible* 452), *nothing* (*everything* 432), *ugly* (*beautiful* 429), *summer* (*winter* 424), *weak* (*strong* 381), *incomplete* (*complete* 365), *uncertain* (*certain* 353), *can* (*cannot* 343).

Creating a Menu

Have students create a dessert menu with descriptions of "rich" desserts.

654 *team*

Other Word Forms, Vocabulary
Skills, Writing Sentences

Have students brainstorm for common other word forms of *team: teams, teamed, teaming, teamster.* Discuss unfamiliar words. Have students write the other word forms in sentences.

Book Tie-In, Writing Descriptions

Use *Team Work: A Picture Essay About Crews and Teams at Work* (George Ancona, Harper, 1983), featuring text and pictures of situations such as mountain climbing, in which working together is important. Have students follow up the reading with writing about a time they used teamwork to accomplish something.

Making a Chart, Forming
Opinions, Writing Reasons

Have student sports fans make a chart of sports teams including pertinent information, such as each team's name, coach, and colors. Ask students to write about their favorite team and why it is the best.

655 *corner*

Idiomatic Usage,
Writing Explanations

Have students explain in writing what they think it means to say these expressions (then discuss):

    to have a corner on something   to corner someone
    to have turned the corner   to cut corners
    to see something out of the corner of your eye

Writing a Definition

Write *corner, coroner, colonel,* and *cornea* on the chalkboard. Have students say the words and look at their letters to note similarities. Then have students write a definition for each of the words.

656 *cat*

Other Word Forms,
Vocabulary Skills

Have students brainstorm for common other word forms of *cat: cats, catty.* Discuss the meaning of *catty,* along with *cattily* and *cattiness.*

Idiomatic Usage,
Writing Explanations

Have students explain in writing what they think it means to say these expressions (then discuss):

> to be a copycat
> Cat got your tongue?
> to let the cat out of the bag
> to look like the cat that swallowed the canary
> to rain cats and dogs
> When the cat's away, the mice will play.

Writing Speculations,
Book Tie-In, Comparing and
Contrasting, Writing a Summary

What are the differences between cats in the wild and domesticated house cats? Ask students to write their ideas. Then explore the answer with *Your Cat's Wild Cousins* (Hope Ryden, Lodestar, 1992) and *Cats* (Cynthia Overbeck, Lerner, 1983), in which domestic and wild cats are compared and contrasted. Have students summarize the differences.

Book Tie-In, Writing a List,
Making Predictions

Use *Big Cats* (Seymour Simon, HarperCollins, 1991). Introduce the book by asking students to list the cats they think might be featured in the picture essay. During the reading, students learn about the lion, tiger, leopard, cheetah, puma, jaguar, and snow leopard.

657 *amount*

Other Word Forms, Vocabulary
Skills, Writing Sentences

Have students brainstorm for common other word forms of *amount: amounts, amounted, amounting.* Discuss unfamiliar words. Have students write the other word forms in sentences. Then have students rearrange the words in each sentence and delete capitals and punctuation. Partners then exchange and unscramble the sentences trying to match the word order of the original sentences.

Sound-Symbol Awareness,
Writing Words

Have students write words with *ou.* Choices may include *thousand* (643), *south* (620), *trouble* (588), *mountain* (526), *hour* (480), *although* (450), *brought* (327), *course* (317), *group* (295), *country* (228), *enough* (209), *should* (156). Note the different sounds the *ou* makes, and help students to conclude that *ou* is an unreliable spelling pattern.

Writing Abbreviations

Have students find and write the abbreviation for *amount* (*amt.*). Then have them find and write more abbreviations. Choices may include *building* (*bldg.*), *chapter* (*chap.*), *department* (*dept.*), *government* (558, *govt.*), *hospital* (*hosp.*), *manager* (*mgr.*), *paid* (*pd.*), *principal* (*prin.*).

658 *garden*

Other Word Forms,
Writing Questions and Answers

Have students brainstorm for common other word forms of *garden: gardens, gardened, gardening, gardener.* Have students write the other word forms in sentences that ask a question. Then have students exchange papers and answer the questions using the same word forms of *garden* in the responses.

Book Tie-In, Writing Directions ❖ Use *A Book of Vegetables* (Harriet Sobol, Putnam, 1984) as a how-to guide for planting and growing a vegetable garden. This book is a good choice for city students far removed from the country farm. *My First Garden Book* (Angela Wilkes, Knopf, 1992) is appropriate for beginning gardeners. Students with gardening skills can write a brief how-to article to supplement this book based on their gardening experiences.

659 *led*

Other Word Forms, Homophone Usage, Hypothesizing ❖ Have students brainstorm for common other word forms of *led: lead, leads, leading, leader.* Discuss the other word form that is a homophone and a homograph (*lead*). Have students write the homophones and homograph in sentences to differentiate them. Then have students write this question and the answer: Why might a grocer use a loss leader? (Have students use a dictionary for the term *loss leader* and ask their local grocer for information about the use of this marketing technique).

Sound-Symbol Awareness, Writing Words, Vocabulary Skills ❖ Have students write *led*. Then have them write new words by changing the beginning letter(s). Choices may include *bed, bled, fed, fled, red* (298), *sled, wed*. Then ask students to identify a common spelling pattern that rhymes with _*ed* (_*ead*). Next, have students list words that are spelled with the _*ead* pattern. Choices may include *read* (165), *head* (212), *ready* (357), *instead* (408), *ahead* (632), *dead, bread, lead*. An irregular spelling pattern is in the rhyming word *said*. Discuss any unfamiliar words.

660 *note*

Multiple Meanings ❖ Brainstorm for meanings of *note*. Then have students check a dictionary for verification. Have students brainstorm for words that can be used in different ways. Have students use the words in oral sentences to illustrate their different meanings.

Other Word Forms, Vocabulary Skills, Spelling Rules, Writing Sentences, Forming Opinions ❖ Have students brainstorm for common other word forms of *note: notes, noted, noting, notation, notable, notably.* Discuss unfamiliar words. Review the spelling rule for adding suffixes to words ending in silent *e* (see *Spelling Sourcebook 1*, page 85). Have students write the other word forms in sentences. Then have students write this question and the answer: What is the most notable school happening so far this school year?

Sound-Symbol Awareness, Sorting Words ❖ Have students write *note* and listen to the long *o* sound. Then have students collect more words with the long *o* sound to note the most frequent spellings for long *o* (most common: *o* [*no*], *o*-consonant-*e* [*those*], *ow* [*show*], *oa* [*coat*], *old* [*cold*], *oe* [*toe*]). Create a list of long *o* words. Have students write the words in categories sorted by the spelling for the long *o*. Have one category for "other" to accommodate less common spellings.

661 *various*

Other Word Forms, Vocabulary Skills, Homophone Usage, Writing Sentences ❖ Have students brainstorm for common other word forms of *various: variously, vary, varies, varied, varying, variety, variation.* Discuss unfamiliar words. Have students point out the other word form of *various* that can be a homophone (*vary*). Have students write the homophone partner (*very* 93). Have students write the other word forms in sentences.

Suffix Practice ❖ Have students find and write more words with *ious*. Choices may include *serious, glorious, notorious.*

662 *race*

Multiple Meanings,
Writing Sentences ❖ Brainstorm for meanings of *race*. Then have students check a dictionary for verification. Review words that can be used in different ways, such as *party* (626), *general* (639), *material* (641), *sign* (644). Have students write the words in sentences to illustrate their different meanings.

Other Word Forms,
Vocabulary Skills, Spelling Rules,
Writing Sentences ❖ Have students brainstorm for common other word forms of *race: races, raced, racing, racer, racy.* Discuss unfamiliar words. Review the spelling rule for adding suffixes to words ending in silent *e* (see **Spelling Sourcebook 1**, page 85). Have students write the other word forms in sentences.

Book Tie-In,
Writing a News Story ❖ Use *Racing Indy Cars* (George Sullivan, Cobblehill, 1992) and the easy-to-read *Racing Cars* (N. S. Barrett, Watts, 1985) for a colorful history of car racing. Follow up with students writing a news story reporting a "big race."

Book Tie-In, Comparing and
Contrasting, Writing Stories ❖ Have students read more than one version of the classic tale of a race, "The Tortoise and the Hare." Ask students to chart the differences and similarities, possibly using a Venn diagram, and then write their own version.

663 *bit*

Multiple Meanings ❖ Brainstorm for meanings of *bit*. Then have students check a dictionary for verification.

Other Word Forms, Vocabulary
Skills, Writing Sentences ❖ Have students brainstorm for common other word forms of *bit: bits, bite, bites, biting, bitten.* Discuss unfamiliar words. Have students write the other word forms in sentences.

Sound-Symbol Awareness,
Writing Words ❖ Ask students to write *bit* and *bite* and note the change in the vowel sound with the addition of the silent *e*. Have students list other word pairs that follow this spelling pattern. Choices may include *at* (20) */ate, can* (38) */cane, hat/hate, mad/made* (81), *past* (403) */paste, tap/tape, hop/hope, dim/dime, kit/kite, pin/pine, fin/fine* (400), *us* (168) */use* (88).

Idiomatic Usage ❖ Have students write equivalents for 2, 4, and 6 bits (25 cents, 50 cents, 75 cents).

664 *result*

Other Word Forms,
Writing Questions and Answers,
Hypothesizing ❖ Have students brainstorm for common other word forms of *result: results, resulted, resulting.* Have students write these questions and the answers:
> What might the results be if saltwater fish are placed in a freshwater aquarium?
> What might result from eating too much fudge cake?
> Where can you read the results of yesterday's national championship game?

665 *brother*

Multiple Meanings,
Writing Sentences ❖ Brainstorm for meanings of *brother.* Then have students check a dictionary for verification. Review words that can be used in different ways, such as *page* (218), *story* (237), *run* (306), *ground* (311). Have students write the words in sentences to illustrate their different meanings.

Other Word Forms, ❖ Have students brainstorm for common other word forms of *brother: brothers,*
Writing Sentences *brotherly, brotherhood.* Discuss unfamiliar words. Have students write the
other word forms in sentences.

Book Tie-In, ❖ Use *The Wright Brothers* (Richard Haynes, Silver, 1992), which includes many
Research and Writing quotations from the brothers' letters. Have students find and write about other
brothers or sisters who excelled. These may include the political leaders John,
Robert, and Edward Kennedy; the storytelling Grimm brothers; the well-known
authors Charlotte and Emily Bronte; the famous actresses Lynn and Vanessa
Redgrave; and the skiers Phil and Steve Mahre.

Antonyms ❖ Ask students to identify the antonym of *brother,* the word *sister,* and predict
its spelling.

666 *addition*

Other Word Forms, Vocabulary ❖ Have students brainstorm for common other word forms of *addition: additions,*
Skills, Writing Sentences *add, adds, added, adding, additional, additionally, additive, addend.* Discuss
unfamiliar words. Have students write the other word forms in sentences.

Homophone Usage ❖ Ask students to identify the homophone of *addition,* the word *edition.* Have
students write sentences to differentiate them.

Antonyms ❖ Ask students to define the antonyms *addition* and *subtraction.*

Writing Math Story Problems ❖ Have students write a math story problem that requires addition. Ask students
to exchange problems and solve them.

667 *doesn't*

Contractions, Homograph Usage ❖ Have students write *doesn't* and *does.* Then have them write the homograph
does in sentences to differentiate the meanings.

Dictation and Writing, ❖ Dictate these partial sentences for students to write and complete:
Writing Speculations If a mountain doesn't get any snow during the winter, then _____ .
If a person doesn't study for a test, then _____ .
If a business doesn't have a sign, then _____ .
If a child doesn't get enough sleep, then _____ .
Next, have students follow the sentence pattern, "If ____ doesn't ____ ,
then . . ." to write sentences for a classmate to complete.

668 *dead*

Other Word Forms, Vocabulary ❖ Have students brainstorm for common other word forms of *dead: deadly,*
Skills, Writing Sentences *deadlier, deadliest, deaden, die, dies, died, death, deathly, deadline.* Discuss
unfamiliar words. Have students write the other word forms in sentences.

Idiomatic Usage, ❖ Have students explain in writing what they think it means to say these
Writing Explanations expressions (then discuss):

as dead as a doornail	to come to a dead end
dead set against something	dead to the world
in a dead heat	dead center
over my dead body	dead wrong

Book Tie-In, Research and Writing, Writing Speculations ❖ Use *Death Is Natural* (Laurence Pringle, Morrow, 1991) as a catalyst for good discussions about death and dying. Have students research and list the current most frequent causes of death for people their age. Then have students write what they think could be done to reduce deaths from this cause.

Book Tie-In ❖ For sensitive fiction that involves the death of a mother, use *The Falcon's Wing* (Dawna Buchanan, Orchard, 1992) for intermediate readers, or *Two Moons in August* (Martha Brooks, Joy Street, 1992) for more mature readers. For treatment of a father's death, have students read *The Fortune Teller in 5B* (Jane Zalben, Holt, 1991).

Antonyms ❖ Ask students to identify the antonym of *dead,* the word *alive,* and predict its spelling.

Writing an Obituary ❖ Have students write an obituary for a book character who died or an important real person.

669 *weight*

Other Word Forms, Vocabulary Skills, Homophone Usage, Writing Sentences ❖ Have students brainstorm for common other word forms of *weight: weights, weigh, weighs, weighed, weighing, weighted, weightless, weightlessness, weighty.* Discuss unfamiliar words. Discuss the homophones *weight* and *wait* (637), *waits* and *weights, way* (86) and *weigh* , *ways* and *weighs.* Have students write the homophones in sentences.

Idiomatic Usage, Writing Explanations ❖ Have students explain in writing what they think it means to say these expressions (then discuss):

> to carry your own weight
> to put on weight
> to throw your weight around
> worth its weight in gold
> to carry the weight of the world on your shoulders

670 *thin*

Other Word Forms, Vocabulary Skills, Spelling Rules, Suffix Practice ❖ Have students brainstorm for common other word forms of *thin: thinner, thinnest, thinly, thins, thinned, thinning.* Discuss unfamiliar words. Review the spelling rule for doubling the final consonant before adding suffixes (see ***Spelling Sourcebook 1**,* page 85). Have students apply the rule to the following words; they must decide whether or not to double the consonant: *spin, grin, win, skin* (622), *flat* (618), *sleep* (586), *trip* (576), *reason* (564), *plan* (544), *map* (497), *begin* (444), *ship* (442), *warm* (412).

Antonyms ❖ Ask students to identify an antonym of *thin,* the word *thick,* and predict its spelling.

671 *stone*

Other Word Forms, Vocabulary Skills, Writing Sentences ❖ Have students find and write synonyms for *stone,* such as rock, boulder, gravel, pebble. Then write about the slight difference in meaning among the words.

Book Tie-In, Research and Writing, Creating a Book	Use *Skara Brae* (Olivier Dunrea, Holiday House, 1985). This description of the Neolithic village north of Scotland tells how the people created efficient houses using stone gathered along the shoreline. Follow up with a class-made book, *Made of Stone,* featuring information about important things made of stone, such as the pyramids, Stonehenge, the Mt. Rushmore monument, and the Vietnam Memorial in Washington, D.C. (see page 138, Creating Classroom Books).

672 *hit*

Other Word Forms, Spelling Rules	Have students brainstorm for common other word forms of *hit: hits, hitting, hitter.* Review the spelling rule for doubling the final consonant before adding suffixes (see *Spelling Sourcebook 1*, page 85). Review the words gathered in the activity for *thin* (670).
Idiomatic Usage, Writing Explanations	Have students explain in writing what they think it means to say these expressions (then discuss):

to hit a snag	hit and miss
to hit bottom	to hit pay dirt
to hit the books	to hit the ceiling
to hit the hay	to hit the high spots
to hit the nail on the head	to hit the jackpot
to hit the spot	to pinch-hit for someone

Book Tie-In, Informational Writing	Provide *Hitting* (Jay Feldman, Simon, 1991) to would-be baseball hitters. It includes advice and opinions on hitting from the best major-league players, along with instructive photographs. Have readers write one new tip they learned from the advice offered in the book.

673 *wife*

Antonyms	Ask students to identify the antonym of *wife,* the word *husband,* and predict its spelling.
Plural Practice, Writing Words	Introduce the plural of *wife, wives* (see *Spelling Sourcebook 1*, page 85). Ask students to find and write more words that follow this spelling rule. Choices may include *life* (208) */lives, leaf/leaves* (460), *half* (297) */halves, loaf/loaves, wolf/wolves, calf/calves, thief/thieves, knife/knives, self/selves, wharf/wharves.*

674 *island*

Other Word Forms, Vocabulary Skills, Writing Sentences	Have students brainstorm for common other word forms of *island: islands, islander.* Discuss unfamiliar words. Have students write the other word forms in sentences.
Book Tie-In, Making Predictions, Writing a List	Use *Swimming With Sea Lions and Other Adventures in the Galápagos Islands* (Ann McGovern, Scholastic, 1992). Before the reading, have students predict in writing what adventures may be included. Following the reading, have students check their predictions. Then have the class create a list of the islands visited and the animals included in the story.

Research and Writing, Sequencing ❖ Have students research and write where these islands are and then sequence the islands by size:
> Greenland (1—North Atlantic), Great Britain (2—off coast of NW Europe), Cuba (3—Caribbean Sea), Newfoundland (4—North Atlantic), and Iceland (5—North Atlantic).

Word Analysis, Writing Words ❖ Have students write *island* and underline the silent *s*. Then dictate these words with silent letters for students to write: *thought* (179), *language* (499), *listen* (507), *guess* (645).

675 *we'll*

Homophone Usage ❖ *We'll* and *wheel* are often pronounced as homophones. Ask students to write sentences to differentiate them.

Writing Contractions ❖ For a timed-write activity (about three minutes), ask students to list contractions. A point is earned for each contraction spelled correctly.

676 *opposite*

Book Tie-In, Writing Poetry ❖ Use *Opposites* (Richard Wilbur, Harcourt, 1973), a book of poems in which the concept of opposite depends on perspective. Students can use the clever poems as a model for their own poetry with plays on words.

Antonyms, Writing Words, Creating a Word Puzzle ❖ Dictate words for which the opposite is a review word. Have students write each word and its opposite. Then have students use the pairs of words to create a crossword puzzle with one member of the pair as the clue. Have students use graph paper or the blackline master grid on page 109 of *Spelling Sourcebook 1*.

Research and Writing, Forming Opinions ❖ Provide students with opinions on current topics. Then have students write the opposite point of view, with substantiating information.

677 *born*

Other Word Forms, Vocabulary Skills, Writing Sentences ❖ Have students brainstorm for common other word forms of *born: bear, bears, bore, bearing.* Discuss unfamiliar words. Have students write the other word forms in sentences.

Other Word Forms, Writing Words ❖ Have students play All in the Family (see *Spelling Sourcebook 1*, page 86) using the other word forms of *born* and selected review words and their other word forms.

Book Tie-In ❖ Use *Being Born* (Sheila Kitzinger, Grosset, 1986), a gentle and enlightening description of the wonder of human birth. This book is appropriate for all ages.

678 *sense*

Other Word Forms, Vocabulary Skills, Spelling Rules, Writing Questions and Answers ❖ Have students brainstorm for common other word forms of *sense: senses, sensed, sensing, senseless, sensory, sensation.* Discuss unfamiliar words. Review the spelling rule for adding suffixes to words ending in silent *e* (see *Spelling Sourcebook 1*, page 85). Have students write the other word forms in sentences that ask a question. Then have students exchange papers and answer the questions using the same word forms of *sense* in the responses.

Book Tie-In, Writing Stories ❖ Use *The Lady Who Put Salt in Her Coffee* (Lucretia Hale, Harcourt, 1989) as a model for "noodlehead" stories in which a lack of common sense makes for a humorous story. Have students collect other examples of these traditional tales. Then have students write one of their own.

Book Tie-In, Research and Writing, Writing a Summary ❖ Use *The Science Book of the Senses* (Neil Ardley, Gulliver, 1992) for projects and experiments with the senses. Have students choose one sense and research it more thoroughly. Sources may include *Smell, the Subtle Sense* (Virginia, Alvin, and Robert Silverstein, Morrow, 1992), a clear, lively discussion of the sense of smell in humans and animals; and *Extraordinary Eyes: How Animals See the World* (Sandra Sinclair, Dial, 1992). Have students write a summary of the information they find.

Homophone Usage ❖ Ask students to identify the homophones of *sense—cents* and *scents*. Have students write sentences to differentiate them.

Writing a Definition ❖ Have students define *common sense*.

679 *cattle*

Plural Practice, Spelling Rules ❖ *Cattle* is the plural of *cows, steers, bulls,* and *oxen* collectively. Have students review spelling rules for plurals (see **Spelling Sourcebook 1**, page 85). Have them write examples of words that follow each plural rule.

Vocabulary Skills ❖ Have students find and write the name for groups of animals, such as *herd* of cattle. Choices may include *sloth* of bears, *flock* of ducks, *pride* of lions, and *pack* of wolves.

680 *million*

Other Words Forms, Vocabulary Skills, Writing Sentences ❖ Have students brainstorm for common other word forms of *million: millions, millionth, millionaire.* Discuss unfamiliar words. Have students write the other word forms in sentences.

Book Tie-In, Writing Descriptions ❖ Use *Make Four Million Dollars by Next Thursday!* (Stephen Manes, Bantam, 1991), the story of Jason, who takes Dr. Silverfish's advice to make big money. Ask students to describe how much money four million dollars actually is. To better understand the concept of a million, use *How Much Is a Million?* (David Schwartz, Lothrop, 1985) and *If You Made a Million* (David Schwartz, Lothrop, 1989).

Visual Skill-Building, Writing Words ❖ Have students find words inside of *million* (*mill, ill, lion, on*). Extend the words-in-words activity to selected review words or words students encounter in other studies.

681 *anyone*

Dictation and Writing, Reference Sources ❖ Dictate these partial sentences for students to write and complete:
Anyone who would like information about oceans could _____ .
If anyone needs to find out about the history of a city, the person should _____ .

When anyone wants to learn how to plant a garden, the person might _____ .

Compound Words, Writing Words ❖ Have students find and write more compound words that use *any* or *one.* Choices may include *everyone, someone, anybody, anyhow, anywhere, anything.* Using these and other compound words, have students play Compound Bingo (see **Spelling Sourcebook 1**, page 87).

682 *rule*

Other Word Forms, Vocabulary Skills, Spelling Rules, Alphabetical Order

❖ Have students brainstorm for common other word forms of *rule: rules, ruled, ruling, ruler.* Discuss unfamiliar words and the various meanings of *ruler, ruled,* and *ruling.* Review the spelling rule for adding suffixes to words ending in silent *e* (see **Spelling Sourcebook 1**, page 85). Have students write the other word forms in alphabetical order.

Idiomatic Usage, Writing Explanations

❖ Have students explain in writing what they think it means to say these expressions (then discuss):

to rule the roost	as a general rule
a hard-and-fast rule	to rule something out

Book Tie-In, Writing Stories

❖ Use the picture-book story *The New Creatures* (Mordicai Gerstein, HarperCollins, 1991), in which grandfather tells how dogs and cats used to rule the world living a life of leisure. To get the world's work done, the animals discovered humans and taught them to do the work. Have students write a follow-up story in which new rulers change the world in another way.

683 *science*

Other Word Forms, Vocabulary Skills, Writing Sentences

❖ Have students brainstorm for common other word forms of *science: sciences, scientific, scientist, scientists, scientifically.* Discuss unfamiliar words. Have students write the other word forms in sentences.

Book Tie-In, Writing a Summary

❖ Use *Wonders of Science* (Melvin Berger, Scholastic, 1991), *Shazam!: Simple Science Magic* (Laurence White and Ray Broekel, Whitman, 1991), and *Amazing Science Experiments with Everyday Materials* (Richard Churchill, Sterling, 1991). Invite students to demonstrate selected science experiments and then have them write summaries of the experiments.

684 *afraid*

Research and Writing, Creating a Book

❖ Ask students to take a poll of their responses to the question "What animals make you feel afraid?" Then have students research those animals noted as most frightening. Point out that knowledge usually helps conquer fear. Two books to dispel myths of danger are *Sharks* (John Wexo, Wildlife, 1983) and *Poisonous Snakes* (Seymour Simon, Four Winds, 1981). Each shows the small risk sharks and snakes pose. Follow up by creating a class-made book, *Reasons Not to be Afraid* (see page 138, Creating Classroom Books).

Book Tie-In, Writing Stories, Oral Reading

❖ To create an eerie, suspenseful mood, use *Hauntings: Ghosts and Ghouls From Around the World* (Margaret Hodges, Little, 1991) and *Seven Strange and Ghostly Tales* (Brian Jacques, Philomel, 1991). Then have students write stories that may make people feel afraid. Dim the classroom lights and have students read their tales orally.

Synonyms, Vocabulary Skills, Writing Sentences

❖ Ask students to research and list synonyms for *afraid.* Choices may include *uneager, hesitant, reluctant, fearful, worried, scared, apprehensive, frightened.* Discuss unfamiliar words and ask students to write them in sentences.

685 *women*

Research and Writing,
Book Tie-In, Creating a Book

Have students read and write about living women who have made contributions. Compile the information into a class-made book, *A Who's Who of Women Today.* Sources may include *Maya Angelou* (Nancy Shuker, Burdett, 1991), *Sandra Day O'Connor: Justice for All* (Beverly Gherman, Viking, 1991), and the easy-reader *Jane Goodall: Friend of the Chimps* (Eileen Lucas, Millbrook, 1992).

Antonyms

Ask students to write the antonym of *women,* the word *men* (148).

Plural Practice

Review irregular plurals (see *Spelling Sourcebook 1*, page 85) using *child* (571) and *children* (200). Have students write the singular of *women, woman* (577). Have students brainstorm for more irregular plurals. Choices may include *foot* (482) */feet, goose/geese, man* (111) */men* (148), *mouse/mice, ox/oxen, tooth/teeth.*

686 *produce*

Homograph Usage

Discuss the two pronunciations and meanings of this homograph. Ask students to write sentences to differentiate them.

Other Word Forms,
Vocabulary Skills, Spelling Rules,
Writing Directions

Have students brainstorm for common other word forms of *produce: produces, produced, producing, producer, productive, productivity.* Discuss unfamiliar words. Review the spelling rule for adding suffixes to words ending in silent *e* (see *Spelling Sourcebook 1*, page 85). Have students write directions for the most productive way to study a spelling word. (See *Spelling Sourcebook 1*, page 27).

687 *pull*

Idiomatic Usage,
Writing Explanations

Have students explain in writing what they think it means to say these expressions (then discuss):

to pull a fast one	to pull a trick on someone
to pull over	to pull yourself together
to pull rank	to pull someone's leg
to pull strings	to pull something out of a hat
to pull the plug	to pull up stakes
to pull the wool over someone's eyes	

Writing Explanations,
Book Tie-In

Have students write an explanation for how a simple machine, the pulley, works. Resources may include *Machines and How They Work* (Harvey Weiss, Harper, 1983).

Antonyms

Ask students to identify the antonym of *pull,* the word *push,* and predict its spelling.

688 *son*

Homophone Usage

Ask students to write the homophone of *son,* the word *sun* (257). Have students write sentences to differentiate them.

Antonyms

Ask students to identify the antonym of *son,* the word, *daughter* and predict its spelling.

689 *meant*

Other Word Forms, Vocabulary Skills, Writing Dialogue

Have students brainstorm for common other word forms of *meant: mean, means, meaning, meaningful, meaningless.* Discuss unfamiliar words. Discuss the two meanings of *mean.* Have students write the other word forms in sentences that include quoted speech. Review the use of quotation marks in dialogue before students begin.

Suffix Practice, Writing Words

Point out the *ful* and *less* suffixes in *meaningful* and *meaningless.* Have students find and write more words that can employ these suffixes. Choices may include *help* (137), *care* (483), *use* (88). Then have them add the *ly* suffix to each word they have made and discuss meanings.

690 *broken*

Other Word Forms, Writing Sentences

Have students brainstorm for common other word forms of *broken: break* (700), *breaks, broke, breaking, breaker.* Have students write the other word forms in sentences.

Sorting Words, Sound-Symbol Awareness

Have students play Word Sorts (see ***Spelling Sourcebook 1***, page 92) using these words: *broken, ride* (648), *bright* (541), *stone* (671), *kind* (214), *no* (71), *boat* (475), *note* (660), *yellow* (625), *wide* (477), *suppose* (555), *wife* (673), *cold* (312), *dry* (438). Then review the long *o* and long *i* spellings.

691 *interest*

Multiple Meanings, Writing Sentences

Brainstorm for meanings of *interest.* Then have students check a dictionary for verification. Have students write *interest* in sentences to illustrate its different meanings.

Other Word Forms, Vocabulary Skills, Writing Questions and Answers

Have students brainstorm for common other word forms of *interest: interests, interested, interesting, interestingly.* Discuss unfamiliar words. Have students write the other word forms in sentences. Then have students write these questions and the answers:

What characteristics make a book interesting?
Why might interest be charged to a credit card account?
What interests do you and your best friend share?

692 *chance*

Other Word Forms, Vocabulary Skills, Spelling Rules, Writing Sentences

Have students brainstorm for common other word forms of *chance: chances, chanced, chancing, chancy.* Discuss unfamiliar words. Review the spelling rule for adding suffixes to words ending in silent *e* (see ***Spelling Sourcebook 1***, page 85). Have students write the other word forms in sentences.

Idiomatic Usage, Writing Explanations

Have students explain in writing what they think it means to say these expressions (then discuss):

by chance	to take a chance
to chance it	a ghost of a chance
to jump at the chance	to stand a chance
once-in-a-lifetime chance	a chance happening

Sound-Symbol Awareness,
Writing Sentences

Have students write *chance*. Then ask them to follow these directions to make new and review words:

Change *chance* to make *change* (264).
Change *chance* to make *dance, romance, prance, stance, glance, trance.* (Discuss unfamiliar words.)
Change *chance* to make *charge*. (Have students write two meanings for *charge*.)

Then have students write a sentence for each word they made.

693 *thick*

Idiomatic Usage,
Writing Explanations

Have students explain in writing what they think it means to say these expressions (then discuss):

as thick as pea soup   as thick as thieves
to lay it on thick   through thick and thin

Antonyms

Ask students to write the antonym of *thick*, the word *thin* (670).

694 *sight*

Idiomatic Usage,
Writing Explanations

Have students explain in writing what they think it means to say these expressions (then discuss):

to buy something sight unseen   to lose sight
to know someone by sight   love at first sight
to lower your sights   to see the sights
Out of sight, out of mind.   a sight for sore eyes

Homophone Usage,
Vocabulary Skills

Introduce the homophones of *sight*, the words *site* and *cite*. Have students check a dictionary to contrast their meanings. Then have students write sentences to differentiate them. Expand the lesson to a review of persistently misused homophones with Mystery Words (see **Spelling Sourcebook 1**, page 89).

Sound-Symbol Awareness,
Sorting Words

Have students write *sight* and listen to the long *i* sound. Then have students collect more words with long *i* to note the most frequent spellings for long *i* (most common: *y* [*my*], *ight* [*right*], *ind* [*kind*], *i*-consonant-*e* [*smile*]). Create a list of long *i* words. Have students write the words in categories sorted by the spelling for the long *i*. Have one category for "other" to accommodate less common spellings.

Visual Skill-Building,
Writing Words

Have students play Word Shapes using grid paper or the blackline master on page 109 of **Spelling Sourcebook 1** (see Letter Grid Games, **Spelling Sourcebook 1**, page 88).

695 *pretty*

Multiple Meanings

Have students write sentences using two different meanings for *pretty*.

Other Word Forms,
Vocabulary Skills, Spelling Rules,
Writing Sentences

Have students brainstorm for common other word forms of *pretty: prettier, prettiest, prettily, prettiness.* Discuss unfamiliar words. Review the spelling rule for adding suffixes to words ending in consonant-*y* (see **Spelling Sourcebook 1**, page 85). Have students write the other word forms in sentences.

Idiomatic Usage,
Writing Explanations
Have students explain in writing what they think it means to say these expressions (then discuss):

as pretty as a picture   to cost a pretty penny
Pretty is as pretty does.   sitting pretty

Synonyms, Writing Words
Have students find and write words that are synonyms for *pretty,* meaning "comely." Choices may include *beautiful* (429), *lovely, attractive, cute, fair.*

696 *train*

Multiple Meanings,
Writing Sentences
Brainstorm for meanings of *train.* Then have students check a dictionary for verification. Review words that can be used in different ways, such as *gold* (486), *rock* (489), *poor* (496), *clear* (510). Have students write the words in sentences to illustrate their different meanings.

Other Word Forms, Vocabulary
Skills, Writing Questions and
Answers, Hypothesizing
Have students brainstorm for common other word forms of *train: trains, trained, training, trainer, trainable, trainee.* Discuss unfamiliar words. Have students write these questions and the answers:

What might you be able to train a dog to do?
Why do you think some animals are better trained than others?

Book Tie-In,
Research and Writing
Use *Train Talk: Guide to Lights, Hand Signals and Whistles* (Roger Yepson, Pantheon, 1983) to explore railroad communications. Ask students to explore and report on other communication codes, including Braille, Chinese kite signals, Morse Code, and signing.

Book Tie-In,
Using Descriptive Language
Models for sensory, descriptive writing are in *Country Crossing* (Jim Aylesworth, Atheneum, 1991) and *The Polar Express* (Chris Van Allsburg, Houghton, 1985). Ask students to find and write favorite descriptive phrases in the books. Then they may create a sensory, descriptive paragraph of their own on any topic.

Book Tie-In, Interviewing,
Writing a Summary
The Wind Warrior: The Training of a Karate Champion (Christopher Goedecke, Four Winds, 1992) offers a photo essay and text that follows the training of a thirteen-year-old karate student. Follow up with students interviewing an athlete about the training for his or her sport. Have students write interview questions beforehand and summarize the interview in writing afterward.

697 *fresh*

Other Word Forms,
Vocabulary Skills, Suffix Practice,
Writing Sentences,
Writing Questions and Answers
Have students brainstorm for common other word forms of *fresh: fresher, freshest, freshly, freshness, freshen.* Discuss unfamiliar words. Point out the *ly* suffix. Ask students to add the *ly* suffix to *general* (639), *late* (584), *natural* (556), *correct* (521), *clear* (510), *possible* (452), *complete* (365), and *certain* (353). Have students write the *ly* words and the other word forms of *fresh* in sentences. Then have students write this question and the answer: What efforts are being made in your community to freshen the air and keep it free from pollution?

Prefix Practice,
Writing a Definition
Have students add the *re* prefix to *fresh.* Discuss how it changes the meaning. Then have them add the *re* prefix to *train* (696), *cover* (640), *forest* (613), *heat* (505), *build* (487). Have students explain in writing what each of the prefixed words means. Have students proofread carefully for their spelling of *again* (141).

Antonyms ❖ Ask students to identify an antonym of *fresh,* the word *stale,* and predict its spelling.

698 *drive*

Multiple Meanings, Writing Sentences ❖ Brainstorm for meanings of *drive.* Then have students check a dictionary for verification. Review words that can be used in different ways, such as *over* (82), *still* (153), *last* (166), *letter* (344). Have students write *drive* in sentences to illustrate its different meanings.

Other Word Forms, Vocabulary Skills, Spelling Rules, Writing Sentences, Research and Writing ❖ Have students brainstorm for common other word forms of *drive: drives, drove, driving, driven, driver.* Discuss unfamiliar words. Review the spelling rule for adding suffixes to words ending in silent *e* (see **Spelling Sourcebook 1,** page 85). Have students write the other word forms in sentences. Then have them write this question and the answer: What requirements must you meet before driving a car in your state?

Book Tie-In, Research and Writing ❖ How and why were many Native Americans driven from their lands? Have students explore the answer with *Trails of Tears: American Indians Driven From Their Lands* (Jeanne Williams, Hendrick, 1992) and *The Tainos: The People Who Welcomed Columbus* (Francine Jacobs, Putnam, 1992). Then have students write an answer to the question.

Word Origins, Writing Words ❖ Introduce students to French spellings of words related to cars and driving: *limousine, garage, route, boulevard,* and *chassis.* Have students find and write more words that the English language has borrowed from French.

699 *lead*

Other Word Forms, Antonyms, Writing Sentences ❖ Have students review common other word forms of *lead: led* (659), *leading, leader.* Ask students to identify the antonym of *leader,* the word *follower.* Have students write the other word forms in sentences.

Homophone Usage ❖ Ask students to write the homophone of *lead,* the word *led* (659). Have students write sentences to differentiate them.

Idiomatic Usage, Writing Explanations ❖ Have students explain in writing what they think it means to say these expressions (then discuss):

All roads lead to Rome.	blind leading the blind
to lead a dog's life	to lead off
to lead the life of Riley	to lead the way
to lead someone down the garden path	

Remember . . .

Develop spelling accountability as students write—see **Spelling Sourcebook 1,** Article 8, page 33. Spelling mastery is achieved ONLY when students can spell and use words consistently correctly in writing.

700 *break*

Multiple Meanings, Writing Sentences ❖ Brainstorm for meanings of *break.* Then have students check a dictionary for verification. Review words that can be used in different ways, such as *caught* (527), *figure* (551), *free* (553), *general* (639). Have students write the words in sentences to illustrate their different meanings.

Other Word Forms, *Writing Sentences*	❖ Have students review common other word forms of *break: breaks, broke, breaking, broken* (690), *breaker.* Have students write the other word forms in sentences.
Idiomatic Usage, *Writing Explanations*	❖ Have students explain in writing what they think it means to say these expressions (then discuss):

at the break of dawn   to break away
Break a leg!   to break even
to break down   to break someone's heart
to break even   to take a break
to break something in   Give me a break.
to break the ice
to get a lucky break (See literature entry below.)

Book Tie-In, *Writing About an Experience*	❖ Use *The Fortunate Fortunes: Business Successes That Begin With a Lucky Break* (Nathan Aaseng, Lerner, 1989), stories of outstanding entrepreneurs whose marketing success began with unusual lucky breaks. Have students follow up with a written description of their "lucky break" experience.
Homophone Usage	❖ Ask students to identify the homophone of *break,* the word *brake.* Have students write sentences to differentiate them.
Antonyms	❖ Ask students to identify an antonym of one meaning of *break,* the word *fix,* and predict its spelling.

701 *sit*

Idiomatic Usage, *Writing Explanations*	❖ Have students explain in writing what they think it means to say these expressions (then discuss):

like a sitting duck   sitting on top of the world
at a sitting   to sit in for someone
to sit on something   to sit tight
Sit up and take notice.   sitting pretty

Spelling Rules, Suffix Practice, *Writing Sentences*	❖ Review the spelling rule for doubling the final consonant before adding suffixes (see **Spelling Sourcebook 1**, page 85). Have students apply the rule to *sit, thin* (670), *skin* (622), *trip* (576), *plan* (544), *begin* (444), *stop* (396). Ask students to write the suffixed words in sentences.

702 *bought*

Other Word Forms, *Writing Sentences*	❖ Have students review common other word forms of *bought: buy* (502), *buys, buying, buyer.* Have students write the other word forms in sentences.
Antonyms	❖ Ask students to identify the antonym of *bought,* the word *sold* and, predict its spelling.
Dictation and Writing, *Making Judgments*	❖ Dictate these partial sentences for students to write and complete: If your friends have bought you a present, you should _____ . If they bought the wrong size, you might be able to _____ .
Sorting Words	❖ Have students play Word Sorts (see **Spelling Sourcebook 1**, page 92) using these words: *bought, daughter, brought* (327), *thought* (179), *caught* (527), *not* (30), *fought, got* (219), *a lot* (4, 597).

703 *radio*

Other Word Forms, Vocabulary Skills, Writing Sentences ❖ Have students brainstorm for common other word forms of *radio: radios, radioed, radioing.* Discuss unfamiliar words. Have students write the other word forms in sentences.

Plural Practice, Writing Words ❖ Have students write the plural of *radio (radios).* Point out that some words that end in *o* become plural with *s,* some with *es,* and some with either *s* or *es,* with one preferred. Words ending in *vowel-o* consistently add *s.* Have students use a dictionary to determine the plural spelling of *patio (s), piano (s), hero (es), potato (es), tomato (es), echo (es), banjo (s, es), zero (s, es), motto (es, s), mosquito (es, s), tornado (es, s).*

Writing a Commercial, Public Speaking ❖ Have students write a thirty-second radio commercial to advertise a product and then deliver their commercial to the class.

Research and Writing, Public Speaking ❖ Have students research one of the following topics, tell about their findings in writing, and then present the information orally to the class:

the five radio stations that have the most listeners in your area and their type of programming

careers in radio and the qualifications to do each

CB radio and how it works

704 *method*

Other Word Form, Vocabulary Skills, Writing Sentences ❖ Have students brainstorm for common other word forms of *method: methods, methodical, methodically.* Discuss unfamiliar words. Have students write the other word forms in sentences.

Writing Descriptions, Writing Reasons ❖ Have students describe in writing a special method they use to do something and tell why it is the best way.

705 *king*

Other Word Forms, Writing Sentences ❖ Have students brainstorm for common other word forms of *king: kings, kingly, kingdom.* Have students write the other word forms in sentences. Then have students exchange papers and rewrite the sentences changing the tense of each.

Book Tie-In, Creating an Invitation ❖ *The King's Day: Louis XIV of France* (Aliki, Crowell, 1989) describes a typical day in the life of this king. Following the reading, ask students to create an invitation to a royal occasion at the palace of King Louis XIV.

Book Tie-In, Writing a Tall Tale ❖ Use *Mike Fink* (Steven Kellogg, Reteller, Morrow, 1992), a tall tale about Mike's career as King of the Keelboatmen. Then have students write a short tall tale using a king as one character.

Writing Explanations, Writing Reasons ❖ Ask students to write an answer to this question: Who was Martin Luther King, Jr., and why do we celebrate his life?

Sound-Symbol Awareness, Writing Words ❖ Have students write *king* and underline the *k.* Then have students write words in which the *k* sound is spelled differently. Help students conclude that the *k* sound can be spelled with *c, ck, qu, ch; ks* can be spelled with *x.* Have students find and write examples of each.

Antonyms ❖ Ask students to identify the antonym of *king,* the word *queen,* and predict its spelling.

706 *similar*

Other Word Forms, Vocabulary Skills, Writing Sentences

❖ Have students brainstorm for common other word forms of *similar: similarity, similarities, similarly, simile*. Discuss unfamiliar words. Have students write the other word forms in sentences.

Writing Similes

❖ Have students write similes such as "quiet as a mouse" and "sleep like a baby."

Book Tie-In, Comparing and Contrasting, Making a Chart

❖ Read *Moss Gown* (Donald Hooks, Clarion, 1987) to students and ask them which familiar story it is similar to ("Cinderella"). Have students create a chart of the similarities and differences of these two stories and other pairs of similar stories. Suggest the use of a Venn diagram.

707 *return*

Other Word Forms, Writing Sentences

❖ Have students brainstorm for common other word forms of *return: returns, returned, returning, returnable*. Have students write the other word forms in sentences.

Prefix Practice, Writing Words, Vocabulary Skills

❖ Have students write *return* and underline the *re* prefix meaning "back." The *re* prefix can also mean "again." Have students find examples of words with the *re* prefix. Choices may include *recall, review, recopy, refresh, recover, reread, rebuild, refine, rewind, replace, regroup, relive, retell, renew*. Then discuss how the *re* prefix changes the meaning of each word.

708 *corn*

Book Tie-In, Informational Writing

❖ Use *Corn Is Maize: The Gift of the Indians* (Aliki, Harper, 1976) for simply written, comprehensive information on corn. Following the reading, have students write one interesting fact they learned about corn.

Research and Writing, Hypothesizing

❖ Have students research popcorn to find out how it is the same and different from the corn we eat from the cob. Ask students to tell how popcorn may have gotten its name.

709 *decide*

Other Word Forms, Vocabulary Skills, Spelling Rules, Writing Sentences, Prefix Practice, Writing Speculations

❖ Have students brainstorm for common other word forms of *decide: decides, decided, deciding, decidedly, decision*. Discuss unfamiliar words. Review the spelling rule for adding suffixes to words ending in silent *e* (see **Spelling Sourcebook 1**, page 85). Have students write the other word forms in sentences. Discuss the *un* and *in* prefixes and have students add them to *decided* and *decision*. Then have students write these questions and the answers:

> Based on an actual recent vote, how do you think the majority of the voters made their decision?
> Why might some people have been undecided on the issue?
> What contributes to indecision when people cast their vote?

Book Tie-In, Writing Explanations

❖ Use *What Should I Do? Learning to Make Decisions* (R. Kunz and J. Swenson, Dillon, 1986). Then ask students to write about a decision that was hard for them to make and how they went about making their choice.

710 *position*

Multiple Meanings, Writing Sentences

Brainstorm for meanings of *position*. Then have students check a dictionary for verification. Review words that can be used in different ways, such as *will* (46), *down* (84), *way* (86), *just* (97), *train* (696), *break* (700). Have students write the words in sentences to illustrate their different meanings.

Other Word Forms, Vocabulary Skills, Writing Sentences

Have students brainstorm for common other word forms of *position: positions, positioned, positioning.* Discuss unfamiliar words. Have students write the other word forms in sentences. Then have students rearrange the words in each sentence and delete capitals and punctuation. Partners then exchange and unscramble the sentences.

Word Analysis, Writing Words

Have students write *position*. Then have them find and write more words with *tion*. Choices may include *sensation* (*sense* 678), *addition* (666), *direction* (619), *objection* (*object* 606), *information* (549), *correction* (*correct* 521). Point out that *sion* less frequently spells the same sound, as in *tension, session, discussion, recession, profession.*

711 *bear*

Multiple Meanings, Writing Sentences

Brainstorm for meanings of *bear*. Then have students check a dictionary for verification. Have students write *bear* in sentences to illustrate the different meanings.

Other Word Forms, Vocabulary Skills, Writing Sentences

Have students brainstorm for common other word forms of *bear: bears, bore, bearing, born* (677), *borne, bearable.* Discuss unfamiliar words. Have students write the other word forms in sentences.

Homophone Usage

Ask students to identify the homophone of *bear,* the word *bare.* Have students write sentences to differentiate them.

Idiomatic Usage, Writing Explanations

Have students explain in writing what they think it means to say these expressions (then discuss):

as hungry as a bear	to bear down
to bear a grudge	to bear in mind
to grin and bear it	to bear with it

Book Tie-In, Creating a Book

Use *Bears* (Ian Sterling, Sierra, 1992), *Seven True Bear Stories* (Laura Geringer, Hastings, 1979) and *Fat Man in a Fur Coat* (Alvin Schwartz, Farrar, 1984) as resources for facts and lore about bears. Follow up by creating a class-made book on bears (see page 138, Creating Classroom Books).

Book Tie-In, Writing Stories

Use *Somebody and the Three Blairs* (Marilyn Tollhurst, Orchard, 1991), a story parallel to "Goldilocks." Let the book be a model for students to write a funny story parallel to a favorite folktale.

Eponyms, Research and Writing, Book Tie-In

Teddy bear is an *eponym,* or word that comes from the name of a person or place. Have students research the origin of *teddy bear* (from Teddy Roosevelt). Have students report in writing. One source for this eponym is *Guppies in Tuxedos* (Marvin Terban, Clarion, 1988).

712 *hope*

Other Word Forms,
Spelling Rules, Writing Dialogue

❖ Have students brainstorm for common other word forms of *hope: hopes, hoped, hoping, hopeful, hopefully, hopeless, hopelessly, hopelessness.* Review the spelling rule for adding suffixes to words ending in silent *e* (see **Spelling Sourcebook 1**, page 85). Have students select words from among the other word forms and write them in sentences that include speakers' exact words. Review the use of quotation marks in dialogue before students begin.

Suffix Practice, Writing Words

❖ Point out this spelling pattern: *hope/hopeful/hopefully/hopeless/hopelessly.* Have students find and write more words that illustrate this pattern. Choices may include *use* (83), *help* (137), *need* (221), *care* (483), *thank, shame, taste, tact.* Review the spelling rule for doubling the final consonant before adding a suffix (see **Spelling Sourcebook 1**, page 85). Have students find and write more words that illustrate this spelling pattern. Choices may include *help* (137), *care* (483), *wish* (573), *force* (627).

713 *song*

Book Tie-In,
Writing Words to a Song

❖ Use *Go In and Out the Window: An Illustrated Songbook for Young People* (Dan Fox, Metropolitan Museum of Art/Holt, 1987), 61 songs with works of art connected to the music. Art and music are linked in a format appropriate for all ages. Follow up by asking students to write the words to a favorite song and then find or create accompanying art.

Dictation and Writing

❖ Dictate these partial sentences for students to write and complete:
The song played on the radio most often now is _____ .
Examples of gold-record songs are _____ .
Probably the most famous song of all time is _____ .
The subject of many songs is _____ .
Two songs that are similar are _____ .
My favorite song is _____ .

714 *engine*

Other Word Forms, Vocabulary
Skills, Writing Sentences

❖ Have students brainstorm for common other word forms of *engine: engineer, engineers, engineered, engineering.* Discuss unfamiliar words. Have students write the other word forms in sentences.

Book Tie-In, Analogies,
Writing Explanations

❖ Use *The Internal Combustion Engine* (Ross Olney, Lippincott, 1982) for a detailed but easy-to-understand explanation of the power source for most vehicles. Analogies aid the explanations. To follow up, ask students to write an explanation using an analogy.

Writing Words, Word Properties,
Writing Reasons

❖ Review the activity "Choose" (see 580, 638). Have students write the words in each row, then choose one word that does not belong, and write why it is different from the others.

engine	change	general	song
bear	corn	fish	horse
garden	lead	wind	object
similar	different	same	alike
train	plane	car	drive

715 *board*

Multiple Meanings, Writing Sentences
Brainstorm for meanings of *board*. Then have students check a dictionary for verification. Review words that can be used in different ways, such as *note* (660), *race* (662), *bit* (663), *rule* (682). Have students write the words in sentences to illustrate their different meanings.

Other Word Forms, Vocabulary Skills, Writing Sentences
Have students brainstorm for common other word forms of *board: boards, boarded, boarding, boarder*. Discuss unfamiliar words. Have students write the other word forms in sentences.

Homophone Usage
Ask students to identify the homophone of *board*, the word *bored*. Have students write sentences to differentiate them.

Compound Words, Writing Words
Have students find and write compound words that contain *board*. Choices may include *cupboard, chalkboard, boardroom, boardwalk, snowboard, skateboard* (see book idea below).

Book Tie-In, Writing a List, Writing Definitions
Introduce *Thrasher: The Radical Skateboard Book* (Kevin Thatcher and Brian Brannon, Random, 1992), a guide for skateboarders. Have students list and define skateboard lingo as a follow-up to the reading.

716 *control*

Other Word Forms, Spelling Rules, Writing Questions and Answers
Have students brainstorm for common other word forms of *control: controls, controlled, controlling, controller*. Review the spelling rule for doubling the consonant before adding a suffix (see **Spelling Sourcebook 1**, page 85). Have students write the other word forms in sentences that ask a question. Then have students exchange papers and answer the questions using the same word forms of *control* in the responses.

Book Tie-In, Writing to Persuade
Use *Gun Control: An Issue for the Nineties* (David Newton, Enslow, 1992) for an objective survey of the challenges associated with this issue. Follow up with students writing persuasive articles for and against gun control using appropriate arguments for each viewpoint.

717 *spread*

Other Word forms, Writing Sentences
Have students brainstorm for common other word forms of *spread: spreads, spreader, spreading, spreadable*. Have students write the other word forms in sentences.

Creating an Advertisement
Have students create a new sandwich spread and develop a magazine advertisement to sell it.

718 *evening*

Other Word Forms, Writing Sentences
Have students brainstorm for common other word forms of *evening: evenings, eve*. Have students write the other word forms in sentences.

Antonyms
Ask students to write the antonym of *evening*, the word *morning* (283). Ask students to write *even* (130) and one of its antonyms, the word *odd*.

Words That Tell When
Point out that *evening* tells "when." Have students write more words that tell the time of day (*sunset, dusk, noon*).

719 *brown*

Other Word Forms, Vocabulary Skills, Writing Sentences

Have students brainstorm for common other word forms of *brown: browns, browner, brownest, brownish, browned, browning.* Discuss unfamiliar words. Have students write the other word forms in sentences.

Book Tie-In, Writing a Sequel

Use books from the *Encyclopedia Brown* series, such as *Encyclopedia Brown's Book of Strange but True Crimes,* (Donald Sobol, Scholastic, 1991), in which Leroy Brown, boy detective, solves mysteries. Have students write a sequel episode to one of the mystery stories.

Writing a List, Color Words

For a timed-write activity (about three minutes), ask students to list color words, starting with *brown.* Let students use a dictionary for a spelling reference. A point is earned for each color spelled correctly. Review the colors students wrote in this activity and introduce color words they didn't use, perhaps *chartreuse, mauve,* or *magenta.* Show color examples of unfamiliar color words.

720 *clean*

Other Word Forms, Writing Sentences, Prefix Practice, Writing Questions and Answers

Have students brainstorm for common other word forms of *clean: cleans, cleaned, cleaning, cleaner, cleanest, cleanly, cleanliness.* Have students write the other word forms in sentences. Discuss the *un* prefix. Then have students write this question and the answer: Would you recommend an unclean restaurant? Why?

Idiomatic Usage, Writing Explanations

Have students explain in writing what they think it means to say these expressions (then discuss):

to clean out	to clean up
to get a clean bill of health	to come clean
to have a clean conscience	to make a clean sweep
to start with a clean slate	to keep your nose clean

Book Tie-In, Research, Writing a Summary, Writing Reasons, Public Speaking

Use *Clean Water* (Karen Barss, Chelsea, 1992) and *Clean Air* (Edward Edelson, Chelsea, 1992), which focus on what to do to solve the pollution crisis. Follow up with students using the *Reader's Guide* to locate one current article about an exemplary program for keeping the earth clean. Have students summarize the program in writing, tell why the program would or would not work for your community, and present the report orally to the class.

Antonyms

Ask students to identify the antonym of *clean,* the word *dirty,* and predict its spelling.

Synonyms, Vocabulary Skills, Writing Sentences

Ask students to find and write synonyms for *clean.* Choices may include *sanitary, immaculate, spotless, unsoiled, pristine, pure.* Discuss the meanings of unfamiliar words and ask students to write them in sentences.

721 *wouldn't*

Dictation and Writing

Dictate these partial sentences for students to write and complete:

One job I wouldn't ever choose is _____ .
I wouldn't want to miss a chance to _____ .
Our teacher wouldn't _____ .

Contractions, Writing Words ❖ Have students write *wouldn't.* Then have them find and write more contractions and then write the words that make up each. Next, have students play Connect the Dots (see **Spelling Sourcebook 1**, page 87) using the contractions.

722 *section*

Other Word Forms, Vocabulary Skills, Writing Sentences ❖ Have students brainstorm for common other word forms of *section: sections, sectioned, sectioning, sectional.* Discuss unfamiliar words. Have students write the other word forms in sentences.

Newspaper Sections ❖ Using local newspapers, students may list the news sections and then tell in which section they would find national weather news, comics, the television viewing schedule, the biggest current news story, world affairs, help-wanted ads, sports scores, recipes, a phone number for placing a classified ad, and movies.

Vocabulary Skills, Writing Explanations ❖ Have students write the word used for a section of a book (*chapter*), a house (*room* 266), the U.S.A. (*state* 371), Canada (*province*). Have students write an explanation for the system used to organize books into sections of a library, the system for how food is organized in a supermarket, or options for organizing the sections of a menu for a restaurant.

723 *spent*

Other Word Forms, Writing Sentences ❖ Have students brainstorm for common other word forms of *spent: spend, spends, spending, spender.* Have students write the other word forms in sentences.

Sound-Symbol Awareness, Writing Sentences ❖ Have students write *spent.* Then ask them to follow these directions to make new and review words:

> Change *spent* to make *sent* (542), *cent, scent.* (Discuss the homophones.)
> Change *spent* to make *rent, dent, lent, pent, tent, vent, went* (143). (Discuss unfamiliar words.)
> Change *spent* to make *spend.*
> Change *spent* to make *serpent.* (Have students define *serpent.*)
> Change *spent* to make *moment* (538).

Then have students write a sentence for each word they made.

724 *ring*

Multiple Meanings, Writing Sentences ❖ Brainstorm for meanings of *ring.* Then have students check a dictionary for verification. Have students write *ring* in sentences to illustrate the different meanings.

Other Word Forms, Vocabulary Skills, Writing Sentences ❖ Have students brainstorm for common other word forms of *ring: rings, rang, ringing, rung, ringer.* Discuss unfamiliar words and the different meanings of *rung.* Have students write the other word forms in sentences.

Homophone Usage ❖ Ask students to identify the homophone of *ring,* the word *wring*; and the homophone of *rung,* the word *wrung.* Have students write sentences to differentiate the homophones.

Idiomatic Usage, *Writing Explanations*	Have students explain in writing what they think it means to say these expressions (then discuss):

to have a familiar ring	to ring someone up
like a three-ring circus	to run rings around someone
to ring in the new year	to toss your hat into the ring

Book Tie-In, Making Inferences,
Writing Reasons

Use *Let Freedom Ring* (Myra Cohn Livingston, Holiday, 1991), a ballad honoring Martin Luther King, Jr. Follow up with students writing why they think the ballad was given that name.

725 *teeth*

Book Tie-In, Writing a Sequel

Use *Dr. De Soto Goes to Africa* (William Steig, HarperCollins, 1992), the humorous story of a mouse dentist who, in this episode, attends to an elephant's ailing tooth. Have students follow up by writing another De Soto episode.

Plural Practice, Writing Words

Review irregular plurals (see **Spelling Sourcebook 1**, page 85) with *child* (571) and *children* (200). Then ask students to write *teeth* and its singular, *tooth*. Have students find and write more irregular plurals. Choices may include *foot* (482) /*feet, goose/geese, man* (111) /*men* (148), *woman* (577) /*women* (685), *mouse/mice, ox/oxen, medium/media, die/dice, cactus/cacti* or *cactuses*.

726 *quiet*

Other Word Forms,
Writing Sentences,
Writing Questions and Answers

Have students brainstorm for common other word forms of *quiet: quieter, quietest, quietly, quietness*. Have them write the other word forms in sentences. Then have students write this question and the answer: In what places is it important to speak and behave quietly? Why?

Antonyms

Ask students to identify the antonym of *quiet*, the word *noisy*.

Word Analysis, Writing Sentences

Have students write *quiet/quite* (447)/*quit*. Contrast the words. Then have students write *maybe* (566)/*may be, already* (411)/*all ready, our* (109)/*are* (15), *then* (53)/*than* (73), *picture* (232)/*pitcher*. Have students write these often-confused words in sentences.

Sound-Symbol Awareness,
Writing Words

Have students find and write words with *q* to note the high reliability of the *qu* spelling pattern. Choices may include *quite* (447), *question* (476), *square* (537), *equal, quick, quart, equinox, equator, aqua*.

727 *ancient*

Book Tie-In,
Research and Writing

Use *The Secrets of Vesuvius: Exploring the Mysteries of an Ancient Buried City* (Sara Bisel, Scholastic, 1991), a part fact, part historical fiction account of the Roman town after the eruption of Mount Vesuvius. Have students follow up by exploring the tools used by archeologists to find out about ancient history. Have students list important tools and tell how they're used.

Book Tie-In, Hypothesizing

For information on dating ancient objects, such as moon rocks, dinosaur bones, and bristlecone pine trees, use *Dating Dinosaurs and Other Old Things* (Karen Liptak, Millbrook, 1992). Then ask students to write an answer to this question: What is the purpose of knowing the age of ancient things?

Book Tie-In, Writing a Sequel ❖ For a guided tour of travels through ancient monuments and lands, use *Let's Go Traveling* (Robin Krupp, Morrow, 1992). Rachel's visits include Stonehenge, the pyramids, the Great Wall of China, and the Mayan ruins. Have students write about Rachel's visit to another ancient site.

Book Tie-In, Writing Reasons ❖ Use *Hieroglyphs: The Writing of Ancient Egypt* (Norma J. Katan, Atheneum, 1981) for an explanation of this ancient communication system. Have students write reasons why this system is not one that people use today.

728 *stick*

Multiple Meanings, Writing Sentences ❖ Brainstorm for meanings of *stick*. Then have students check a dictionary for verification. Review words that can be used in different ways, such as *party* (626), *sand* (635), *general* (639), *material* (641), *bear* (711), *ring* (724). Have students write the words in sentences to illustrate their different meanings.

Other Word Forms, Writing Sentences, Writing a List ❖ Have students brainstorm for common other word forms of *stick: sticks, stuck, sticking, sticker, sticky, stickier, stickiest*. Have students write the other word forms in sentences. Then have them list things that feel sticky.

Idiomatic Usage, Writing Explanations ❖ Have students explain in writing what they think it means to say these expressions (then discuss):

to get the short end of the stick	to stick out like a sore thumb
Stick 'em up!	to stick to your guns
to stick around	to stick together
to stick by someone	to stick up for someone
to stick your neck out	a stick-in-the-mud

729 *afternoon*

Dictation and Writing ❖ Dictate these partial sentences for students to write and complete:
This afternoon after school I may decide to _____ .
The weather this afternoon _____ .
My friend and I once spent a whole afternoon _____ .

Compound Words, Writing Words ❖ Have students write *afternoon* and underline the two word parts. Dictate these compound words for students to write: *something* (178), *however* (250), *upon* (286), *outside* (420), *everyone* (430), *themselves* (443). Then dictate these compounds (each element is a review word): *airplane, breakfast, headlight, driveway, football, cattail, greenhouse, bookcase, playground, homework, classroom, fireplace, sandpaper, copyright, seashell, waterfall, weekend*. Then have students play Password (see **Spelling Sourcebook 1**, page 89) using these and other compounds.

730 *silver*

Multiple Meanings, Writing Sentences ❖ Brainstorm for meanings of *silver*. Then have students check a dictionary for verification. Review words that can be used in different ways through a timed-write activity (about three minutes). One point is earned for each word listed that has more than one meaning and is correctly spelled. Then select words for students to write in sentences to illustrate their different meanings.

Book Tie-In, Rhyming Words ❖ Use the poetry collection *There Is No Rhyme for Silver* (Eve Merriam, Atheneum, 1962). Ask students if there are other words for which there are no rhymes.

Color Words, Writing Words ❖ Review the color words generated in the activity with *brown* (719). Then have students play Spelling Baseball (see ***Spelling Sourcebook 1***, page 91) using color words and their other word forms.

731 *nose*

Other Word Forms, Vocabulary Skills, Writing Sentences, Writing Questions and Answers, Hypothesizing ❖ Have students brainstorm for common other word forms of *nose: noses, nosed, nosing, nosy, nosier, nosiest*. Discuss unfamiliar words. Review the spelling rule for adding suffixes to words ending in silent *e* (see ***Spelling Sourcebook 1***, page 85). Have students write the other word forms in sentences. Then have students write these questions and the answers:

What might a nosy person do?
What might a noisy person do?

Idiomatic Usage, Writing Explanations ❖ Have students explain in writing what they think it means to say these expressions (then discuss):

can't see beyond the end of your nose
to count noses
to cut off your nose to spite your face
to follow your nose
to have your nose in a book
to keep your nose to the grindstone

to nose around
to take a nose dive
to turn your nose up at something
to win by a nose
on the nose

Book Tie-In, Making Predictions ❖ Use *The Badger and the Magic Fan* (Tony Johnston, Putnam/Whitebird, 1990), in which a magic fan makes noses grow and shrink. Before the reading, ask students to write predictions of what they think the magic fan can do. Provide *nose* as a hint.

Book Tie-In, Creating a Book ❖ Use *Breathtaking Noses* (Hana Machotka, Morrow, 1992), an appealing set of simple lessons about animal noses. Ask students to use this book as a model to create a silly book, such as *Unheard of Ears* or *Tales to End all Tails* (see page 138, Creating Classroom Books).

Homophone Usage ❖ Ask students to identify the homophone of *nose*, the word *knows*. Review *no* (71) and *know* (100). Have students write sentences to differentiate the homophones.

732 *century*

Vocabulary Skills, Research and Writing ❖ Ask students how many years there are in a century (100), a decade (10), and a score (20). Ask students to write how many years "four score and seven years ago" was (87). Then have them write the significance of this phrase (from the start of Lincoln's Gettysburg Address).

Spelling Rules, Plural Practice, Writing Words ❖ Review the spelling rule for making plurals of words ending in consonant-*y* (see ***Spelling Sourcebook 1***, page 85). Have students make plurals of *century, party* (626), *copy* (612), *history* (567), *baby* (559), *body* (285), *city* (273), *story* (237), *country* (228). Then have students find and write more words that follow this spelling pattern.

Research and Writing, ❖ Have students research one of the following topics, tell about their findings in
Public Speaking writing, and then present the information orally to the class:

> what they think are the most significant innovations of the twentieth
> century
>
> the changes in lifestyle predicted for the twenty-first century

733 *therefore*

Dictation and Writing ❖ Dictate these partial sentences for students to write and complete:

> I couldn't think of a good reason to explain why I was late; therefore
>
> _____ .
>
> The snow was deep on the roads; therefore travel _____ .
>
> The evening was especially dark and quiet; therefore _____ .

Homophone Usage, ❖ Have students write the homophones for *there* (37) and *fore: their* (42), *they're,*
Writing Sentences *for* (12), *four* (211). Review these and other persistent homophone errors with
Mystery Words (see **Spelling Sourcebook 1**, page 89).

734 *level*

Multiple Meanings, ❖ Brainstorm for meanings of *level.* Then have students check a dictionary for
Writing Sentences verification. Have students write *level* in sentences to illustrate the different
meanings.

Palindromes, Writing Words, ❖ Discuss palindromes, words that are spelled the same forward and backward.
Book Tie-In, Writing Riddles Have students collect palindromes, beginning with *level.* Choices may include
eye (578), *noon, nun, kayak, peep, did* (83), *rotator, Anna, Bob, repaper, deed.*
Introduce the palindrome sentences, *Pull up if I pull up* and *Was it a car or a
cat I saw?* and *Step on no pets.* Then use *Too Hot to Hoot: Funny Palindrome
Riddles* (Marvin Terban, Clarion, 1985). Have students create their own silly
palindrome riddles.

735 *you'll*

Homophone Usage ❖ Introduce the homophone of *you'll,* the word *yule.* Have students write
sentences to differentiate them and the often-confused words *your* and *you're.*

Contractions, Writing Words ❖ Have students write *you'll* and the words from which the contraction was made
(*you* 8, *will* 46). Have students list more contractions that use *you* or *will* and
then write the words from which they are made. Choices may include *you're*
(552), *you'd, you've, we'll* (675), *they'll, there'll, she'll.*

736 *death*

Other Word Forms, ❖ Have students brainstorm for common other word forms of *death: deaths,*
Writing Sentences *deathly.* Have students write the other word forms in sentences.

Book Tie-In, Writing a Letter ❖ Use *The Kids' Book About Death and Dying* (Eric Rofes, Little, 1985), which
offers a discussion held by the author, a teacher, and the teacher's eleven- to
fourteen-year-old students. Also use the 1978 Newbery Medal book *Bridge to
Terabithia* (Katherine Paterson, Harper, 1987), which tells how Jess struggles
with the death of his friend Leslie. Have students write a kind letter to Jess.

Antonyms ❖ Ask students to write the antonym of *death,* the word *life* (208).

737 *hole*

Other Word Forms, Vocabulary Skills, Writing Sentences

Have students brainstorm for common other word forms of *hole: holes, holed, holey*. Discuss unfamiliar words. Have students write the other word forms in sentences.

Homophone Usage

Ask students to identify the homophone of *hole*, the word *whole* (259). Discuss the homophones *holey, holy,* and *wholly*. Have students write sentences to differentiate the homophones.

Idiomatic Usage, Writing Explanations

Have students explain in writing what they think it means to say these expressions (then discuss):

an ace in the hole	Money burns a hole in your pocket.
a hole in one	to pick holes in something

738 *coast*

Multiple Meanings, Writing Sentences

Brainstorm for meanings of *coast*. Then have students check a dictionary for verification. Review words that can be used in different ways, such as *lot* (597), *store* (589), *iron* (587), *trip* (576) *silver* (730), *level* (734). Have students write the words in sentences to illustrate their different meanings.

Other Word Forms, Vocabulary Skills, Writing Questions and Answers

Have students brainstorm for common other word forms of *coast: coasts, coasted, coasting, coaster, coastal*. Discuss unfamiliar words. Have students write the other word forms in sentences that ask a question. Then have students exchange papers and answer the questions using the same word forms of *coast* in the responses.

Book Tie-In, Research and Writing, Making a Poster

Along the coast of Australia within the Great Barrier Reef, puzzling animals have escaped scientific explanation. Have students explore these coastal animals using *The Great Barrier Reef: A Living Laboratory* (Rebecca Johnson, Lerner, 1992). Then have students make a poster showing an illustration and facts about a giant clam or dugong or other strange animal.

Sound-Symbol Awareness, Sorting Words

Have students write *coast* and listen to the long *o* sound. Then have students collect more words with the long *o* sound to note the most frequent spellings for long *o* (most common: *o* [*no*], *o*-consonant-*e* [*those*], *ow* [*show*], *oa* [*coat*], *old* [*cold*], *oe* [*toe*]). Create a list of long *o* words. Have students write the words in categories sorted by the spelling for the long *o*. Have one category for "other" to accommodate less common spellings.

Synonyms, Vocabulary Skills

Have students write *coast* and synonyms for the noun. Choices may include *beach, bank, seashore, shore, shoal*. Discuss unfamiliar words.

739 *cross*

Multiple Meanings, Writing Sentences

Have students brainstorm for meanings of *cross*. Then have students check a dictionary for verification. Have students write *cross* in sentences to illustrate the different meanings.

Other Word Forms, Spelling Rules, Plural Practice, Writing Words

Have students brainstorm for common other word forms of *cross: crosses, crossed, crossing, crossings, crossly*. Review the spelling rule for making nouns plural (see **Spelling Sourcebook 1**, page 85). Have students write the plurals for *business* (595), *wish* (573), *grass* (560), *watch* (436), *glass* (488), *class* (391), *box* (388), *tax, church, lunch, dish, dress, witch, inch, speech, success, ditch, fox, match, boss*.

740 *sharp*

Multiple Meanings, Art ❖ Brainstorm for meanings of *sharp*. Then have students check a dictionary for verification. Review words that can be used in different ways, such as *bear* (711), *board* (715), *ring* (724), *stick* (728). Have students illustrate the different meanings of the words on art paper.

Other Word Forms, ❖ Have students brainstorm for common other word forms of *sharp: sharper,*
Writing Questions and Answers *sharpest, sharpen, sharply, sharpness.* Have students write these questions and the answers:

What might make someone speak sharply to another?
What are ways you can sharpen your spelling skills?

Antonyms ❖ Ask students to identify an antonym of *sharp,* the word *dull.* Review another antonym for *dull,* the word *bright* (541).

741 *fight*

Other Word Forms, ❖ Have students brainstorm for common other word forms of *fight: fights, fought,*
Word Analysis, Writing Sentences *fighting, fighter.* Have students make *fought* into *bought* (702), *brought* (327), *taught.* Contrast the spellings. Then have students write the words in sentences.

Book Tie-In, Writing ❖ Use *That's Exactly the Way It Wasn't* (James Stevenson, Greenwillow, 1991), a
Explanations, Solving Problems humorous picture book that focuses on sibling fights. Ask students to write about the one thing that causes the most trouble between them and their siblings and/or friends. Then have them pose a solution to the discontent.

Sound-Symbol Awareness, ❖ Have students write *fight* and listen to the long *i* sound. Then have students
Sorting Words collect more words with long *i* to note the most frequent spellings for long *i* (most common: *y* [*my*], *ight* [*right*], *ind* [*kind*], *i*-consonant-*e* [*smile*]). Create a list of long *i* words. Have students write the words in categories sorted by the spelling for the long *i*. Have one category for "other" to accommodate less common spellings.

Visual Skill-Building, ❖ Write *fight* on the chalkboard, and draw an outline around it to accentuate its
Writing Words shape. Provide students with graph paper (or use the blackline master on page 109 of ***Spelling Sourcebook 1***). Have students write the word in the boxes and outline its shape (see Letter Grid Games on page 88 of ***Spelling Sourcebook 1***). Then have students make word shapes for review words, exchange papers with a partner, and see if the partner can fill in the boxes with the appropriate words.

742 *capital*

Multiple Meanings, ❖ Brainstorm for meanings of *capital*. Then have students check a dictionary for
Writing Sentences verification. Have students write *capital* in sentences to illustrate the different meanings.

Other Word Forms, ❖ Have students brainstorm for common other word forms of *capital: capitals,*
Vocabulary Skills, Capitalization *capitalize, capitalized, capitalizing, capitalization.* Discuss unfamiliar words. Have students write sentences that include examples of capitalization: in direct quotations, at the beginning of a sentence, for *I,* and more.

Homophone Usage ❖ Introduce the homophone of *capital,* the word *capitol.* Have students write sentences to differentiate them.

Book Tie-In, Research and
Writing, Hypothesizing

❖ Use *A Capital for the Nation* (Stan Hoig, Cobblehill, 1990), and *A Capital Capital City* (Suzanne Hilton, Atheneum, 1992), which describe the official capital city and its history. Follow up with students researching and writing about their state capital. Have them hypothesize why their capital city was chosen.

743 *fill*

Idiomatic Usage,
Writing Explanations

❖ Have students explain in writing what they think it means to say these expressions (then discuss):

to fill in for someone	to fill someone in
to fill someone's shoes	to fill something out
to fill the bill	to fill the gap
to get your fill of something	

Analogies, Writing Words,
Writing Sentences

❖ Review analogies (568, 614, 643). Then have students write these analogies and complete them with words of frequencies 723–743 or their other word forms:

bored : board :: capitol : _____ (capital)
wife : wives :: tooth : _____ (teeth)
mined : mind :: whole : _____ (hole)
modern : ancient :: life : _____ (death)
shore : coast :: angry : _____ (cross)

Have students write the answer words in sentences.

744 *deal*

Multiple Meanings,
Writing Sentences

❖ Brainstorm for meanings of *deal*. Then have students check a dictionary for verification. Have students write *deal* in sentences to illustrate the different meanings.

Other Word Forms, Vocabulary
Skills, Alphabetical Order

❖ Have students brainstorm for common other word forms of *deal: deals, dealt, dealing, dealer.* Discuss unfamiliar words. Have students write the other word forms in alphabetical order.

Idiomatic Usage,
Writing Explanations

❖ Have students explain in writing what they think it means to say these expressions (then discuss):

a great deal (two meanings)	to make something into a big deal
to deal someone in (or out)	to get a raw deal
to deal with something	It's a deal!

Sound-Symbol Awareness,
Homophone Usage,
Writing Sentences

❖ Have students write *deal*. Then ask them to follow these directions to make new and review words:

Change *deal* to make *heal.* (Discuss *heal* and *heel.*)
Change *deal* to make *peal.* (Discuss *peal* and *peel.*)
Change *deal* to make *dear.* (Discuss *dear* and *deer.*)
Change *deal* to make *meal, real* (454), *seal, teal, veal, zeal.* (Discuss unfamiliar words.)
Change one letter of *deal* to make *deaf.*
Change one letter of *deal* to make *dead* (668).

Then have students write a sentence for each word they made.

745 *busy*

Other Word Forms,
Spelling Rules, Writing Sentences

Have students brainstorm for common other word forms of *busy: busier, busiest, busies, busied, busying, busily.* Review the spelling rule for adding suffixes to words ending in consonant-*y* (see *Spelling Sourcebook 1*, page 85). Have students write the other word forms in sentences.

Book Tie-In,
Writing Tongue Twisters

Use *Busy Buzzing Bumblebees* (Alvin Schwartz, Harper, 1982) for terrific tongue twisters to twist and tangle talkers. Have students follow up by writing original tongue twisters for their classmates to say.

746 *beyond*

Idiomatic Usage,
Writing Explanations

Ask students to explain in writing what they think it means to say each of these expressions (then discuss):

    beyond your means   beyond words

    beyond a reasonable doubt   It's beyond me.

    above and beyond the call of duty (See activity below.)

Writing Descriptions

Have students describe in writing what they've done that was "above and beyond the call of duty."

Word Analysis, Writing Words,
Vocabulary Skills

Have students list *be____* words, beginning with *beyond.* Choices may include *because* (127), *between* (154), *below* (176), *began* (215), *before* (332), *became* (334), *become* (336), *behind* (342), *begin* (444), *beside* (590), *believe, beneath, belong, belittle, betray, belabor, befriend, bestow.* Discuss unfamiliar words.

747 *send*

Other Word Forms,
Word Analysis, Writing Words

Have students brainstorm for common other word forms of *send: sends, sent, sending, sender.* Discuss the use of *sent* instead of "sended." Have students write more words that have a changed past-tense spelling instead of the *ed* ending. Choices may include *made* (81), *thought* (179), *came* (122), *went* (143), *found* (152), *saw* (177), *meant* (689), *spent* (723), *stuck* (*stick* 728), *fought* (*fight* 741).

Addressing an Envelope

Review with students how to address an envelope. Then have them write addresses for three people to whom they may send mail.

Antonyms, Writing Words

Have students identify an antonym for *send,* the word *receive.* For a timed-write activity (about three minutes), ask students to list antonym pairs. Let students use a dictionary for a spelling reference. A point is earned for each pair spelled correctly.

748 *love*

Other Word Forms, Spelling
Rules, Using Descriptive Language

Have students brainstorm for common other word forms of *love: loves, loved, loving, lovely, lovelier, loveliest, lovable.* Review the spelling rule for adding suffixes to words ending in silent *e* (see *Spelling Sourcebook 1*, page 85). Have students write their description of the loveliest weather day using vivid, descriptive words.

Book Tie-In,
Comparing and Contrasting

Use *Somebody Loves You, Mr. Hatch* (Eileen Spinelli, Bradbury, 1992). Ask students to write how Mr. Hatch changes from the beginning of the story to the end.

Antonyms ❖ Ask students to identify the antonym of *love*, the word *hate*, and predict its spelling.

Visual Skill-Building, Writing Words, Creating a Word Puzzle ❖ Play the Word Look-Alike game. Ask students to circle the words in each row that are like the underlined word. Then they turn the paper over, picture the underlined word, and write it.

<u>love</u>	live	line	love	dove	glove	lone
<u>capital</u>	carnival	capitol	castle	capital	capped	captain
<u>coast</u>	coast	cost	boast	cast	coat	coal
<u>quiet</u>	quick	quite	quit	quack	quiet	queen
<u>section</u>	session	action	section	sanction	sector	section

Next, have students create more look-alike word sets for a classmate to complete.

749 *cool*

Other Word Forms, Writing Sentences ❖ Have students brainstorm for common other word forms of *cool: cools, cooled, cooling, cooler, coolest, coolly, coolness.* Have students write the other word forms in sentences.

Book Tie-In, Writing a Summary ❖ Use *A Chilling Story: How Things Cool Down* (Albert Stwertka and Eve Stwertka, Messner, 1991), which includes experiments for understanding refrigeration. Have students write summaries of the experiments demonstrated in class.

Antonyms ❖ Ask students to write the antonym of *cool,* the word *warm* (412).

Synonyms, Vocabulary Skills, Sequencing ❖ Have students write words that describe cold. Choices may include *chilly, frosty, nippy, arctic, icy, freezing.* Then have students sequence the words from the coldest to the least cold using their judgment of the words' connotations.

750 *cause*

Other Word Forms, Spelling Rules, Research and Writing ❖ Have students brainstorm for common other word forms of *cause: causes, caused, causing.* Review the spelling rule for adding suffixes to words ending in silent *e* (see **Spelling Sourcebook 1**, page 85). Have students write these questions and the answers:
What causes steam?
What do you think caused dinosaurs to disappear?

Research and Writing ❖ Introduce the word *effect* and provide examples of cause and effect. Then ask students to write the causes of population increases or decreases in your community or state and the effects the changes have had on the people there.

Visual Skill-Building ❖ Have students write *because* (127) and underline *cause.*

751 *please*

Other Word Forms, Spelling Rules, Writing Questions and Answers, Making Judgments ❖ Have students brainstorm for common other word forms of *please: pleases, pleased, pleasing, pleaser, pleasant, pleasantly.* Review the spelling rule for adding suffixes to words ending in silent *e* (see **Spelling Sourcebook 1**, page 85). Have students write this question and the answer: From what you know about the tastes of people your age, which movie, library book, TV show, and after-school activity would be most pleasing to them?

Writing a List, Book Tie-In, Hypothesizing

❖ Have students make a list of "polite" words, beginning with *please* and *thank you*. Then introduce *Mind Your Manners* (Peggy Parish, Greenwillow, 1979). Have students write why they think Peggy Parish chose this title for her book. What other titles might have worked as well?

Word Origins, Vocabulary Skills

❖ Introduce the word *etiquette*, a French word. Explain that many French spellings use *ette: silhouette, dinette, gazette, rosette, marionette*. Discuss unfamiliar words. Expand the lesson to the French spelling *que* (*antique, unique, technique, critique, picturesque, physique*).

752 *meat*

Homophone Usage, Book Tie-In, Creating a Book

❖ Ask students to identify the homophone of *meat*, the word *meet* (610). Have students write sentences to differentiate them. The homophone *mete* could also be discussed. Then use *A Chocolate Moose for Dinner* (Fred Gwynne, Holt, 1987) for a humorous look at homophones and the multiple meanings of words. Students can use this book as a model to write and illustrate their own silly homophone book (see page 138, Creating Classroom Books).

753 *lady*

Spelling Rules, Plural Practice, Writing Words

❖ Review the spelling rule for making plurals of words ending in consonant-*y* (see **Spelling Sourcebook 1**, page 85). Have students apply this rule to *lady* and *century* (732). Then ask them to find and write other consonant-*y* plurals.

Book Tie-In, Drawing Conclusions

❖ Use *The Old Ladies Who Liked Cats* (Carol Greene, HarperCollins, 1991), a funny story that teaches a lesson to people of all ages. Following the reading, ask students to write the lesson the ladies in the story teach the reader—a lesson about mutual need and support.

Research and Writing, Book Tie-In, Comparing and Contrasting

❖ Have students research and write about a former First Lady, the wife of a U.S. president. Sources may include *Stateswoman to the World: A Story About Eleanor Roosevelt* (Maryann Weidt, Carolrhoda, 1991) and *Barbara Bush: First Lady* (Rose Blue and Corrine Naden, Enslow, 1991). Then ask students to compare and contrast the First Lady they researched with the current First Lady.

Antonyms

❖ Ask students to identify the antonym of *lady*, the word *gentleman*, and predict its spelling.

754 *west*

Other Word Forms, Vocabulary Skills, Writing Sentences

❖ Have students brainstorm for common other word forms of *west: western, westward, westerly*. Discuss unfamiliar words. Have students write the other word forms in sentences.

Book Tie-In, Writing Jokes

❖ Use *Westward Ho Ho Ho!: Jokes From the Wild West* (Victoria Hartman, Viking, 1992) as a model for students to write their own Old West jokes.

Book Tie-In, Comparing and Contrasting

❖ Use *Ride Western Style: A Guide for Young Riders* (Tommie Kirksmith, Howell, 1991) with students interested in horseback riding. Have students research the English style of riding and the Western style and then compare and contrast the two in writing.

Antonyms, Writing Descriptions ❖ Ask students to identify the antonym of *west,* the word *east.* Have them write *north* (581) and *south* (620). Then have students write a description of what lies to the north, south, east, and west of their school.

755 *glad*

Other Word Forms, Spelling Rules, Suffix Practice, Writing Explanations ❖ Have students brainstorm for common other word forms of *glad: gladder, gladdest, gladly, gladden, gladness.* Review the spelling rule for doubling the final consonant before adding suffixes (see **Spelling Sourcebook 1**, page 85). Have students find and write words to which they can apply the rule. Then have them explain how to gladden a sick or sad friend.

Synonyms, Vocabulary Skills, Writing Sentences ❖ Ask students to research and list synonyms for *glad.* Choices may include *delighted, pleased, elated, happy, exuberant.* Discuss the meanings of unfamiliar words and ask students to write them in sentences.

756 *action*

Book Tie-In, Making a Poster ❖ Use *Action* (Kim Taylor, Wiley, 1992) for science experiments that introduce students to motion. Have students follow up by creating a poster that features a fact learned in the book, its explanation, and an illustration.

Prefix Practice, Writing Definitions ❖ Have students add prefixes to *action* and *active.* Then have them write definitions for the resulting words (*reaction, reactive, interaction, interactive, inactive, underactive, hyperactive, proactive, retroactive*).

757 *pass*

Multiple Meanings, Writing Sentences ❖ Brainstorm for meanings of *pass.* Then have students check a dictionary for verification. Review words that can be used in different ways, such as *blue* (407), *mind* (419), *game* (433), *watch* (436), *level* (734). Have students write the words in sentences to illustrate their different meanings.

Other Word Forms, Writing Questions and Answers, Hypothesizing ❖ Have students brainstorm for common other word forms of *pass: passes, passed, passing, passer, passable, passage, passenger.* Have students write these questions and the answers:

Why might an overpass be constructed on a highway?
What might make a road impassable?
When might a passenger need a ticket?

Idiomatic Usage, Writing Explanations ❖ Have students explain in writing what they think it means to say these expressions (then discuss):

to come to pass	in passing
to pass out	to pass on
to pass away	to get passed over
to pass something up	to pass the buck
to pass the hat	to pass the time of day

758 *type*

Multiple Meanings, Writing Sentences ❖ Brainstorm for meanings of *type.* Then have students check a dictionary for verification. Have students write *type* in sentences to illustrate the different meanings. Then write an explanation for why a typewriter may become obsolete.

Other Word Forms,
Vocabulary Skills, Spelling Rules,
Suffix Practice, Writing Words

❖ Have students brainstorm for common other word forms of *type: types, typed, typing, typist*. Discuss unfamiliar words. Review the spelling rule for adding suffixes to words ending in silent *e* (see **Spelling Sourcebook 1**, page 85). Review suffix additions to *please* (751), *cause* (750), *love* (748), *nose* (731), *hope* (712), *decide* (709), *drive* (698), *race* (662), *practice* (634), *force* (627), *trouble* (588), *measure* (523), *leave* (431), *change* (264). Have students use these words with their suffixes in Bingo (see **Spelling Sourcebook 1**, page 87).

759 *attention*

Other Word Forms,
Vocabulary Skills,
Writing Questions and Answers

❖ Have students brainstorm for common other word forms of *attention: attend, attends, attended, attending, attendance, attentive, attentively, attendant*. Discuss unfamiliar words. Have students write these questions and the answers:
   What does a parking attendant do?
   What might the advantages be for perfect school attendance?

Prefix Practice, Writing Questions
and Answers, Speculating

❖ Have students write *attention* and add the prefix that makes the word mean its opposite (*in*). Have students write this question and the answer: Why might a student be inattentive?

Prefix Practice, Writing Questions
and Answers

❖ Have students add the *in* prefix to *active* (action 756), *complete* (365), *direct*. Then have students write these questions and answers:
   Is an inactive volcano dangerous? Why?
   What happens if your homework is incomplete?
   Why might you take an indirect route home from school?

Suffix Practice, Writing Words

❖ Prepare the game Suffix Boxes (see **Spelling Sourcebook 1**, page 89) with *attend* and selected review words.

Remember . . .

Develop spelling accountability as students write—see **Spelling Sourcebook 1**, Article 8, page 33. Spelling mastery is achieved ONLY when students can spell and use words consistently correctly in writing.

760 *gas*

Other Word Forms,
Writing Sentences

❖ Have students brainstorm for common other word forms of *gas: gases, gassed, gassing, gaseous, gasoline*. Have students write the other word forms in sentences.

Plural Practice, Writing Words

❖ Review the spelling rule for making nouns plural (see **Spelling Sourcebook 1**, page 85). Have students write the plurals for *pass* (757), *business* (595), *wish* (573), *grass* (560), *watch* (436), *glass* (488), *class* (391), *box* (388), *tax, church, punch, dish, dress, witch, inch, speech, success, fox, patch*.

Clipped Words, Writing Words

❖ *Gas* is a "shortcut" word, or clipped word, for *gasoline*. Have students brainstorm for other clipped words and their longer forms. Choices may include *plane* (561) */airplane, bike/bicycle, math/mathematics, teen/teenager, gym/gymnasium, auto/automobile, limo/limousine, phone/telephone*.

Book Tie-In, Writing Questions,
Informational Writing,
Creating a Classroom Book

❖ Use *Oil and Natural Gas* (Betsy Kraft, Watts, 1982) for an introduction to these energy sources. Ask students before the reading to list questions about how these energy sources are located, mined, and transported. Then have them read for the answers. Follow up with a class-made question-and-answer book about oil and natural gas (see page 138, Creating Classroom Books).

Research and Writing, ❖ Have students research one of the following topics, tell about their findings in
Public Speaking writing, and then present the information orally to the class:

the factors that influence the price of gas at the gas station

the advantages and disadvantages of using oxygenated gasoline fuel

761 *kitchen*

Writing a List, Sorting Words ❖ Have students list things often found in a kitchen cupboard, such as plates,
cups, bowls, pans, cereal, and sugar. Then have students sort the items in some
way. Students may go on to list and sort kitchen appliances, such as stove,
microwave oven, coffee-maker, and refrigerator.

Hypothesizing ❖ The electric kitchen range, or stove, was invented in 1890, but few Americans
were interested in getting one. Have students hypothesize in writing why they
think this might have been (few homes had electricity).

Creating a Checklist ❖ Have students write a checklist for cleaning the kitchen after dinner that would
be used by a younger sibling.

762 *pick*

Other Word Forms, ❖ Have students brainstorm for common other word forms of *pick: picks, picked,*
Writing Sentences *picking, picker, picky, pickier, pickiest.* Have students write the other word
forms in sentences.

Multiple Meanings, ❖ Brainstorm for meanings of *pick.* Then have students check a dictionary for
Writing Sentences verification. Review words that can be used in different ways, such as *last*
(166), *left* (169), *might* (173), *sound* (175). Have students write the words in
sentences to illustrate their different meanings.

Idiomatic Usage, ❖ Have students explain in writing what they think it means to say these
Writing Explanations expressions (then discuss):

to have a bone to pick   to pick a fight

to pick at someone   to pick on someone

to pick up the tab   to pick holes in something

Word Properties, Writing Words ❖ Have students have fun with word properties with the Picky Family of
activities (see ***Spelling Sourcebook 1***, page 88).

763 *scale*

Multiple Meanings, ❖ Brainstorm for meanings of *scale.* Then have students check a dictionary for
Writing Sentences verification. Have students write *scale* in sentences to illustrate the different
meanings.

Other Word Forms, ❖ Have students brainstorm for common other word forms of *scale: scales,*
Spelling Rules, Writing Sentences *scaled, scaling, scaly.* Review the spelling rule for adding suffixes to words
ending in silent *e* (see ***Spelling Sourcebook 1***, page 85). Have students write
the other word forms in sentences. Then have students rearrange the words in
each sentence and delete capitals and punctuation. Partners then exchange and
unscramble the sentences.

Writing a Story ❖ Have students play Finish the Story (see ***Spelling Sourcebook 1***, page 88) to
reinforce *scale* and selected review words.

764 *basic*

Other Word Forms, Vocabulary Skills, Writing Sentences

❖ Have students brainstorm for common other word forms of *basic: basics, basically, base* (525), *bases, based, basing*. Discuss unfamiliar words. Have students write the other word forms in sentences.

Analogies, Writing Words, Other Word Forms

❖ Review analogies (614, 643, 743). Then have students write these analogies and complete them with words of frequencies 744–764 or their other word forms:

glad : pleased :: standard : _____ (basic)
busy : inactive :: east : _____ (west)
airplane : plane :: gasoline : _____ (gas)
bird : feather :: fish : _____ (scale)
silver : color :: beef : _____ (meat)

Have students write other word forms of the answer words.

765 *happen*

Dictation and Writing

❖ Dictate these partial sentences for students to write and complete:

One thing people said would never happen that did happen was _____ .
Something almost everyone said would happen that didn't happen was

_____ .

Other Word Forms, Writing Words

❖ Have students brainstorm for common other word forms of *happen: happens, happened, happening, happenings*. Have students play All in the Family (see *Spelling Sourcebook 1*, page 86) using these and other word forms of selected review words.

766 *safe*

Multiple Meanings, Writing Sentences

❖ Brainstorm for meanings of *safe*. Then have students check a dictionary for verification. Review words that can be used in different ways, such as *silver* (730), *level* (734), *coast* (738), *cross* (739). Have students write the words in sentences to illustrate their different meanings.

Other Word Forms, Spelling Rules, Prefix Practice, Writing Questions and Answers

❖ Have students brainstorm for common other word forms of *safe: safer, safest, safely, safes, safety*. Review the spelling rule for adding suffixes to words ending in silent *e* (see *Spelling Sourcebook 1*, page 85). Discuss the *un* prefix and have students add it to *safe*. Have students write these questions and the answers:

Why are there laws to require wearing safety belts in cars?
Why is it unsafe to drive at the posted speed in icy weather?

Book Tie-In, Making a Poster

❖ Use *Play It Safe: The Kids' Guide to Personal Safety and Crime Prevention* (Kathy Kyte, Knopf, 1983), advice for kids of all ages. Following the reading, ask students to make a poster for safety or crime prevention.

Writing a List

❖ Have students make a list of bicycle safety tips.

767 *grown*

Other Word Forms, Writing Questions and Answers

❖ Have students review common other word forms of *grown: grow* (337), *grows, grew, growing, growth, grower*. Have students write the other word forms in sentences that ask a question. Then have students exchange papers and answer the questions using the same word forms of *grown* in the responses.

Homophone Usage, Writing Words
❖ Ask students to identify the homophone of *grown*, the word *groan*. Have students write sentences to differentiate them. Then have students play Race Track Spelling (see **Spelling Sourcebook 1**, page 90) using persistently misused homophones.

768 *cost*

Other Word Forms, Writing Questions and Answers
❖ Have students brainstorm for common other word forms of *cost: costs, costing, costly*. Have students write this question and the answer: Why are designer clothes often more costly?

Research and Writing, Making a Chart, Public Speaking
❖ Have students research one of the following topics, tell about their findings in writing, and then present the information orally to the class using a self-made chart as a visual aid:
    items that have a significant cost difference at various stores
    an example of the effect of consumer demand on the cost of an item

Synonyms
❖ Have students write synonyms for *cost*. Choices may include *price, value, worth, fee, charge*.

769 *wear*

Other Word Forms, Homophone Usage
❖ Have students brainstorm for common other word forms of *wear: wears, wore, wearing, worn, wearer*. Discuss the homophones *wore* and *war, wears* and *wares, worn* and *warn*. Have students write the homophones in sentences to differentiate them.

Informational Writing, Writing Reasons
❖ Have each student create a school dress code for students and teachers and write why the guidelines are appropriate.

Homophone Usage
❖ *Wear* and *where* are sometimes pronounced as homophones. Ask students to write sentences to differentiate them. Expand the lesson to *witch* and *which* (41).

770 *act*

Multiple meanings, Writing Sentences
❖ Brainstorm for meanings of *act*. Then have students check a dictionary for verification. Have students write *act* in sentences to illustrate the different meanings.

Other Word Forms, Homophone Usage, Writing Sentences
❖ Have students brainstorm for common other word forms of *act: acts, acted, acting, active, activity, action, actor, actress*. Discuss the homophones *acts* and *axe*. Then have students write the homophones and the other word forms in sentences.

Prefix Practice, Writing Definitions
❖ Have students add the *re* prefix to *act*. Ask them to write a description of a mature way to react to an unkind remark made about them. Have them add the *re* prefix to *action* (756), *fill* (743), *position* (710), *fresh* (697), *train* (696), *store* (589). Have students explain in writing what each prefixed word means.

Idiomatic Usage, Writing Explanations
❖ Have students explain in writing what they think it means to say these expressions (then discuss):
    to act high and mighty   to act your age
    an act of faith   to act up
    an act of war   to put on an act
    a tough act to follow   to read the riot act

771 *hat*

Book Tie-In,
Reasoning, Sequencing

❖ Use *Anno's Hat Tricks* (Anno Mitsumasa and Akihiro Nozaki, Philomel, 1985), puzzles requiring deductive reasoning and ranging from easy to challenging. Have students write the steps for the solution of one hat trick.

Book Tie-In,
Drawing Conclusions

❖ Ask students to write what significance the hat has in the picture book *My Grandfather's Hat* (Melanie Scheller, McElderry, 1992).

Writing a List

❖ Have students list kinds of hats and the people who wear them (crown/royalty, football helmet/football player).

Idiomatic Usage,
Writing Explanations

❖ Have students explain in writing what they think it means to say these expressions (then discuss):

at the drop of a hat	to pull something out of a hat
to be old hat	to take your hat off to someone
to keep something under your hat	to toss your hat into the ring
to pass the hat	to wear more than one hat

772 *arm*

Multiple Meanings,
Writing Sentences

❖ Brainstorm for meanings of *arm*. Then have students check a dictionary for verification. Review words that can be used in different ways, such as *sharp* (740), *capital* (742), *deal* (744), *pass* (757). Have students write the words in sentences to illustrate their different meanings.

Other Word Forms,
Vocabulary Skills, Spelling Rules,
Plural Practice

❖ Have students brainstorm for common other word forms of *arm: arms, armed, arming, armor, army, armory*. Discuss unfamiliar words. Have students change *army* to its plural (*armies*) and write the spelling rule they applied (see **Spelling Sourcebook 1**, page 85). Dictate these words and have students write the plurals: *lady* (753), *century* (732), *party* (626), *copy* (612), *baby* (559), *body* (285), *city* (273), *story* (237), *country* (228).

Prefix Practice,
Writing Definitions

❖ Have students add the *un* prefix to *armed* and the *dis* prefix to *arm*. Discuss how the prefix changes the meaning. Explain that the prefixes *in, im, dis,* and *un* can mean "not" or "the opposite of." Then have them add one of these prefixes to *active* (*act* 770), *safe* (766), *clean* (720), *decided* (*decide* 709), *similar* (706), *human* (575), *reasonable* (*reason* 564), *natural* (556), *happy* (540), *correct* (521), *clear* (510), *possible* (452), *certain* (353), *able* (346), *do* (45), *agree, continue, comfortable, mature, honest*. Have students check a dictionary if they are uncertain which prefix to use. Then have students write what each prefixed word means.

Idiomatic Usage,
Writing Explanations

❖ Have students explain in writing what they think it means to say these expressions (then discuss):

armed to the teeth	to twist someone's arm
to cost an arm and a leg	arm in arm
to keep at arm's length	up in arms
to receive with open arms	to put the arm on someone

Book Tie-In, Writing a Summary

❖ Use *Polly Vaughn: A Traditional British Ballad* (Barry Moser, Little, 1992), a retelling of the English tale teaching the dangers of firearms. Follow up with students finding and summarizing a current event that involves the danger of firearms.

773 *believe*

*Other Word Forms,
Spelling Rules, Writing Sentences*
❖ Have students brainstorm for common other word forms of *believe: believes, believed, believing, believer, believable.* Review the spelling rule for adding suffixes to words ending in silent *e* (see ***Spelling Sourcebook 1***, page 85). Have students write the other word forms in sentences.

Book Tie-In, Writing Reasons
❖ Use *Super Stitches: A Book of Superstitions* (Ann Nevins, Holiday, 1983). Follow up with students writing reasons for personal superstitions.

Word Analysis, Writing Words
❖ *Believe* is spelled with *ie.* Have students find and write more *ie* words, such as *piece* (392), *field* (472), *friend* (498), *science* (683), *quiet* (726), *ancient* (727).

774 *major*

*Multiple Meanings,
Writing Sentences*
❖ Brainstorm for meanings of *major.* Then have students check a dictionary for verification. Have students write *major* in sentences to illustrate the different meanings.

*Other Word Forms, Vocabulary
Skills, Writing Explanations*
❖ Have students brainstorm for common other word forms of *major: majors, majored, majoring, majority.* Discuss unfamiliar words. Have students write to tell how *majority* and *democracy* are related.

*Antonyms, Homophone Usage,
Writing Sentences*
❖ Ask students to identify the antonym of *major,* the word *minor.* Discuss meanings of *minor.* Then discuss the homophone of *minor,* the word *miner.* Have students write the words in sentences.

775 *gray*

British Spellings
❖ Note with students the British spelling of *gray,* the word *grey.*

*Book Tie-In,
Writing a Bibliography*
❖ Use *The Moon of the Gray Wolves* (Jean Craighead George, HarperCollins, 1991), which tells about the life of the gray wolf in Alaska. Have students create a bibliography of additional resources for information about the gray wolf.

*Sound-Symbol Awareness,
Sorting Words*
❖ Have students write *gray* and listen to the long *a* sound. Then have students collect more words with long *a* to note the most frequent spellings for long *a* (most common: *ay* [*play*], *ai* [*train*], *a*-consonant-*e* [*same*]). Create a list of long *a* words. Have students write the words in categories sorted by the spelling for the long *a.* Have one category for "other" to accommodate less common spellings.

776 *wonder*

*Other Word Forms,
Writing Sentences*
❖ Have students brainstorm for common other word forms of *wonder: wonders, wondered, wondering, wonderful, wonderfully, wondrous.* Have students write the other word forms in sentences.

*Book Tie-In,
Comparing and Contrasting*
❖ Use *Natural Wonders and Disasters* (Billy Goodman, Little, 1991), which includes information and striking photography on natural phenomena, such as volcanoes and hurricanes; and *The Seven Natural Wonders of the World* (Celia King, Chronicle, 1991), a pop-up book appropriate for middle-grade readers. Then introduce students to man-made wonders with *Explore the World of Man-Made Wonders* (Simon Adams, Golden, 1991), which includes Stonehenge. Have students compare and contrast natural and man-made wonders in writing.

777 *include*

Other Word Forms, Vocabulary Skills

Have students brainstorm for common other word forms of *include: includes, included, including, inclusion, inclusive.* Discuss unfamiliar words.

Antonyms, Prefix Practice, Writing Definitions

Ask students to identify the antonym of *include,* the word *exclude.* Have students write this question and the answer: When might a person feel excluded? Then have them write definitions of *preclude* and *conclude.*

778 *describe*

Other Word Forms, Prefix Practice, Writing Definitions

Have students brainstorm for common other word forms of *describe: describes, described, describing, description, descriptive.* Then have them write the words and meanings of *prescribe, subscribe, inscribe, transcribe.*

Using Descriptive Language

Have students find authors who use descriptive language, copy examples, and read the examples to the class. Then have students write one sentence that illustrates their own best use of descriptive language.

779 *electric*

Other Word Forms, Vocabulary Skills, Writing Sentences

Have students brainstorm for common other word forms of *electric: electricity, electrical, electrician.* Discuss unfamiliar words. Have students write the other word forms in sentences.

Book Tie-In, Writing Explanations

Use *Electricity* (Neil Ardley, New Discovery, 1992), *How Electricity Is Made* (C. L. Boltz, Facts on File, 1985), and *Simple Electrical Devices* (Martin Gutnik, Watts, 1986) as resources for students to write an explanation for how electricity works.

Visual Skill-Building, Writing Words, Writing Sentences

Write *electric* and *basic* (764) on the chalkboard, and draw an outline around each to accentuate its shape. Provide students with graph paper (or use the blackline master on page 109 of ***Spelling Sourcebook 1***). Have students write the words in the boxes and outline their shape (see Letter Grid Games on page 88 of ***Spelling Sourcebook 1***). Then have students make word shapes for review words, exchange papers with a partner, and see if the partner can fill in the boxes with the appropriate words. Next have students write sentences using these words.

780 *sold*

Other Word Forms, Homophone Usage, Writing Sentences

Have students brainstorm for common other word forms of *sold: sell, sells, selling, seller.* Discuss the homophones *sell* and *cell, seller* and *cellar.* Have students write the homophones in sentences to differentiate them.

Antonyms, Writing Words

Ask students to write the antonym of *sold,* the word *bought* (702). Expand the lesson by saying these words and asking students to write the opposite word: *minor* (*major* 774), *life* (*death* 736), *modern* (*ancient* 727), *dirty* (*clean* 720), *stale* (*fresh* 697), *thin* (*thick* 693), *behind* (*ahead* 632), *was* (*wasn't* 623), *north* (*south* 620), *unnecessary* (*necessary* 615).

781 *visit*

Other Word Forms, Vocabulary Skills, Writing Sentences
❖ Have students brainstorm for common other word forms of *visit: visits, visited, visiting, visitor, visitation.* Discuss unfamiliar words. Have students write the other word forms in sentences. Then have students rearrange the words in each sentence and delete capitals and punctuation. Partners then exchange and unscramble the sentences trying to match the word order of the original sentences.

Book Tie-In, Creating a Book
❖ Use *Visiting a Village* (Bobbie Kalman, Crabtree, 1991), a book from the *Historic Communities* series that explores the everyday life of early Canadian settlers. Have students use the book as a model to write a class-made book, *Visiting Our School* (see page 138, Creating Classroom Books).

782 *sheep*

Book Tie-In, Writing Stories
❖ Use *Sheep in a Shop* (Nancy Shaw, Houghton, 1991), a silly story of sheep shopping in the local general store; and the companion books *Sheep in a Jeep* (Houghton, 1986) and *Sheep on a Ship* (Houghton, 1989). Have students write a story about the senseless sheep that would complement Shaw's series.

Vocabulary Skills, Writing Words
❖ Ask students what we call young *sheep* (*lambs*). Then have students find and write the names of animal offspring. Choices may include *bear/cub, cat/kitten, cow/calf, dog/puppy, goat/kid, kangaroo/joey, rabbit/bunny, swan/cygnet, turkey/poult, whale/calf.* Then have students play the All-Play Spelling Bee (see **Spelling Sourcebook 1**, page 86) using this information.

783 *I'd*

Homophone Usage
❖ Ask students to identify the homophone of *I'd*, the word *eyed*. Have students write sentences to differentiate them.

Contractions
❖ Have students write other contractions made with *would*, such as *we'd, they'd, she'd, he'd, who'd.*

784 *office*

Other Word Forms, Vocabulary Skills, Writing Sentences
❖ Have students brainstorm for common other word forms of *office: offices, officer, official, officially.* Discuss unfamiliar words. Have students write the other word forms in sentences.

Writing a List, Sorting Words
❖ Have students list things that are in the school office. Choices may include desks, telephones, pencils, flag. Make a cumulative class list. Then have the school secretary verify the items. Next, have students sort the items on the list in some way.

Career Awareness, Writing a Summary
❖ Ask students to find out the education and qualifications necessary to be a police officer in your community. Have students summarize the information in writing.

785 *row*

Homophone Usage
❖ Have students write the homophones of *rowed*, the words *rode* and *road* (406). Have students write the words in sentences to differentiate them.

Homograph Usage,
Writing Words

❖ Introduce *row* as a homograph. Have students check a dictionary for the two pronunciations and three meanings for *row*. Then have students write the word in sentences to illustrate the different meanings. Next, have students find and write more homographs, such as *use* (88), *does* (128), *read* (165), *live* (217), *close* (328), *wind* (341), *present* (543), *object* (606), *minute* (608), *record* (611), *produce* (686), *lead* (699). Have students use these and other homographs to play Spelling Baseball (see ***Spelling Sourcebook 1***, page 91).

786 *contain*

Other Word Forms,
Vocabulary Skills, Prefix Practice,
Writing Sentences

❖ Have students brainstorm for common other word forms of *contain: contains, contained, containing, container.* Discuss unfamiliar words. Then write and discuss *pertain, retain, detain, maintain, sustain.* Have students write these words and the other word forms of *contain* in sentences.

Analogies, Writing Words,
Writing Sentences

❖ Review analogies (743, 764). Then have students write these analogies and complete them with words of frequencies 766–786 or their other word forms:

act : actor :: contain : _____ (container)
cub : bear :: lamb : _____ (sheep)
help : helpful :: wonder : _____ (wonderful)
bought : sold :: minor : _____ (major)
acts : axe :: groan : _____ (grown)

Have students write the answer words in sentences.

787 *fit*

Multiple Meanings,
Writing Sentences

❖ Brainstorm for meanings of *fit*. Then have students check a dictionary for verification. Have students write *fit* in sentences to illustrate the different meanings.

Idiomatic Usage,
Writing Explanations

❖ Have students explain in writing what they think it means to say these expressions (then discuss):

fit as a fiddle   to fit in with others
fit for a king   to fit like a glove
fit to be tied   to throw a fit
If the shoe fits, wear it.   survival of the fittest

Book Tie-In,
Creating an Advertisement

❖ To promote fitness, introduce *Looking Good, Eating Right* (Charles Salter, Millbrook, 1991), which emphasizes exercise and nutrition. Have students follow up by writing an advertisement for a real or make-believe fitness product.

Spelling Rules, Suffix Practice,
Writing Sentences

❖ Review the spelling rule for doubling the final consonant before adding suffixes (see ***Spelling Sourcebook 1***, page 85). Have students apply the rule to *fit, sit* (701), *hit* (672), *thin* (670), *skin* (622), *flat* (618), *trip* (576), *plan* (544), *step* (570), *map* (497), *begin* (444), *ship* (442), *stop* (396), *shop, trap, skip, forget, drop, quit.* Have students write the suffixed words in sentences.

788 *equal*

Other Word Forms, Vocabulary
Skills, Writing Sentences

❖ Have students brainstorm for common other word forms of *equal: equals, equaled, equaling, equally, equality.* Discuss unfamiliar words. Have students write the other word forms in sentences.

Exploring Symbols ❖ Have students write the symbol that means equal (=). Then have students find and write more symbols and write what they mean. Choices may include @, #, $, %, +, −, ?.

Sorting Words, Writing Words ❖ Have students play Word Sorts (see **Spelling Sourcebook 1**, page 92) using these words: *equal, enough* (209), *square* (537), *quite* (447), *eye* (578), *question* (476), *eight* (602), *especially* (614), *liquid, quarter, expect, east.*

789 *value*

Other Word Forms, *Vocabulary Skills,* *Spelling Rules, Suffix Practice* ❖ Have students brainstorm for common other word forms of *value: values, valued, valuing, valuable, valueless.* Discuss unfamiliar words. Review the spelling rule for adding suffixes to words ending in silent *e* (see **Spelling Sourcebook 1**, page 85). Have students brainstorm for words that end in silent *e* to which they can apply this rule. Have students write the words with selected suffixes.

Book Tie-In, *Writing Explanations, Evaluating* ❖ To help students learn the value of money, introduce *The Kids' Complete Guide to Money* (Kathy Kyte, Knopf, 1984), which includes comparison shopping and advertising. Have students follow up by choosing two different brands of a product and writing why one is the better value.

790 *yard*

Multiple Meanings, *Writing Sentences* ❖ Brainstorm for meanings of *yard.* Then have students check a dictionary for verification. Review words that can be used in different ways, such as *country* (228), *story* (237), *course* (317), *fire* (356), *spring* (515), *pick* (762), *scale* (763), *safe* (766), *arm* (772). Have students write the words in sentences to illustrate their different meanings.

Other Word Forms, Vocabulary *Skills, Writing Sentences* ❖ Have students brainstorm for common other word forms of *yard: yards, yardage.* Discuss unfamiliar words. Have students write the other word forms in sentences.

Measurement Words, Sorting *Words, Writing Explanations* ❖ Have students write measurement words, such as *yard, hour* (480), *day* (114), *foot* (482). Make a cumulative list on the chalkboard. Next, have each student sort the measurement words in some way. Then students exchange sorted lists and explain in writing how their partner sorted their words.

791 *beat*

Multiple Meanings, *Writing Sentences* ❖ Brainstorm for meanings of *beat.* Then have students check a dictionary for verification. Have students write *beat* in sentences to illustrate the different meanings.

Other Word Forms, *Writing Questions and Answers* ❖ Have students brainstorm for common other word forms of *beat: beats, beater, beating, beaten, beatable.* Have students write the other word forms in sentences that ask a question. Then have students exchange papers and answer the questions using the same word forms of *beat* in the responses.

Prefix Practice,
Writing Words, Vocabulary Skills

❖ Have students add the *un* prefix to *beatable*. Have students write a description of a team that is unbeatable. Review that the prefixes *in, im, dis,* and *un* can mean "not" or "the opposite of." Then have students add one of these prefixes to *equal* (788), *fit* (787), *describable* (*describe* 778), *believable* (*believe* 773), *armed* (*arm* 772), *active* (*act* 770), *safe* (766), *passable* (*pass* 757), *clean* (720), *controlled* (*control* 716), *decided* (*decide* 709), *similar* (706), *afraid* (684), *human* (575), *reasonable* (*reason* 564), *natural* (556), *planned* (*plan* 544), *happy* (540), *correct* (521), *explained* (*explain* 513), *clear* (510), *possible* (452). Have students check a dictionary if they are uncertain which prefix to use. Then discuss the meanings of the newly made words.

Homophone Usage,
Writing Descriptions

❖ Ask students to identify the homophone of *beat*, the word *beet*. Have students write a description of a beet.

Idiomatic Usage,
Writing Explanations

❖ Have students explain in writing what they think it means to say these expressions (then discuss):

to beat a dead horse	to beat someone up
to beat around the bush	to beat someone to the draw
to beat the band	to have your heart skip a beat
off the beaten track	to beat your head against a wall
to beat a path to your door	

792 *inch*

Spelling Rules, Plural Practice

❖ Review the spelling rule for making *inch* plural (see **Spelling Sourcebook 1**, page 85). Have students write the plurals for *gas* (760), *cross* (739), *business* (595), *wish* (573), *grass* (560), *watch* (436), *glass* (488), *class* (391), *box* (388), *tax, church, lunch, dish, dress, witch, speech, success, fox, search, six, address, bus, match.*

Writing Words,
Word Properties, Writing Reasons

❖ Review the activity "Choose" (580, 638, 714). Have students write the words in each row, then choose one word that does not belong, and write why it is different from the others.

inch	yard	year	value
contain	equal	quiet	square
row	office	wind	does
gray	yellow	light	blue
I'd	don't	won't	can't
arm	nose	eye	hat
believe	piece	wonder	friend

793 *sugar*

Other Word Forms,
Writing Sentences

❖ Have students brainstorm for common other word forms of *sugar: sugars, sugared, sugaring, sugary.* Have students write the other word forms in sentences.

Research and Writing, ❖ Have students research one of the following topics, tell about their findings in
Public Speaking writing, and then present the information orally to the class:

> spellings for the *sh* sound with examples and information about which is
> the most and least common (most common is *sh;* least common is *s* as in
> *sure* [251] and *sugar*)
>
> the differences among sugars such as granular sugar, sugar substitutes,
> honey, powdered sugar, sucrose
>
> how and where sugar is grown and refined

794 *key*

Multiple Meanings, ❖ Brainstorm for meanings of *key.* Then have students check a dictionary for
Writing Sentences verification. Have students write *key* in sentences to illustrate the different
meanings.

Book Tie-In ❖ Use *The Keys to My Kingdom: A Poem in Three Languages* (L. Dabcovich,
Lothrop, 1992), in which English, French, and Spanish texts can create
multilingual interest as well as provide a catalyst for writing about other keys
that can unlock the imagination.

Spelling Rules, Plural Practice ❖ Review the spelling rule for making *key* plural (see **Spelling Sourcebook 1**,
page 85). Have students write the plurals for *monkey* and *valley.*

795 *product*

Other Word Forms, Vocabulary ❖ Have students brainstorm for common other word forms of *product: products,*
Skills, Writing Sentences, *production, productive, productivity.* Discuss unfamiliar words. Have students
Prefix Practice, Evaluating write the other word forms in sentences. Next, have students add the *un* prefix
to *productive.* Then have them write this question and the answer: If your study
time has been unproductive, what might have made it more productive?

Book Tie-In, Writing Stories ❖ Introduce *Mistakes That Worked* (Charlotte Jones, Doubleday, 1991), which
tells how products such as cola, doughnuts, and popsicles were discovered.
Then have students write about a time they made a mistake that led to a
productive ending.

Book Tie-In, Writing a Letter ❖ Use *Better Mousetraps: Product Improvements That Led to Success* (Nathan
Aaseng, Lerner, 1990), a book in the series *Inside Business.* Following the
reading, have students write a letter to a company suggesting how one of its
products can be improved.

796 *desert*

Homograph Usage, ❖ Discuss the two pronunciations and meanings of this homograph. Then ask
Homophone Usage students to identify the homophone of *desert,* the word *dessert.* Have students
write sentences to differentiate the homophones and homographs.

Other Word Forms, Vocabulary ❖ Have students brainstorm for common other word forms of *desert: deserts,*
Skills, Making Comparisons *deserted, deserting, deserter, desertion.* Discuss unfamiliar words. Have
students write how the words *abandoned* and *deserted* are alike.

Book Tie-In, Creating a Book ❖ Use *A Desert Year* (Carol Lerner, Morrow, 1991) and *Deserts* (Keith Lyle,
Silver, 1987) for a survey of the earth's deserts, their climates, and their plant
and animal life. Follow up with students writing a class-made book of desert
trivia (see page 138, Creating Classroom Books).

Book Tie-In, Writing a Sequel ❖ Use the folktale *Winning Scheherazade* (Judith Gorog, Atheneum, 1991), which follows the heroine on a desert adventure. Then have students write a sequel to the story.

Research and Writing, Writing Descriptions ❖ Have students research and list deserts in the United States, such as Great Salt Lake, Mojave, and the Painted Desert. Then have students write a description of desert terrain for someone who has never seen a desert.

797 *bank*

Multiple Meanings, Writing Sentences ❖ Brainstorm for meanings of *bank*. Then have students check a dictionary for verification. Review words that can be used in different ways, such as *caught* (527), *figure* (551), *free* (553), *general* (639), *act* (770), *arm* (772), *major* (774), *row* (785). Have students write the words in sentences to illustrate their different meanings.

Homophone Usage, Writing Speculations, Word Origins ❖ Ask students to hypothesize in writing why a pig is the animal of choice for a bank in which to save coins. Have students speculate about other appropriate animal choices for banks (dogs hide away bones, squirrels "squirrel away" food). Then share with them that pygg was the clay from which pots and jars were made in the Middle Ages. People placed valuables in the pygg jars and called them *pygg banks*. That was the beginning of pig-shaped piggy banks.

798 *farther*

Word Analysis, Word Usage, Writing Sentences ❖ Have students write *farther, further,* and *father* (229). Discuss usage of *farther* (when meaning physical distance) and *further* (when physical measurement is not possible). Review *quiet* (726) /*quite* (447) /*quit, maybe* (566) /*may be, already* (411) /*all ready, our* (109) /*are* (15), *then* (53)/*than* (73), *picture* (232) /*pitcher.* Contrast the look-alike words. Have students write these often-confused words in sentences.

Writing City and State (or Province) Names, Map Skills ❖ Play the game "Which is Farther?" Give students several small slips of paper. Have students write the name of one city and its state or province on each paper. Place all slips in a box. Then have students take turns to draw two slips of paper each. Students can use a map to decide which of the two cities is farther away from them. Have students write their answer. Continue play with another draw of two slips of paper each.

799 *won*

Homophone Usage, Writing Number Words ❖ Ask students to write the homophone of *won*, the word *one* (28). Then have them find and write other homophones that include number words: *to* (5), *two* (65), *too* (112); *for* (12), *fore, four* (211); *eight*(602), *ate*. Have students write the homophones in sentences to differentiate them.

Homophone Usage, Writing Sentences ❖ Have students play Mystery Word to reinforce homophones in context (see **Spelling Sourcebook 1**, page 89). Include *won* and other homophones that are a persistent spelling challenge.

Antonyms ❖ Ask students to write the antonym of *won*, the word *lost* (514).

Research and Writing ❖ Have students research the answers to these questions:

Who won the U.S. presidential election in 1988?
Who won the Canadian election for prime minister in 1993?
Who won a gold medal in the most recent Olympic Games?
Who won a Nobel Peace prize?
Who won the most recent Caldecott Medal?
Who won the most recent Newbery Medal?
Who won an Oscar?

Creating an Award, Writing Reasons ❖ Have students design their own award, tell what it is for, and then choose a winner. Have students write why their winner most deserves to have won the award.

800 *total*

Other Word Forms, Suffix Practice, Book Tie-In, Creating a Book ❖ Have students brainstorm for common other word forms of *total: totals, totaled, totaling, totally.* Review the *ly* suffix and reinforce it with *A Snake Is Totally Tail* (Judi Barrett, Aladdin, 1983). Use it as a model for a students' class-made book using the same pattern—a crocodile is mostly mouth, a kangaroo is partially pocket (see page 138, Creating Classroom Books).

Word Analysis, Vowel Practice, Writing Words ❖ Write *t__t__l* on the chalkboard. Ask students to add the vowels to make *total.* Point out the difficulty in determining the vowel(s) in the unaccented syllable. Have students play the vowel fill-in game with other words with vowels in an unaccented syllable: *children* (200), *second* (235), *several* (263), *certain* (353), *hundred* (374), *surface* (393), *problem* (422), *pattern* (466), *bottom* (492), *travel* (516), *human* (575), *modern* (592), *practice* (634), *garden* (658), *broken* (690), *engine* (714), *capital* (742), *kitchen* (761). Have students fill in the vowel(s) and then write the whole word.

Creating Classroom Books

A Reading and Writing Partnership

Spelling Sourcebook 3 contains many suggestions for class-made and student-made books. The catalysts for the book-making projects are often books themselves—literature references are abundant in these activities. By reading, thinking, writing, creating their own books and reading them too, students are experiencing the full circle of language. And within that circle are varied language-building opportunities, including spelling and proofreading.

In a class-made book, each student participates in writing the book. Perhaps each student writes one page in the book. Perhaps students work in small groups to produce the book. Or a third strategy for making a class book is to have the class as a whole develop the story together, as an experience chart might be made in the primary grades. The final product in a class-made book is the result of input from the whole class. However, a student-made book is an individual's original book. A single student is the author. It is likely to be shorter than a class-made book.

When writing pieces are "published," such as in the production of class-made and student-made books, a writing-as-a-process approach is often used. This kind of writing, as opposed to everyday writing, strives for error-free final copies. There are various writing process models. Each model progresses through several stages of refinement to the published, perfectly proofread piece.

The class-made and student-made published books should resemble "actual" library books as closely as possible. They might include a section "about the author(s) or illustrator(s)," illustrations, a table of contents, page numbers, chapter titles, an index, a library card, and a cover.

The books can be assembled by the students, a teacher, or volunteer helpers. A school or classroom publishing house may be an efficient way to do this. With all the materials at hand, the books can be bound with ease.

Convenient bindings include construction paper and staples, report folders, file folders, poster board (railroad board) and tape, wallpaper and staples or tape, fabric and heavy thread or yarn. The paper books last longer if they are laminated or covered with clear, adhesive shelf-lining paper.

Novelty-style books include "accordion" books, "canned" books, and "shape" books. An accordion book is easy to make by taping pages accordion-pleated-fashion and attaching cover paper to the two end pages. Canned books are written on narrow paper, such as cash register tape, wound, and fitted inside a clean soup can that announces its title on a decorated paper label. Shape books have covers and pages cut into a shape appropriate for the book's content. For example, a book explaining the history and myth of Halloween might be shaped like a jack o' lantern.

The books produced at school can be cataloged in a classroom or school library, each with a library card for check-out. Some of the books could have an accompanying audio tape of the story text for check-out. Students can make these audio tapes. In fact, trying to record well-read stories on tape sharpens students' oral reading skills. But people other than students can read the stories on tape. For example, the school principal or office secretary can become the occasional audio tape story reader. Students enjoy having different familiar voices on the tapes.

The value of read-aloud time in the classroom is undisputed. Students of all ages who are afforded read-aloud time show growth in reading skills, writing development, and related language learning that can be attributed to the oral reading. The literature suggestions in *Spelling Sourcebook 3* can be shared orally, or parts of them can be. But the students' class-made and student-made books should also be chosen for read-alouds.

Story readers can be students, school personnel, or community visitors invited to the classroom to be readers. The community readers might be "special" personalities, such as the local newscaster, a fire fighter, or the mayor. These special read-alouds might be video-taped for replay. Students can invite the readers through written invitations . . . and thank them for being a guest through written thank-you letters— authentic examples of writing with built-in reasons to spell and proofread with accuracy.

Book-making activities provide one of many possibilities for reading and writing partnerships in the classroom. The marriage of reading and writing in the instructional program affords gains in student skill development, as well as increased student interest in both reading and writing. Combine the two through an ongoing production of class-made and student-made books in your classroom!

word	page	word	page	word	page	word	page
hat	128	level	116	office	131	result	93
he's	78	listen	43	oil	71	return	107
heart	25	longer	16	opposite	97	rich	90
heat	42	lost	45	outside	15	ride	89
heavy	17	lot	72	pair	83	ring	112
held	12	love	120	party	81	road	11
history	62	low	36	pass	123	rock	37
hit	96	machine	56	past	10	round	9
hole	117	main	31	pattern	30	row	131
hope	109	major	129	pay	69	rule	99
hour	34	map	40	period	89	safe	126
huge	88	mark	42	pick	125	sand	84
human	65	material	86	plan	55	sat	24
I'd	131	maybe	62	plane	60	scale	125
I've	80	meant	101	please	121	science	99
ice	21	measure	47	poor	39	section	112
inch	134	meat	122	position	108	seem	52
include	130	meet	76	possible	24	send	120
information	56	method	106	power	15	sense	97
instead	11	middle	63	practice	84	sent	54
interest	101	milk	67	present	54	seven	68
iron	70	million	98	pretty	102	shape	74
island	96	mind	14	problem	16	sharp	118
isn't	87	minute	75	produce	100	sheep	131
itself	32	miss	29	product	135	shell	20
job	41	modern	71	pull	100	ship	22
key	135	moment	53	question	33	sight	102
king	106	moon	14	quiet	113	sign	87
kitchen	125	mountain	48	quite	23	silver	114
lady	122	mouth	63	race	93	similar	107
language	40	music	41	radio	106	simple	26
late	69	natural	59	rain	26	single	44
lay	28	necessary	77	rather	55	sit	105
lead	104	nor	89	reach	72	size	28
least	33	north	68	reading	39	skin	80
leave	19	nose	115	real	25	sky	30
leaves	28	note	92	reason	61	sleep	69
led	92	object	75	record	76	snow	26
length	55	ocean	59	region	89	soft	74

word	page	word	page	word	page
soil	65	thus	52	wonder	129
sold	130	tiny	34	wood	50
someone	31	total	137	wouldn't	111
son	100	train	103	wrong	83
song	109	travel	46	wrote	46
south	79	trip	66	yard	133
speak	73	trouble	70	yellow	81
speed	56	type	123	you'll	116
spent	112	understand	13	you're	58
spread	110	unit	78	yourself	52
spring	45	value	133		
square	52	various	92		
stay	32	village	75		
step	63	visit	131		
stick	114	wait	85		
stone	95	walked	30		
store	70	wall	75		
straight	48	war	51		
strange	64	warm	12		
street	61	wasn't	80		
subject	80	watch	20		
suddenly	27	we'll	97		
sugar	134	wear	127		
summer	13	weather	29		
suppose	59	week	44		
system	20	weight	95		
tail	84	west	122		
tall	38	whose	47		
teacher	53	wide	33		
team	90	wife	96		
teeth	113	wild	28		
temperature	82	window	42		
test	82	winter	16		
themselves	22	wish	65		
therefore	116	within	21		
thick	102	woman	66		
thin	95	women	100		
third	23	won	136		
thousand	87	won't	73		

Rebecca Sitton's
Spelling Sourcebook Series

Sourcebook 1: Guidelines for Developing and Implementing Your Own Language-Integrated Spelling Program—17 How-To Chapters, Multiple References Including 1200 High-Use Words Listed by Frequency, and Blackline Masters for Practice Procedures and Record Keeping

Sourcebook 2: Activity Ideas for Words with Frequencies 1–400

Sourcebook 3: Activity Ideas for Words with Frequencies 401–800

Sourcebook 4: Activity Ideas for Words with Frequencies 801–1200

Videotape Programs Turn page for info...

Here's how to order . . .

Spelling Sourcebook 1 (the guidelines for developing your own spelling program and much more!)

1–49 copies $26.50 each . . . . . . number of copies _____ Total $ _____

50 or more* $21.50 each . . . . . . number of copies _____ Total $ _____

Spelling Sourcebook 2 (activities for words 1–400)

1–49 copies $26.50 each . . . . . . number of copies _____ Total $ _____

50 or more* $21.50 each . . . . . . number of copies _____ Total $ _____

Spelling Sourcebook 3 (activities for words 401–800)

1–49 copies $26.50 each . . . . . . number of copies _____ Total $ _____

50 or more* $21.50 each . . . . . . number of copies _____ Total $ _____

Spelling Sourcebook 4 (activities for words 801–1200)

1–49 copies $26.50 each . . . . . . number of copies _____ Total $ _____

50 or more* $21.50 each . . . . . . number of copies _____ Total $ _____

Subtotal $_____

* Any combination of *Sourcebooks* *1, 2, 3,* and *4* totaling 50 copies

Add tax 8.25% in CA, 8.10% in WA $ _____

Add postage: 8% in USA, 15% in Canada $ _____

(Payment must be in US funds) **TOTAL** $ _____

Choose your payment method:

_____ Bill school/district: Purchase order # _____

_____ Check enclosed (Prepay personal orders—pay in US funds)

Authorized signature _____

Bill to (please print):	*Ship to (if different):*
District _____	Name_____
Address _____	Address _____
City _____	City _____
State _____ Zip _____	State _____ Zip _____
Phone _____	Phone _____

Mail US orders to: Northwest Textbook
17970 SW McEwan Road
Portland, OR 97224
503-639-3194   FAX 503-639-2559

Mail Canadian orders to: Walt's Mailing
East 9610 1st
Spokane, WA 99206
509-924-5939   FAX 509-924-6923

Schedule a fast-paced, exciting *seminar* with Rebecca Sitton, the ***Sourcebook*** author. Prepare teachers to let go of tired, traditional workbook spelling. Open the door to the refreshing possibilities that language-integrated spelling offers! Contact Rebecca Sitton for information: South 2336 Pittsburg, Spokane, WA 99203 509-535-5500

Rebecca Sitton's
Spelling Sourcebook
Video Series

Tape I   Introduction to Teachers (70 minutes)
Rebecca introduces educators to the commonsense methodology and research-based strategies outlined in the *Sourcebooks* for developing, implementing, and authentically assessing a language-centered spelling curriculum. This tape is a "must" for educators who are considering developing their own spelling program (one without student books) or for beginning users of the methodology.

Tape II   Introduction to Parents (40 minutes)
In this video, Rebecca visits with parents about the challenge of teaching students to spell and proofread in their writing every day, *not* just on Friday Spelling Tests! She assures parents that the focus of the *Sourcebook* approach to spelling growth parallels real-world use of spelling… spelling well in daily writing… and outlines the steps for achieving it.

Tape III   Management and Record Keeping Options (70 minutes)
Rebecca offers multiple how-to suggestions for organizing the daily use of the *Sourcebook* methodology. This video includes a comparison of Core Words and Priority Words, considerations for identifying Priority Words, selecting and marking everyday writing papers for spelling performance and feedback, grading, time-effective record keeping, and managing the Individualized List to complement learning.

Here's how to order . . .

Tape I   Introduction to Teachers $150.00 . . . . number of tapes _____ Total $ _____

Tape II   Introduction to Parents $100.00 . . . . number of tapes _____ Total $ _____

**Tape III   Management and
        Record Keeping Options** $150.00 . . . . number of tapes _____ Total $ _____

Tape Set (one of each tape) $350.00 . . . . number of sets _____ Total $ _____

Tape Set (ten or more tape sets) $300.00 . . . . number of sets _____ Total $ _____

Subtotal $ _____

Contract for Special Broadcast and Duplication
Rights for Copyright Videos: Contact R. Sitton,
South 2336 Pittsburg, Spokane, WA 99203
Phone 509-535-5500

Add tax 8.25% in CA, 8.10% in WA $_____
Add postage: 8% in USA, 15% in Canada $_____
(Payment must be in US funds) **TOTAL** $_____

Choose your payment method:

_____ Bill school/district: Purchase order # _____

_____ Check enclosed (Prepay personal orders—pay in US funds)

Authorized signature _____

Bill to (please print):

District _____

Address _____

City _____

State _____ Zip _____

Phone _____

Ship to (if different):

Name _____

Address _____

City _____

State _____ Zip _____

Phone _____

Mail US orders to: Northwest Textbook
17970 SW McEwan Road
Portland, OR 97224
503-639-3194
FAX 503-639-2559

Mail Canadian orders to: Walt's Mailing
East 9610 1st
Spokane, WA 99206
509-924-5939
FAX 509-924-6923